Eliza Fowler Haywood
Memoirs of a Certain Island Adjacent to the Kingdom of Utopia, Volume 1

Women Philosophers Heritage Collection

English Version and Introduction

Edited by
Ruth Edith Hagengruber

In Cooperation with
Antonio Calcagno, Priyanka Jha, Rodney Parker

Volume 2/1

Eliza Fowler Haywood

Memoirs of a Certain Island Adjacent to the Kingdom of Utopia

Volume 1

Edited and Introduced by
Sina Menke

DE GRUYTER

This publication is based on:
Eliza Fowler Haywood, *Memoirs of a Certain Island Adjacent to the Kingdom of Utopia*, vol. 1, 2nd edition, London: Printed, and sold by the booksellers of London and Westminster, 1726/1724.

ISBN 978-3-11-114950-9
ISSN 2510-9243

Library of Congress Control Number: 2024935275

Bibliographic information published by the Deutsche Nationalbibliothek
The Deutsche Nationalbibliothek lists this publication in the Deutsche Nationalbibliografie; detailed bibliographic data are available on the Internet at http://dnb.dnb.de.

© 2024 Walter de Gruyter GmbH, Berlin/Boston
Cover image: Ruth Edith Hagengruber

www.degruyter.com

Contents

Introduction —— 1
1 Biographical Notes —— 1
2 Contextualizing Memoirs of a Certain Island —— 9
2.1 Factions and Parties —— 9
2.2 The South Sea Crisis —— 11
3 Memoirs of a Certain Island —— 14
3.1 Media History and Patronage —— 14
3.2 A Brief Comment from the Editor —— 17
3.3 Summary —— 18
4 Haywood's Philosophical Method(s) —— 24
4.1 The Hillarian Circle and Sublimity —— 24
4.2 Desire and Haywood's Contemporaries —— 28
4.3 Love as a Historical Constant: The Divine Historian —— 31
4.4 Love as an Other-directed Passion: From Self to Community —— 33
5 Brief Outlook —— 35
 Bibliography and Further Reading —— 35
 Timeline —— 39

Editorial Notes —— 41
 Problems of Haywood Editions —— 41

Memoirs of a Certain Island Adjacent to the Kingdom of Utopia:
Volume 1 —— 43
 The Story of the Enchanted Well —— 46
 The History of *Graciana* —— 51
 The History of the Chevalier *Windusius*, and the fair, false *Wyaria* —— 87
 The History of *Cesaria*, Marchioness del Keisar —— 116
 The History of *Hortensia* —— 120
 The History of *Masonia*, Count *Marville*, and Count *Riverius* —— 137
 The History of Count *Orainos*, and Madam *Del Millmonde* —— 156
 The History of the Chevalier *Beaujeune*, and the Beautiful *Olivia* —— 165
 The History of the Duke and Dutchess *de Marbien* —— 168
 The History of the Chevalier *Blantier, Olimpia,* and the unfortunate *Silenia* —— 176
 The History of the Chevalier *Le Brune, Cleander,* and the fair *Euphelia* —— 191

The History of the Count *Montreville*, *Martasinda*, and Madam *de Fautmille* —— **202**
A. Key —— **218**

Index of Names —— 221

Index of Subjects —— 222

Introduction

1 Biographical Notes

"Unskill'd in Science, in rude Ign'rance bred; Unhappy that I am."
(Haywood 1742: 262; from a dispute with Scottish poet Walter Bowman of the Hillarian Circle)

"Enjoy the virtues you have so well expressed / Nor blessing others, be thyself unblessed / Believe in jumble innocence thou'lt know / Delights, which pompous vice could never bestow."
(Haywood 1724: 186; from *Letter to the Ingenious RIVERIUS, on his writing in the Praise of Friendship*)

Eliza Haywood, neé Fowler, was certainly born in 1693, potentially in London, and perhaps died in Westminster in 1756. During most of her lifetime, England was under Hanoverian rule, although Haywood initially grew up under Queen Anne, the last Stuart monarch. Most details known about Haywood have been unearthed by scholars since the 1970s, who helped raise her from being relatively unrecognized and by no means canonized to, at least in the realms of English literary Studies[1] and Early Modern History, a more familiar but still all too often disregarded female author. Still, considering the recognition that her works and her skills received during her lifetime, she remains far too unknown today.

Given the lack of information about her life, there are numerous versions of Haywood, and the following can only be another one of them. It is believed that Haywood's father worked "in the Mercantile Way," which would put her somewhere in what would later become the English middle class (Earle 1989). As such, she would not have been under scrutiny for publishing for money, as high-born women would have been, and she would have lived in a "social milieu that valued study and self-improvement" (Schellenberg 2015: 41). Between 1660 and 1780, as Schellenberg argues, there was a considerable change towards the acceptance of women as literary authors, publishers, who could make a living – possibly even a comfortable living – from their writing (42). Thus, at the beginning of her career but also throughout, Haywood could certainly have been able to earn her living through a combination of writing poetry, her acting, and her work in the print business. Despite this, it appears that the money she made never did allow her to live comfortably. Thus, it would likely be erroneous to imagine Haywood living the lavish life of a celebrated author – it is far more probable that her circum-

---

[1] Those scholars usually focused on Haywood as part of one of the dominant questions of the 1960s and 1970s: "What were eighteenth-century novels?" (Bowers 2009: 54).

stances were humble and her income unstable.² This appears to have been true throughout her life, as even close to her death Haywood worked on her periodical *The Young Lady*, a largely pecuniary project, which however proved unsuccessful. Still, while she did not have a financially stable life, she was exceptionally successful in having her works published in print, most often publishing them herself.³ Despite the budding acceptance of female authorship, publishing in print was not a common occurrence for women at the beginning of the eighteenth century: Most, but not all, writing that women took part in revolved around the "culture of letter writing and manuscript exchange" (Schellenberg 2015: 45). There are other exceptions to this rule such as Aphra Behn (1640?–1689) and Elizabeth Carter (1717–1806), but the majority – and especially high-born women – did not publish in print.

There is evidence that Haywood might have had two children, but the details are yet again muddled: One version holds that both died young, while another supposes that she raised both children on her own, without the help of the husband whose last name she took. Beyond this name, little is known about her husband – which has supported the proliferation of colorful stories, like the long-canonized fiction of the 'runaway clergyman's wife', in which Haywood was said to have married, and dramatically left, the Reverend Valentine Haywood. Since Christine Blouch has quashed this rumour, many guesses have been formulated, none of which have proven fitting. Those clues that are available, at most indicate that her husband must either have passed away or vanished "before she embarked upon her public career."⁴

It will have become evident by now that too little is known with any certainty how the real Eliza Haywood passed her days. She remains a figure that has invited conjecture and animated imaginations, who is constructed 'from the outside in,' through an external view that begins with stereotypes and hearsay, and often relies all too heavily on the testimony of those contemporaries she associated with, whether deliberately or otherwise.

The following is thus what we do know about Haywood's life. Her first theatrical role is documented as having been in the *Dublin's Smock Alley*, a small Irish theater which first opened in 1662, known for its great acoustics but terrible con-

---

2 Rough estimates of Haywood's income have been calculated by Spedding (2004: 76–64).
3 "In addition to briefly operating as a pamphlet-shop proprietor and minor publisher at the Sign of Fame in Covent Garden …, she produced advice literature for servants, husbands, and wives" (Schellenberg 2015: 45).
4 For the quest to identify Haywood's husband, see King (2012).

struction, collapsing only eight years later.[5] This means that while she spent most of her life in London, she also travelled and lived in Ireland for some time. The character she played was that of Shakespeare's Chloe, which, as Kathryn King describes, is a typical beginner's role, perhaps one level above an extra: "[T]he only role for which records have survived, was the bit part of Chloe in Shadwell's adaptation of *Timon of Athens*. This confirms that she was there as a novice to learn her craft. Chloe mostly stands around on stage, now and then delivering a line of little import such as 'Madam! Your father is come in'" (King 2012: 19).

Eliza Haywood gathered a wide circle of friends, acquaintances, and collaborators throughout her acting years, a trend that would continue with her joining the Hillarian Circle as one of its first members. She would later leave the diverse group of poets and writers with a bang following the publication of the first part of *Memoirs of a Certain Island*. While the image of "two Haywoods" is prevalent in modern scholarship on the author, viewing her divided into Haywood the writer and Haywood the actress, I suggest a more intimate connection in place of this forced dichotomy, wherein acting might have indeed paved her way to becoming an acknowledged writer.[6] Not dissimilar from contemporary artistic communities, actors in the early modern period often possessed a wide-reaching network in which they associated with other writers, actors, poets and directors, a frequently employed resource to aid one's own profession.[7] This extends beyond the more direct financial benefits of acting: As Hammond argues, the theater "was temporally prior to the publishing industry in affording a living to imaginative writers" because of its "direct and often brutally frank" connection of playwrights and audiences (Hammond 1997: 48–49, 55–69). How much both acting and writing are connected in Haywood's life can again be seen by her choice of patrons, prime among them Aaron Hill – namesake of the Hillarian Circle – who had "a life-long passion" for both acting and the theater (Gerrard 2003: 25). By 1709, Hill was *Drury Lane*'s general manager, and by 1721, the new *Little Theatre* had hired him to instruct performers.

Despite having built a network and establishing herself as an actress, Haywood was never as successful in her acting as she was in her writing. Nevertheless, she was an accomplished playwright, and her theatrical oeuvre includes plays such

---

[5] Joseph Ashbury, an officer in Ireland during the Protectorate, notes that the theater collapsed in December 1670 and killed (at least) one young girl (Jeffares 1982).

[6] For an earlier biographical account criticizing the foregone idea of the "two Haywoods," see Blouch 1991.

[7] Backscheider writes that "Aphra Behns *Oronooko* (1688), Deariver Manley's *romans à clef*, and Eliza Haywood's political allegory, *The Adventures of Eovaai* (1736), attracted the same audience as their plays" (1987: 245–262).

as *The Fair Captive* (1721) and *A Wife to be Lett* (1723), and she continued to act in different roles throughout her lifetime. While her acting likely cannot be seen divorced from financial necessity, it certainly belies a profound interest in the theater, which in turn influenced her writing. At roughly 40 or 50 years of age, Haywood began to establish herself as a novelist, increasingly devoting her time to the craft. This line of work proved to be extensively fruitful for her, so much so that she "outsold nearly all of her rival novelists in the early eighteenth century" (Hollis 1997: 43). Yet, she is often mentioned last when it comes to the so-called "fair Triumvirate (of Wit)," a term coined in the early eighteenth century by Irish poet and cleric John Sterling, who writes "Pathetic[a] Behn, or Manley's greater Name / Forget their Sex, and own when Haywood writ / She clos'd the Fair triumvirate of Wit," placing Haywood with eighteenth- and seventeenth-century writers Delariviere Manley and Aphra Behn (see Anderson 1936). Indeed, she appears to often have been laid aside, especially for her alleged lack of political writing, a charge which, as the fiercely political *Memoirs of a Certain Island* demonstrates, is not tenable (see Hollis 1997).

A similar disregard is visible in terms of her philosophical thinking, which Haywood scholarship has touched upon, principally, as a sidenote. One of the reasons for the prevailing lack of research concerning her political and philosophical thought may, however, be reasonably mundane: Most Haywood scholars originate from an English or literary studies background, meaning that their primary focus comes from a perspective that, while it has allowed for great strides to be made in interpreting Haywood's intricate writing, does not routinely prioritize political philosophy. Beyond the previous, largely marginal discussion of Haywood's attention to philosophical problems, there has been an increase in attention to her philosophical leanings: In this regard, Rebecca Tierney-Hynes points out that, as a counterbalance to the eighteenth-century stereotype of the "impressionable woman reader," Haywood concerned herself with the practice of reading, especially philosophical reading. Simultaneously, she showed interest in theoretical treatises about love and desire, which inspired her to produce a "history of philosophical discourse of the passions" (Tierney-Hynes 2010: 154). Acknowledging a "third Haywood" as a philosopher, however, clearly reveals the necessity of reading Haywood not as an isolated thinker, and more against the backdrop of other philosophers like René Descartes and his *Passions of the Soul* (1646).

Simultaneously, while Haywood concerned herself with political, philosophical, and economic problems, her career as a publisher and editor of her very own periodical flourished, though always framed by her work as an actress and novelist. Her first periodical, a one-woman job, was *The Female Spectator*, named after the successful periodical *The Spectator* by English essayist and poet Joseph Addison, and Anglo-Irish essayist, playwright, and politician Richard Steele.

The Female Spectator is especially significant as it is often named as the first periodical solely run by a woman. Different from other early periodicals that followed stricter gender divides, however, its intended readership was not confined to women, but to both high-born women and men (Wright and Newman 2006: 18f.).[8] This approach quickly proved successful: When the first edition was launched in April 1744, it gained a vast readership.[9] It is further speculated that Haywood launched her periodical "perhaps partly as an effort to make a go of the bookselling business she had established at the *Sign of Fame* in Covent Garden, where she specialized in selling her own works" (Wright and Newman 2006: 13).

What may initially appear as an at times tumultuous and financially insecure but otherwise safe life was disrupted by Haywood's arrest and detainment in 1750. While the circumstances surrounding this are lost to time, it has been established that, in 1750, Haywood was placed "under arrest on suspicion of producing a seditious pamphlet," the obliquely titled *A Letter from H——G——g ... to a Particular Friend Esq.* (1749) (King 2012: 11). There is, however, some speculation as to whether Haywood was the true author of the *Letter*, despite her arrest, as she denied authorship of it. As was often the case, the *Letter* was only externally assigned to her by "Ralph Griffiths, founder and editor of the *Monthly Review*" (King 2012: 181). It appears that despite her self-description as an author who "never wrote any thing in a political way," this claim of innocence did not succeed in absolving her of suspicion (King 2012: 1).

A Letter should not be read in isolation, appears to have been done by past scholars such as Carnell and MacKenzie, who interpreted it as clearly in favor of Jacobitism. King instead argues that "Jacobitism ... supplied her with a language to express opposition without necessarily implying support for an actual Stuart restoration" (King 2012: 181). What does she mean by this? In the second half of the 1740s, many writers exploited "the glow of romance and mystery 'surrounding the glamorous, melancholy figure of Prince Charles Edward himself' in the aftermath of the failed rebellion" (King 2012: 181). *A Letter* or, as King calls it, *The Goring Pamphlet*, thus similarly portrays Charles Edward Stuart as an amatory hero who travels with his companion, Henry Goring. If we follow the assumption of Haywood's authorship of the pamphlet, it indicates that she used the mystery surrounding the incognito travels of Charles to capitalize on that very "glow." Simultaneously, the pamphlet openly plays with political positions, often merging Charles and Frederick, Prince of Wales, into one person. As can be seen in other romances such as

---

8 As an example of a specifically female audience, see Mary Astell's works which are usually dedicated to her female friends.
9 Wright and Newman have extensively carved out (among others) the relevance, themes, and politics of *The Female Spectator* (Wright and Newman 2006).

Ascanius; or, The Young Adventurer. A True History (1746), written by English publisher and journal editor Ralph Griffiths, the government was clamping down on any perceived expression of Jacobitism. Haywood, it appears, doubly endangered herself: She was deliberately unclear by not openly opposing Jacobitism, but also actively obscured divergent political positions, implementing a form of "strategic Jacobitism" (King 2012: 71). Her play with political stances becomes more prominent in her later writings, where she begins to "oppose every administration and consistently write on the side of exiles, outsiders and those excluded from power or, in the case of the Jacobites, those harassed or worse by power" (King 2012: 71). In the end, though, the *Letter* was much less dangerous than it was made out to be by the government, there being other, far more critical texts, including many by Haywood, especially from 1744/1745 onwards. Concerning its actual tameness, King points to Griffith's observation about Haywood's arrest, who remarks in the *Monthly Review* that had the government not arrested Haywood, the pamphlet would surely have been "turned into waste-paper" (King 2012: 185).

Masterful in obscuring positions in her texts, Haywood was also masterful in obscuring information about herself. Thus, numerous versions of Haywood exist not due to an abundance of information on her, but due to a lack thereof (see Blouch 1991; Spedding 2017). While Haywood seemed to have been externally defined as a typical writer of scandal novels, she most certainly was playing with this ascription, too. Due to the explicit self-presentation of Haywood as an author of scandalous fiction, it cannot be said with certainty what part of these fabrications were her own doing. This kind of attention, of her being treated as a controversial and even scandalous figure, has arguably proven to be beneficial – it may not simply be disadvantageous for an author to be noticed and talked about. It would therefore likely be too simple to solely frame Haywood as a victim of undue scandalization. In turn, exclusively regarding Haywood as an author of scandalous fiction again distracts from her multifaceted identity as an author, distracting from the impressive range of her philosophical, economic, and political works. The total number of her retrieved works is currently estimated at around 70, but additional pieces of writing continue to be (re)discovered.

Her significance as an author of multiple genres is being (re)discovered by the ever-growing scholarship on her works, life, and significance during her own lifetime. There are Haywood scholars who have meticulously carved out parts of her life over the last years and decades, among those King, Spedding, Barchas, Creel, Backscheider, Ingrassia, and Howard. They have used various methods to try to capture something of Haywood's life by studying engravings, portraits, and mentions made by other writers and poets. Even though Haywood herself was born and raised in London, a majority of contemporary Haywood research originates in the United States, with the exception of Kim Simpson, and a small number of continental European scholars, like French cultural studies scholar Orla Smyth. The only biographical information about Haywood that we have from around her own lifetime is "David E. Baker's brief 1764 biographical account" (King 2008: 722). This void of information has proven especially intriguing given its stark contrast to the very clear ideas circulated about Haywood's life and talent (or perceived lack thereof) by some of her contemporaries: Especially in the eighteenth century, defamations of Haywood appear much more popular than her actual works. This has led to the assumption that the frequency and magnitude of such defamation may have forced Haywood to disappear from public life or cease publishing new texts, with Haywood the writer becoming Haywood the myth, only graspable through the – often more than unkind – perspectives of others. The truth, however, as excavated by King, paints a more resilient picture: Haywood not only survived but prospered throughout the period of defamation; her career was far from stifled.

One especially forceful literary insult has survived until today and, even without acquiescing to overly external portrayals of Haywood, it is difficult to imagine writing about her without mentioning Alexander Pope. His unflattering portrayal of her in his *Dunciad* (1727/1728) reads:

> See in the circle next Eliza placed,
> Two babes of love close clinging to her waist;
> ...
> The Goddess then: 'Who best can send on high
> The salient spout, far-streaming to the sky,
> His be yon Juno of majestic size,
> With cow-like udders, and with ox-like eyes (Pope 1728)

Perhaps fearing the English middle-class had lost their sense of taste, Pope casts Haywood as "Juno of majestic size," a lustful bovine creature with two illegitimate children. Jonathan Swift's insult is more revealing: "Mrs. Heywood I have heard of as a stupid, infamous, scribbling woman, but have not seen any of her productions" (Swift 1701: 153). There is a surprising number of contemporaries who published similar opinions of her, such as Lord Dover joining Pope in calling her "a voluminous writer of indifferent novels." Indeed, the impressive number of denunciations has led to Haywood researcher and collector Patrick Spedding compiling them in what he calls his "Wall of Shame" (see Spedding 2015).

Beyond these somewhat crude depictions, we find both praise and more nuanced critique. Richard Savage, poet and permanent member of the Hillarian Circle, delivered one of the most glowing commentaries of her work and person. His poem to Haywood is a comment on *The Rash Resolve*, indicating, unlike Swift, close familiarity with her work: "In thy full Figures, Painting's Force we find / As Music fires, thy Language lifts the Mind. ... Eliza, still impaint Love's po'rful Queen! / Let Love, soft Love! Exalt each swelling Scene" (Savage 2013/1726: 162). Spedding adds that "it is possible that the ornament following Richard Savage's poem in praise of Haywood's Rash Resolve may have been intended as an idealized representation of Haywood" (Spedding 2017: 348). Indeed, his adoring portrayal had many scholars insinuate an affair between the two, even attributing Haywood's two, if we believe Pope, illegitimate children to Savage. This fiction, befitting the tendency to ancillary scandalizations of her life, appears to have taken a longer route already in the nineteenth century, originating in English poet Charles Whitehead's *Richard Savage: A Romance of Real Life* (1841), wherein he imagined a love affair between Savage and Haywood. (see Savage 1896: 185). As King has shown, this does not hold true, and is most likely based on a, albeit very cautious, reading of Whitehead by Blouch (King 2008: 723). Rather than any romantic interest in Savage, Haywood appears to have been interested in the eponymous initiator of the Hillarian Circle, Aaron Hill. While there is no verifiable information whether this interest led to a relationship, it does offer a better explanation for Haywood's dispute with Martha Sansom (maiden name Fowke), as Sansom quite openly professed her love for Hill (see Sansom 1997).

It is perhaps not surprising that Haywood's life and potential lovers have lent themselves to a degree of speculation, especially so for an author of amorous fiction and scandal novels and, even more so, one with a deliberately obscure biography. Yet while some fictions are evidently just that, there is still work to be done for the biographical cause, as to learn more about Haywood's life may lead to further keys into her work.[10]

Much like the continued interest in her life, there appears a continuity in the interest in, and reception of, her work. Haywood was not just praised by her contemporaries. At the beginning of the nineteenth century, in *On the Origin and Progress of Novel Writing*, poet and essayist Anna Letitia Barbauld writes: "Mrs. Haywood was a very prolific genius: her earlier novels are in the style of Mrs. Behn's, and Pope has chastised her in his *Dunciad* without mercy or delicacy; but her later works are by no means void of merit" (Barbauld, n.d.).

Therefore, to reconstruct Haywood as a person and a philosophical thinker means concentrating on her friends and acquaintances instead, as King and Spedding have begun to do. Haywood was not a singular, isolated thinker at the beginning of the eighteenth century but a lively, well-connected and, through her numerous works, very much a 'public' person.

---

[10] Among those potential lovers were Henry Fielding, William Hatchett, and Aaron Hill, just to name a few.

2 Contextualizing Memoirs of a Certain Island

2.1 Factions and Parties

The idea of the isolated thinker is not exclusively, but frequently attached to the image of the isolated philosopher. However, the image of an erudite recluse, detached from society at large, does not appear to hold up to historical scrutiny. This is no less true for women philosophers who often shifted between 'private' and 'public' spaces, which were in general much less separate than has long been assumed.[11] Following from this, as well as the fluidity of women philosophers, their philosophical problems and questions transcended the academic realm, especially when it came to aspects that concern wider society, with political upheaval proving no exception.

At the beginning of the eighteenth century, English society was in turmoil: There was talk of a 'factionalization' of England, and the rise of political parties was at the core of English civil discourse. Both common folk and intellectuals were debating in the streets, in salons, and in their homes, deliberating the danger posed, or potential offered, by the emergence of political parties. Early on, it appears, the majority condemned the rise of parties, as "division was seen as posing an existential threat to the political community" (Skjönsberg 2021: 27). It is no coincidence, then, that on the second page of Haywood's *Memoirs*, the island is praised for its serenity, where "no tumults, no Noise, no stormy Tongues of Faction ... seemed ever to have disturbed the Quiet of this happy Shore" (Haywood 1724: 2). Both faction and party were used interchangeably by most early modern writers, but for those instances in which one term would nevertheless be used instead of the other, Skjönsberg has illustrated three distinct properties that the term faction may, specifically, convey:

> First, it could denote the Whig and Tory factions, in other words be interchangeable with party. Second, it could mean something akin to "interest group," notably an economic interest. Third, it could refer to a party connection purely motivated by ambition and self-interest, with little or no interest in principles or opinions. ... Finally, it could imply the even more negative connotation of a conspiracy within the state to destroy the constitution. Frederick Barlow's *Dictionary* (1772) defined faction as "a tumult, discord, confusion or dissension". (Skjönsberg 2021: 16)[12]

---

[11] For a classification of the intersection of public and private in the early modern period, see Schmidt-Voges (2019); Eibach, et al. (2015); Burton (2019); Wunder (2022).

[12] Interest is another fundamental aspect of *Memoirs of a Certain Island*, to the extent that it does not merely remain an abstract concept, but is personified or deified as one of the two guardians of the enchanted well, Pecunia, Goddess of Interest.

In *Memoirs of a Certain Island*, 'faction' is portrayed through its absence: The Noble Youth, arriving on the isle, is pleased to find that there are in fact "no stormy Tongues of Faction." Following the Noble Youth's description, Haywood's use of 'factions' would fit the third and fourth category proposed by Skjönsberg. Thus, 'faction' would be a description with an explicitly negative connotation, as Haywood's use adds it to the enumeration of "tumults," "noise," and "stormy Tongues." Note, however, the distinction between "no Factions" and "no stormy Tongues of Faction." It is not just the factions whose absence is celebrated, but the absence of the debate or talk about them, as there is no discord disturbing the "Quiet of this happy Shore" (Haywood 1724: 2).

In her rather negative use of factions, Haywood aligns with many of her contemporaries. Both Swift and John Trenchard argue strongly against party politics, cautioning against blindly trusting political factions, with Swift claiming that freely given trust in parties would be "below the Dignity both of Human Nature, and Human Reason" (Swift 1701: 56). As the emergence of parties in England was a relatively singular occurrence throughout the seventeenth and eighteenth centuries, many English and Scottish philosophers like David Hume and Edmund Burke, but also non-English philosophers such as Paul de Rapin, discussed the potential problems and chances that parties might bring (Burke 1791: 416; see Rapin 1732). Unlike Swift and Trenchard, they did not espouse as openly a final judgement: Hume is an especially illustrative example, as he was very much invested in the analysis of party politics and their historical realization. Whereas today he is most well-known for his *A Treatise of Human Nature* (1739–1740), he was recognized more for his collection, *Essays, Moral Political and Literary* (1777) during his own lifetime. In one of the essays, *Of Parties in General* and *Of the Parties of Great Britain* (1741), Hume takes on the role of a historian who explores the genesis of party politics in Britain, beginning with the founding of the two-party system consisting of monarchy and republicanism, lasting until the Glorious Revolution in 1688, and illustrating parallels and differences between Tories and Whigs. In short, he argues that while the founding parties of Great Britain were based and focused on principles, the Tory/Whig government was solely focused on interest and, therefore, weak.

Haywood's line of argumentation displays some similarities to that employed by Hume. She mentions the term "party" mostly in conjunction with the necromancer Lucitario and potentially the most villainous character in the whole text, Romanus, who King has identified as John Trenchard.[13] In *Memoirs of a Cer-*

---

[13] Both Trenchard and Haywood shared their critique concerning the South Sea Scheme and the

tain Island, Lucitario does not act as a singular person, it is "Lucitario's party" which uses "images of wizardry and enchantment [to] deliver a powerful vision of a society undone at every level, rich and poor, old and young, by failure to resist the seductive promise of easy wealth" (King 2012: 39). Haywood's writing is thus deeply rooted in the ravages of her time, as the primary allegation was one of herd mentality, whereby the people would blindly follow the party leaders as sheep follow their shepherd, echoing the charges brought by Trenchard and Swift (Skjönsberg 2021: 28). King describes Haywood's relationship to party politics as belonging to a discursive patriotic mix of the first half of the eighteenth century in which "political manoeuvrings at mid-century were based on 'complex alliances between Jacobites, Whigs, Patriots and Tories' that inevitably blurred the ideological boundaries between these groups" (King 2012: 8).

2.2 The South Sea Crisis

As the previous passages have begun to illustrate, Haywood was not solely occupied with party politics, but also with a problem of an economic, financially speculative nature emerging at the beginning of the eighteenth century, which was closely linked to party politics. The activities of the joint stock venture, the *South Sea Company*, was a hotly discussed issue when Haywood wrote the first of her two-part work, an issue that, for many, proved difficult to fully grasp. When *Memoirs of a Certain Island* was published, England was already feeling the aftermath of that company's collapse (see King 39). According to King, *Memoirs of a Certain Island* is not considered a central work in discussions about the South Sea scheme, despite it being one of the most detailed contemporary descriptions of the financial crash. This holds especially true for her attention to the various financial entanglements of the investors, although her description of the various impacts of the crash must be approached with a degree of caution.

Founded in 1711 by an Act of Parliament, the *South Sea Company*'s primary directive was to promote trade with "Spanish America" to reduce the looming national debt. The company operated under the assumption that the War of Spanish Succession would end with a treaty allowing this trade. Indeed, in 1713, the Spanish Crown granted a monopoly of trade in the region to Queen Anne, part of which

---

ministerial machinations. The precise reasons for her attack, in which she simultaneously praises Romanus for his wit and intelligence, are not clear. King suggests personal reasons (2012: 42).

was the Asiento,[14] which promoted the trade of African slaves with the Spanish and Portuguese empires.[15] Anne transferred the contract to the *South Sea Company*, which in turn agreed to assist with the partial reform of the national debt. This approach, which had proven profitable in the past, initially appeared similarly lucrative. In July 1711, the *South Sea Company* signed agreements with the *Royal African Company* to provide Jamaica with the requisite number of African slaves. In the first year, the company shipped at least 1,200 slaves, although the total number was likely higher, from Jamaica to the Americas. In total, the number of slaves transported by the *South Sea Company* is estimated at around 34,000. For a long time, historians have described the undertakings of the *South Sea Company* as financially unsuccessful, but this no longer appears to have been the case.[16] What did follow from the focus on whether or not the deal had been lucrative or not, however, is the almost complete ignorance of the fate of the "thousands of people [who] were transported across the Atlantic by the South Sea Company" (Paul 2011: 11).

Beyond questions of financial viability, however, The final chapters of the *South Sea Company* are well researched: The deal with the Spanish Crown collapsed in September 1720, and even a simplified description of events can paint a familiar picture of what followed – share prices began to fall and, seeing others incur heavy losses, many pulled out entirely, leading to an increasing spiral of dis-

---

14 Asiento, which comes from the Spanish verb *sentar*, which means 'to sit', can also mean "settlement, establishment" or "consent" in Spanish. It denotes a "contract, trading agreement" in a business setting.
15 For more background on the economic situation of England during the 17th century, see Pohl: "Whilst late feudalism and mercantilism were essentially domestic economies, the late seventeenth century saw the decline of monopolies, of regulations for domestic industries, and the succession of small-scale merchant companies by expanding colonial companies. Scientific and geographical discoveries which in themselves facilitated the acquisitions of new, natural resources, profitable foreign markets, and commercial opportunities such as slave trade and plantations, advanced the development of a successful consumer economy. This development might be seen to culminate in the institution of the Bank of England in 1694 which became symbolic for the shift from a mercantile economy rule by the principle of state regulation and 'balance of payments' to commercial capitalism with no restrictive regulation of domestic industry, growth of competition and a system based on credit. Palladianism in its uniformity and regularity, as Cynthia Wall suggests, became one counterpoint to the social and economic destabilization, especially in London" (Pohl 2017: 8).
16 The prospect of a lucrative outcome for the Company and for the English population did not come out of nowhere. The South Sea Company initially offered an interest rate of as much as six percent to those who bought shares, so there were indeed good reasons from the English people's point of view to invest in the South Sea Company and the slave trade had proven to be lucrative in the past. Under King George, people from all walks of life, whether nobility or farm laborers invested in the Company's shares.

investment, which in turn made share prices plummet even more drastically. Finally, "the South Sea stock fell to such an extent that it ... stood below the value at which most of the government debtholders had converted" (Paul 2011: 50). Even though the Bank of England terminated the contract with the company, share prices recuperated somewhat, only to then ultimately, and lastingly, crash.

It is often believed that this collapse led to one of the largest financial crashes and instabilities of English history, but this is only partially accurate. The factual effects of the crash, and its post hoc narrativization, were not too dissimilar to those of the Tulip Mania in the years between 1634 and February 1637, whose actual impact was convincingly unpacked by Goldgar (2008). Both the South Sea Bubble crash and the Tulip Mania appear to have been overly mystified as immense financial catastrophes, betraying "a gap between rhetoric and the way in which society actually functions" (Paul 2011: 14).

During Haywood's lifetime, there appear to have been many writers who viewed the stock market as unethical and immoral. Moral philosophers, such as Lord Shaftesbury or Francis Hutcheson, were arguing that "stock market gains were ... made at the expense of others (e.g., honest citizens)" (Paul 2001: 13). In many of their treatises, the metaphor of gambling[17] is used as a way of asserting the egotism and ruthlessness seen as inherent in the concept (ibid.). Another frequently condemned aspect of speculation was the untouchability of speculative finance, which subsequently led to comparisons invoking magic, alchemy, and other dark and unholy arts: Gerrard points to Haywood's "analogy between the South Sea Bubble scam and ministerial alchemy," which, in *Memoirs of a Certain Island*, is displayed most directly in the devilishly named necromancer Lucitario, who is identified by King as James Cragg.[18] Almost every citizen suffers under the "infatuation of *Lucitario's* Magick," which he disperses through the omnipresent enchanted well.

The image is openly satirical: Unwittingly, people 'invest' in the well and, having thrown their money into it under false promises of reward, eventually must find ways to recoup their losses (Haywood 1724: 15). In desperation, they often turn to shady means, spinning intrigues or fabricating inheritance swindles. The typology of associating influential ministers with sorcery and evil spells goes

---

[17] Paul points to the eighteenth-century context of terms such as 'gambling', 'risk', and 'rationality'. In terms of gambling, she explains that it could also mean "simply an event with two or more outcomes" or refer to "games of skill" or even just "card games" (Paul 2011: 16).
[18] King, instead of associating Lucitario with Walpole, claims that "Lucitario corresponds far more closely to James Craggs senior, the Postmaster-General whom an authoritative modern account describes as 'the last, and one of the least popular, victims of parliamentary vengeance'" (2012: 36).

back to the seventeenth century and experiences its peak during the time of Queen Anne (cf. Gerrard 2011: 175).[19] Adapting depictions from the seventeenth century of influential men and women as wizards, alchemists or witches was common, although such adaptation was subject to variation. More intangible forms of currencies such as stocks, for instance, were often compared to witchcraft. The painter and pictorial satirist William Hogarth depicts the English as having been influenced by "moneys magick power,"[20] while Haywood warns of new forms of currencies as dangerous alchemy. The people associated with speculation, rather than "being manifestations of powerful malevolent forces, witchcraft and magic came instead to be linked with mundane trickery and deception" (Daniell 2023: 118).[21] Haywood merges both approaches, ostensibly resorting to seventeenth-century descriptions of powerful magic, while deriding those individuals associated with the bursting South Sea Bubble as charlatans – issuing an emphatic warning of, as she envisions it, the future of England's emerging financial system.

3 Memoirs of a Certain Island

3.1 Media History and Patronage

Haywood published the first part of her satirical utopia, *Memoirs of a Certain Island Adjacent to the Kingdom of Utopia*, in September 1724, followed by the second part a year later, in October 1725 (see Carnell 2014: 111). Both parts were published in London, and it is remarked that they were "printed and sold by the booksellers of London and Westminster" (see title page). In a slight deviation from established customs, Haywood does not mention a patron or addressee in either of the two parts. They were published shortly before she returned to acting, when her tragedy "*Frederick, Duke of Brunswick-Lunenburgh* was staged at Lincoln's Inn Fields" (King 2012: 55). Given what we know of eighteenth-century publishing practices, it is plausible that, prior to their publication, the parts either circulated as earlier versions of the prints or were initially released as separate parts.

Even before its official publication, *Memoirs of a Certain Island* caused a stir; especially inside the Hillarian Circle. The cause, as suggested by Gerrard, was a

---

[19] A good example of the amalgamation of magic and philosophy is alchemist and neo-Platonist (after Marsilio Ficino) John Dee.
[20] William Hogarth refers to "moneys magic power" underneath his engraving *The South Sea Scheme*, printed in 1722.
[21] This holds especially true for the changes that came about in 1736, when the new Witchcraft Act eliminated the harsh laws enacted in 1604.

particularly harsh iteration of Haywood's customarily sharp-tongued literary portrayals, this time not directed at a political party or personage, but towards the poet Martha Sansom. Likely aggravating the insult, it is evident that Sansom knew of the defamatory passages prior to the publication of the first part, possibly from other members of the Hillarian Circle (Gerrard 2003: 88). Therein, Haywood portrays her as having had an incestuous relationship with her father. In *Memoirs of a Certain Island*, the disparagingly named character of Gloatitia represents Sansom, who is introduced as the daughter of the Chevalier Del Gloatus. It is from him that she supposedly "learn'd those deluding Arts, she has since practis'd, to the Ruin of as many Women as she could get acquainted with their Lovers or their Husbands" (Haywood 1724: 43). Cupid does add a seeming caution, "whether this Report be true, I will not pretend to determine," but immediately adds "for my pure and hallow'd Fires would sicken at a sight so horrible, so shocking as an Act of Incest" (Haywood 1724: 44). Sansom, in retaliation, famously affords Haywood the moniker "The Scorpion" in her autobiography *Clio* (Sansom 1997). The exact reasons for the conflict are unknown, with most speculations supposing either a clichéd catfight, or Haywood's exasperation with Sansom's straightforwardness when it came to sexuality and/or desire.[22]

While it appears that, considering the grotesques in Pope's *Dunciad*, extravagant literary insults were not uncommon, this does not imply that they were without consequence: Even though the details and interpersonal background of the scandal are still debated, it is certain that *Memoirs of a Certain Island* was the text that disrupted ties not just with Sansom, but with the entire Hillarian circle and, especially, Richard Savage.[23] At the time of the publication of *Memoirs of a Certain Island*, Haywood was no longer officially associated with Aaron Hill or the Hillarians. She was now in a position where it was more difficult to finance her writings or support herself through her acting, and the end of her association with Hill and thereby evidently the patronage of the English aristocrat and writer Lady Mary Wortley Montague,[24] meant yet another loss of security and standing.

In the early eighteenth century, authors did not receive royalties, instead being paid once per manuscript, often necessitating the financial support of a patron. Yet, the fact that "Haywood did not dedicate either of her encrypted secret histories to a potential patron" renders more difficult the task of identifying who financed the two-part work (Carnell 2014: 111). There is, however, one individual whom Haywood might have focused on as financer of her works. In *Memoirs of*

---

22 On her open desire towards Aaron Hill, see Gerrard (2003: 89).
23 *Mr. S—e*, is portrayed as a "duped tool" of Sansom by King (2008: 731).
24 Montagu is mentioned and thanked several times as a patron by members of the Hillarian Circle.

a Certain Island, there is a list of abbreviated names of which many have been reconstructed mostly through the work of Kathryn King, but many remain unsolved. One of the most commonly referred to names in *Memoirs of a Certain Island* is that of the 1st Earl of Orford, First Prime Minister of Britain, Robert Walpole, but commonly referred to through the abbreviated version of his name, Walpole.

Whereas a majority of Haywood scholars subscribe to the notion that Haywood satirizes Walpole in her work, King highlights that Haywood's strikingly reverent eulogy of Walpole as a "Greatly noble Patriot, whose only Care, whose only Aim, is how to serve his Country, shows he despises all those sordid Views by which his Contemporaries are sway'd, looks down on Titles, and chuses to be great in Worth alone" are meant sincerely (Haywood 1724: 277). It is unclear whether Haywood supported Walpole politically, but there are indications that Haywood, just like many other writers at the beginning of the eighteenth century was interested in his patronage. King argues that "her attentiveness to the basic requirements of patronage seeking is neatly illustrated in the way she coordinated her compliments with changes of personnel in the royal household" (King 2012: 38). In the early 1720s, Walpole did not yet possess the almost mythologically powerful status later afforded him but was instead regarded as a connoisseur and appreciator of the liberal arts.[25] Many of her contemporaries also applied for Walpole's patronage, among them Swift, Pope, and Fielding, lending a degree of credibility to the assumption that Haywood may have followed suit.

Throughout her literary life, Haywood experimented with diverse genres and styles, variously directed at different patrons. As I have already suggested, the dichotomous image of "two Haywoods," of Haywood the actress and Haywood the writer, fails to adequately capture her. This is not only because of her interrelated utilization of different media, but because she consistently mixed genres, as she does in *Memoirs of a Certain Island*. This has led to some attempted genre classifications appearing forced, the most frequent misclassification reading the *Memoirs* as a *roman à clef*, potentially due to a perceived similarity to *Memoirs and Manners of Several Persons of Quality, of both Sexes. From the New Atalantis, an Island in the Mediterranean* by Delarivier Manley (1709). However, *Memoirs of a Certain Island* is not, like *New Atalantis*, an exclusively partisan history of scandal, for to classify Haywood's utopia in this way is to lose much of her engagement with the 'ordinary people.' While the first part of *Memoirs of a Certain Island* already concerns itself with people from the lower or middle classes the second part goes far beyond this. According to King, *Memoirs of a Certain Island* has "more in common with the work of Pope and Swift than either of her fellow satirists

---

25 For more on Walpole as a patron, see Mount (2006: 167–184).

cared to admit" (King 2012: 43). As elements of satire, romantic and scandal novel, political commentary, moral philosophy, and theater are all encompassed in *Memoirs of a Certain Island*, it is likely best described as a satirical utopia. As utopian writing bore an intimate relationship to censorship, a practise that was beginning to be relaxed due to the Copyright Act of 1709 called *The Statute of Anne*, this classification should not be understood as unequivocal, but as a reader's aid.

3.2 A Brief Comment from the Editor

Reading Haywood's *Memoirs of a Certain Island* comes with an immense number of prerequisites. It is not an easy work to read – or to edit. This is not intended to oversell the editors' work, but to act as a potentially useful guide: The text features over 16 stories, which are often long and, given the frequency of repetitions, may even appear mildly tedious at times. It introduces almost 100 different characters, some of whom are modelled after Haywood's contemporaries, while others are likely purely fictitious. Oftentimes, the stories' highly dramatized form and salacious details may appear overly pontifical. However, in case one gets lost in Haywood's world and prose, we are reminded of the potential reward by philosopher Daniel-Pascal Zorn, who writes that "those who have understood the problem of a philosopher can understand why [their] work often follows the tortuous paths that seem so incomprehensible to us at first glance" (2018: 39).[26] There are, then, those tools and pieces of advice that can render this path less tortuous when retracing *Memoirs of a Certain Island*: As a work by a writer not exclusively known for novels but for her stage plays, it is best read out loud. Imagine it being intoned in a salon, in front of a small audience not entirely unlike those that Haywood would have come to customarily address as an actress. In this way one can let the lyrical qualities of the text shine more truly, and vastly improve its understanding. To aid the process of compiling this edition, I have recorded the text for myself as an audiobook, which drastically changed my perception of it. Despite reoccurring observations of the "death of rhetoric" in the eighteenth century, this cannot be said about Haywood's utopian satire – like ancient rhetoric, it was shaped by the stage, and this is where it attains its full oratorial force.

The similarity runs deeper than the ideal setting for a reading, however. Studying *Memoirs of a Certain Island* through the lens of rhetoric highlights its careful

---

[26] "Wer das Problem eines Philosophen verstanden hat, kann nachvollziehen, warum sein Werk oft die verschlungenen Wege geht, die uns auf den ersten Blick so unverständlich scheinen" (translated by the author).

construction, including but not limited to the theatrical frame of the text, its initial and final chapters. While it must not be applied as a strict analytical mould into which to press the *Memoirs*, rhetoric can offer a vantage point from which to approach the arguments developed in the text. Arriving on a certain island, guided by Cupid's foreword, we can easily recognize elements reflecting the *exordium* in classical rhetoric: The scene is set, the problem introduced, and the immediate condemnation of greed and avarice offers more than a hint of the judgement to come. In Haywood's – or rather Cupid's – multifaceted 'narrations,' then, we may come across recurring themes and *topoi*, which are dramatized through distinctly varied settings, illustrating at the very least that the dichotomies of base or noble passion, love, and wild desire, and *communitas* or selfishness, apply not to a select few, but to all, bringing reward or ruin in turn. When these stories come to a close, the two founding forces of the island, its divine patron and its exiled King of the Isle, begin their deliberative dialogue of the island's fate, the vices and virtues of its citizenry, and the source of its ruin. And when they finally settle their dispute, with judgement rendered with wand and sword, the *topoi* developed in the many stories told before converge in a resounding conclusion to the argument.

3.3 Summary

The full title of both parts, *Memoirs of a Certain Island Adjacent to the Kingdom of Utopia*, can already be taken as a guide for what is to follow. The first part of the titles invokes a temporal reference to the inner past of the text, being a memoir, but the novel's geographical locus is, at first, less evident. We set foot on a "certain island" which remains undefined beyond its proximity to another, slightly more familiar island. Through this proximity, it supplies a crucial piece of information, immediately laying bare what the place is not: It is not "Utopia," it is not a "no-place" or a "good place," at least not currently. However, its adjacency not only prepends that the two islands are non-identical but represents a relational linkage between them. The island is thus inherently related to the Kingdom of Utopia.

While the title simultaneously remains specific and vague, it shows knowledge of 'utopian conceptions.' Haywood implements an interesting twist to utopian writing, as the reader never learns how the supposed protagonist, the noble youth, arrives on the island. The only known aspect of their travels is the aim of "pleasure and improvement" (Haywood 1724: 1). In other utopian texts, such as Tommaso Campanella's *La Citta del Sole* (1602), in which "he organizes a model of mutual accomplishment" (Hagengruber 2020: 49) for both men and women, or Margaret

Cavendish's *The Blazing World* (1666),²⁷ the path to the place far away is a significant part of the plot. Simultaneously, *Memoirs of a Certain Island* operates on two timelines. The first, mirroring the South Sea crash and its consequences is synchronous with Haywood's own time, while the second one is located in the distant past, to which Cupid nostalgically refers.²⁸

The text begins with a description of the locale, which is framed in a mythological setting typical for "fictional speech."²⁹ The "noble youth" reaches an island that they, with admiring eyes, perceive as an island of science near perfection, undisturbed by "stormy tongues of faction" (Haywood 1724: 2). Almost immediately, the youth casts eyes on the deity Cupid who, leaning more towards the classical Greek than later cherubic depictions, is described as a small, angelic boy. After being admired by the youth, Cupid compares him to the citizens of the island and decides that the latter are much less noble. The islanders, Cupid charges, have ceased all admiration and celebration of his divinity, and instead worship a false God, a demon who has usurped the role of Cupid. The island, the reader now learns, is not the perfect image of utopia, as that one is long gone. In accordance with the function of an *exordium*, Cupid appeals to the reader by telling them right at the beginning how depraved the islanders now are and how virtuous they were in the past. Here his role as a chronologist of the island initially becomes evident, with his view of the island spanning past, present, and future. Once, at Cupid's behest, the people were blessed by the most important deities:

> *Mars* gave them Courage to subdue their foreign Foes! *Minerva* Wisdom, to discover and circumvent home-bred Conspiracies! *Bacchus* enriched their Vintage! *Ceres* bless'd their Harvest! *Venus* gave Beauty to their Nymphs, and my Companion *Honour* influenced their Swains! *Hymen* assisted at their Marriages! Even *Jupiter*, and the Ocean's God heard my Entreaty. (Haywood 1724: 4)

One could hardly imagine a more extensively blessed populace: courageous and astute, well-nourished, fertile, honorable, and devoted, with most of the pantheon extending their favors. But despite all the gifts bestowed upon them, the islanders have given in to corruption. From the outside, their home might yet look enchanting, sublime even, if one were to believe the erstwhile impression shared by the noble youth. But while it once possessed divine protection and military strength,

---

27 In Cavendish's case, for instance, the Empress of the Isle is kidnapped by "a merchant travelling into a foreign country". See Cavendish (1666: 125).
28 Reminiscent of Plato's *Symposium*, there is a diegetic distance from the events significant to the work, realized as a retelling (in terms of the *Symposium*: after the drinking bout).
29 Fictional speech (in German *behauptende Rede*) is one method of contextual strategic mediation often used in philosophical texts.

all that remains now are false statues and vices, rampant "wild desires, impatiencies and perplexities" (Haywood 1724: 30).

The cause of the corruption, and a core element of *Memoirs of a Certain Island*, is introduced next: "[T]hey [now] endeavour not to merit, but to obtain." Greed, be it financial or sexual, has corrupted the island throughout and placed avarice at its heart. To open the youths' eyes to the island's moral decline, Cupid ushers them to the heart of the island, revealing the central image of the narrative: the enchanted well. It is guarded by two grand statues, depicting Pecunia, goddess of interest, and Fortuna, goddess of luck and fortune. The surrounding statues show that moral corruption penetrates the entire *société d'ordres*. Dukes, Madams, Duchesses, Counts, Chevaliers, and Marchionesses – no one escapes the seduction of this bottomless pit.

The well, the noble youth learns, was first discovered by a necromancer bearing the name Lucitario. Closely working with the sovereign of the island, Lucitario spread the myth that whoever casts money into the well will multiply their fortune – symbolizing investment and the promise of profit. The only ones profiting from this scheme are, of course, Lucitario and the sovereign.

Having established the scene surrounding the enchanted well, Cupid, the personified narrator of *Memoirs of a Certain Island*, begins to tell the story of the islanders. He explains how they lost not only their wealth, but their morality and principles to the well, stressing the extent of their decline. Thus, reminiscent of the *narratio*'s inherent perspectivity, the stories function as a partial description of a situation, they are distinctly told from Cupid's perspective – and readers can only rely on his claim to truth. Personifying their interjections, the Noble Youth occasionally asks questions and comments on the stories. Cupid's *narratio* begins with Graciana, a wealthy islander about to marry Romanus, a young utopian in exile. The young utopian quickly reveals his ambitions, gaining access to the senate by using Graciana's father, a leading senator, who dies shortly before his daughter's wedding. Cupid attempts to prevent a marriage contract – without success. Romanus, realizing that he no longer has any advantages from marrying Graciana but that he signed the contract, drafts an escape plan. He meets with Graciana, attempts to seduce her, fails, and instead rapes her, and subsequently forces her to move into private lodgings. From within these lodgings, she is instructed to write letters to a Cheavlier D'Eshart, so that it would appear she was having an affair with another man. This fabricated scandal allows for the dissolution of the marriage contract. Graciana repeatedly attempts suicide, but is protected through divine intervention, as the gods are convinced that her destiny is not yet fulfilled. The Noble Youth interrupts Cupid at this point, asking why Romanus was not punished for his foul deeds. Cupid answers that "his time of Punishment is not yet arriv'd; and tho' that which I have related (monstrous as it is) is not the greatest of his Crimes, he is allow'd to continue in them" (Haywood 1724: 19).

Most stories[30] follow this or a similar structure: An individual, sometimes a man sometimes a woman, already starts out as being a morally questionable person. They are greedy, perverted, superficial, vain and if they are not, then they marry someone who is. Usually, the life of the person spirals downwards quickly, especially once they are in any way involved with an investor, or an acquaintance of Lucitario. In the end, they often fall ill, die, or lose their loved ones, but do not blame themselves for their own failures, but love. "For," Cupid cries out, "among all these monstrous Passions, there is not one who lays not all the blame of their Mismanagement on Love" (Haywood 1724: 198). Again, approaching the text through a rhetorical lens can help identify its structures. As it is the main aim of the *narratio* to benefit and prepare the case to be made in the argument, Cupid's reference to a false or bad love (or use of it) can be read as preparing the argument to follow.

Once Cupid ends his last tale, the tragedy of the young Martasinda, the novel enters one of its most critical acts, developing the argumentation in a godly dispute. Just as the noble youth sets out to reply to Cupid's last story, both are interrupted by a "Mist so thick, it darken'd all the Air" (Haywood 1724: 272). The cloud is accompanied by a light so radiant that "even the bright Glories which darted from the God of Love, were for a while obscur'd" (Haywood 1724: 272). This sublime appearance initiates the first part of the 'spirit exorcism' when the false Cupid, the "hideous Phantom flew, and in a distant Chasm, beyond the ken of mortal Sight, conceal'd his horrid Shape" (Haywood 1724: 273). Instead of the daemon, the "Genius of the Isle" appears, later revealed as the King of the Isle, supported by Astrea, goddess of justice, and Reason. Reminiscent of the popular folklore motif represented in Arthurian legend, and the Kyffhäuser tale, in which Emperor Barbarossa descends from the mountain, the Genius of the Isle returns to retake his crown. The King of the Isle who, as the reader learns, did not leave by his own volition but was exiled, is now presented with two gifts. Astrea bestows upon him a Sword to destroy the false idols erected by the islanders, and the Wand of Truth is given to him by Reason.

Once the two deities leave, the King of the Isle and Cupid begin their dialogue, which is structured in such a way that one might easily imagine it being set on stage. The Noble Youth does not partake in their exchange, only listening and looking on in awe. Cupid no longer appears as a gentle god or patient guide, but his

---

30 The focus here will not be on the individual stories and their historical reference points. This is important work which others have already done very thoroughly. See King (2012) and Paul (2023).

"sparkling Eyes sho[o]t Beams of angry Fire" (Haywood 1724: 275), as he chastises the King of the Isle for having abandoned his people. Cupid charges:

> The Name of Cupid is despise'd, and Lust and Avarice, those undoing Harpys, honour'd and rever'd by one, the innocent and unwary Virgin is seduced; by the other, the experienced Matron is betray'd to a forgetfulness of her first Vows, and yields herself a Prey to mercenary Slavery. Even Nature is depress'd by these two Fiends, and has no more the power to operate. Where sordid Interest points the means of Gain, or Passion actuates the tempestuous Will, Sons against Fathers rise, Fathers renounce the Babes they lately blest; Brother with Brother vies with inveterate Strife. The Power of Blood and Kin, all Alliances, all Ties of Relative, or Obligations lose their force; their Desires self-centred, aim only at self-service, let 'em then enjoy it, 'till Fate and Jupiter shall, by the glare of some unlock'd-for Woes, force them at once to see their Crime and Punishment. (Haywood 1724: 274)

Cupid's bleak image of decay concerns both women and men, and even nature is afflicted. Driven by interest and base passions, discord and ruin pervade the island. Divine retribution is sure to follow, affecting everyone, be it man, woman or child. In this example, the lack of earthly justice is especially striking, a recurring element of Haywood's critique. As a writer who deliberately employed scandalous elements in her work, she was acutely aware that many scandals never reach the public eye, especially those involving influential figures. Her image of the decline of English society, with party politics sowing division, culminating in a state of civil war, is a sentiment previously expressed by "[Thomas] Hobbes and [William] Temple in the seventeenth century, [as] many in the eighteenth-century associated party conflict with civil war" (Skjönsberg 2021: 27).

The King of the Isle confirms the suspicion that once love is gone, all vices, "Lust and Avarice" first and foremost, come to the fore. Realizing the island's dire future, he begs Cupid for forgiveness, while accepting that justice must be done. Ending on a hopeful note, he asks that love return once punishment is dealt (Haywood 1724: 275). He underlines this plea by proclaiming that not all citizens are afflicted by the lure of the well, and that there are still those of virtue among the islanders. For instance, there is Cleomenes, "[t]hat greatly noble Patriot" (Haywood 1724: 277) whom King has identified as Walpole, or Nelsus, who is "bred up to Arts and Sciences" (Haywood 1724: 278) but also knowledgeable in warfare and military matters. He is not self-centered, as his priorities are to give to others. The King of the Isle, humbled by Cupid's judgement, sets out to redeem both himself, and those islanders still worthy of divine support. Following his speech on the good citizens of the isle, he destroys the false statues and the enchanted well and thus completes the second act of the 'spirit exorcism'.

Its final act begins after the end of Cupid's speech, and thus near the end of *Memoirs of a Certain Island*. After the destruction of the well, all citizens wake up from their collective enchantment to realise their dual folly – not only have they fallen prey to Lucitario's scam but have fooled themselves by not seeing the enchanted well for what it is, namely, a simple, common well. Their reactions to this uncomfortable realization differ. Those who have lost everything are described as follows:

> [N]o dependance, no hope of Support, or even Sustenance for themselves and miserable Families .... What was now the Estate of these unhappy Wretches! How truly dreadful their Condition! Long beguil'd with pleasing Dreams of coming Happiness, Prosperity, Plenty, to be waked at once to such a Certainty of Penury, Disgrace, and all the Miseries which make consummate Ruin. To have no hope, no expectation left, and to know that they had lost all this by an Infatuation .... [W]ith Guilt and Shame opprest, with Fear and Wonder stupified, they stood as riveted in Earth, and seem'd so many Monuments of Misery, known but by their horror-darting Eyes to have any Remains of Life. (Haywood 1724: 285)

The citizens who lost a considerable sum but are still wealthy are less bothered: "[T]he young gay Coquette, tho' she lost great part of her Pertness, still flirted her Fan, and perhaps affected more than felt a real Terror. The well-dress'd powder'd Beau, shaking back his Ruffle, and gently rapping with his ring'd Fingers his Snuff-Box-Lid, cry'd, Gad, tis wondrous strange!" The King of the Isle, in turn, discounts their affectations: "They are a sort of Butterfly; pretty, little, unhurtful, insipid Insects, who when they have play'd away their Season here, are translated into some other World to buzz about, incapable of meriting either Heaven or Hell" (Haywood 1724: 286).

Cupid executes an important differentiation here. Those who have lost everything are ready to repent, while those able to continue their decadence merely "*affected more than felt a real terror*" (Keating 2015: 58f.; Haywood 1724: 286), unable or to unwilling to redeem themselves in the face of divine justice. They do not care, as they can continue their lives as they did before.

These cases, and the stories told by Cupid, are thus examples for the larger criticism developed in the utopian work. Having finished his work and acknowledging the strenuous and overwhelming nature of a discussion between two (almost) godly characters, Cupid lulls the Noble Youth into a deep slumber, marking the end of the first volume, the second thus beginning with the youth waking up refreshed and prepared not merely for new adventures, but also to continue the old ones.

4 Haywood's Philosophical Method(s)

The South Sea Scheme, the political scandals, the intrigues, and the debate about the goodness or evil of party politics, all taken together provide the context of Haywood's writing. They are the political themes of *Memoirs of a Certain Island*, and they are precisely rooted in eighteenth-century discourse. However, there is another level to understanding her writing, one less concerned with specific themes, but with 'how' she writes about them. The 'how,' or method, becomes important when considering that even though censorship had officially been minimized, if not altogether abandoned, with the introduction of *The Statute of Anne*, Haywood's arrest in 1750 shows that caution was still advisable. This is one of the reasons why the gist of Haywood's argument is veiled across almost 300 pages (or, if counting both parts together, 600 pages), much less likely to have been thoroughly examined for seditious or otherwise inflammatory sentiment. In a method common to those seeking to avoid danger, she uses her knowledge of theatrical play[31] and rhetoric, which are of course already intertwined, and stages a specific setting interwoven with mythological compounds, humor, and eroticism.[32] This knowledge is applied precisely in these philosophical or philosophically adjacent methods that I call 'the sublime,' 'the passions,' and 'the divine historian.'

4.1 The Hillarian Circle and Sublimity

> "o'er our Souls the Lov'd Hillarius reigns" (Haywood 1726: 41)

As has been established, Haywood was a well-connected writer and actress. As such, she was surrounded by people who inspired her, offered discussion, and introduced her to various philosophical possibilities. Not only is she methodologically informed by early eighteenth-century academic philosophers, but one need not look very far outside her immediate biographical context to find that she was heavily influenced by her lettered friends within the Hillarian Circle.[33]

---

[31] For a thorough analysis of the influences of theatrical performance in Haywood's texts, see Howard (2015).

[32] This leads to, in part, absurd conversations between the introduced citizens, such as the story of Wyaria, in which she exclaims "Oh! I have the Cramp ... in the upper part of my Thigh; I cannot bear the Torment; chase it with your warm Hand, for Heaven's sake" (Haywood 1726: 74).

[33] "The Hillarian circle primarily provided a meeting point for literary friendships, support, discussion, and the incessant circulation of poetic manuscripts" (Gerrard 2003: 76).

While *Memoirs of a Certain Island* was published shortly after Haywood cut ties with the group that centered around Aaron Hill, she had been influenced by the formative exchanges of ideas offered by meetings of the Hillarian Circle, and the close friendships she entertained for years with some of its members. King emphasizes that her "hope is that makers of new biographical narratives, whatever direction their own desires and guesswork may take them, will at least attend more closely to the Hillarian context of her early career" (King 2012: 739). Seemingly following King's plea, recent scholars such as Genevieve Howard have been more attentive to Haywood's intimate connection with the circle and have therein enabled current interpretations of her work to move into a much more informed and comprehensive direction.

The Hillarian Circle or Group was first and foremost a project of its founder, Aaron Hill (1685–1750), who was already well known for being simultaneously involved in a multitude of projects, such as managing the Theatre Royal, Drury Lane, and founding the periodical *The Plain Dealer*. Despite its relatively short life, the Circle proved to be one of his most successful projects. It served much like a salon, allowing writers, mathematicians, poets, and actors to meet and exchange ideas. For many of them, it further served as a stepping stone to the publication of their works. It was intrinsically designed as "one of the few centres of coterie writing within a dominant print culture in London" and, highly encouraged by Hill, promoted "collaborative authorship" in which thinkers would work and write as a collective (Gerrard 2003: 74).

After deciding against acting as a primary profession, Haywood entered the literary circle around 1719 (King 2005: 263). Group membership fluctuated, but a number of principle figures can be identified. Among these was poet and Jacobite Richard Savage, who had a strong literary connection not only with Haywood, but with poet and Catholic Martha Sansom, with whom he published works together. Sansom, conversely, enjoyed an intensive, but not necessarily friendly relationship with Haywood, punctuated by a final falling out prior to the publication of *Memoirs of a Certain Island*. There was also Scottish poet and professor of mathematics Walter Bowman, who acted as a mathematical tutor to Hill, and a cherished sparring partner for Haywood, leaving her to complain about her lack of learnedness in comparison to his 'genius.' Scottish poet and dramatist David Mallet in turn brought along Whig politician James Thomson, as well as a number of theater figures such as a "'Mr. Fielding (probably the actor, not the playwright)" (King 2012: 59). Omnipresent throughout the lifespan of the Circle were numerous writing women such as the wife of Aaron Hill, Margaret ('Miranda'), and others who used pseudonyms such as 'Daphne,' 'Evandra,' 'Aurelia,' and 'Ophelia' (Gerrard 2003: 75). The omnipresence of women was marked by another social factor which set it apart from the mostly male-connotated coffeehouses. The Hillarians are described as a group of "tea-drinkers," a practice more closely associated with women during the end of the seventeenth and beginning of the eighteenth centuries (see Ellis 2019). They did not principally describe themselves as philosophers, preferring to style themselves as a literary circle. What brought the diverse group together was their interest in engaging in debates as a form of philosophical exercise, be it in oral or literary form. In this, their meetings are not too different from the more 'academic' realm of eighteenth-century philosophy. They would frequently comment on current events, building on socially or politically significant incidents to develop philosophical problems and thought experiments. Those problems frequently related to social affairs, such as the role of women in marriage, or friendship between men and women (see Howard 2015).

One of the most central aspects of their meetings, however, was to ask themselves: What makes an effective text and, specifically, great poetry?[34] They found their answer in a concept "often discussed ... in philosophical aesthetics, literary theory, and art history," in the sublime or, more specifically, the Longinian sublime (Doran 2015: 1). In rhetoric, the sublime, or *genus sublime*, is the highest level of a stylistic form to arouse strong emotions, or pathos. More specifically, the Longinian sublime, named after the assumed author of a Roman-era Greek work of literary criticism, Cassius Longinus, can be achieved with "great thoughts, strong emotions, certain figures of thought and speech, noble diction, and dignified word arrangement" (Leitch 2001: 136). A good text, here, is predicated on the idea that experience – intense, visceral, and sensory experience – is the foundation upon which language can be used to construct works of art and/or powerful writing. Confronted with nature in its splendour or austerity, like looking on a vast mountain, the observer may be struck with awe, feeling immensely powerful and vanishingly small at the same time. The sublime as a literary concept precisely describes this mixture of being "*overwhelmed* or *overawed*" and "*exalted* or *elevated*" (Doran 2015: 4).

The Longinian sublime was "the dominant affective theory of the early eighteenth century" (Tierney-Hynes 2010: 159), which eighteenth-century philosophers and writers merged with the dominant eighteenth-century theory of emotions or, as they were called, passions. Aaron Hill and David Mallet both claimed that the sublime could be invoked most effectively in the form of poetry, awing the reader into feeling momentous and insignificant at the same time, enabling a self-detached immediacy. Haywood diverged from Mallet and Hill in terms of which literary form would be most adept at invoking passionate imme-

---

[34] See, for example, Behn in her *Love-Letters between a Nobleman and His Sister* (1684).

diacy, and instead experimented with the sublimity of passions in her satirical utopian prose (Ashfield and de Bolla 1998: 11).³⁵ In *Memoirs of a Certain Island*, the *genus sublime* is used methodically, to invoke immediacy in the reader in order to draw their attention to her philosophical problem. As a method of aesthetic writing, when applied successfully, the sublime is innately critical precisely because it denies self-importance in favor of a sharpened focus. To borrow from Descartes, the passions function like a magnifying glass, which "cause the goods they represent, as well as the evils, to appear much greater and more important than they are" (Descartes 1649: 138). An example of how the sublime denies self-importance is the presentation of a woman who accommodates Duke de Conbree, after he had lost everything to the enchanted well. After providing him with a roof and by urging him to take back the money he once gave to her, she explains:

> When you bestow'd on me (said she) this lavish Testimony of your Love, I accepted it with an infinity of pleasure, because I knew such Offerings come not but from the Heart! by that I found your Passion; but in restoring it, I have an opportunity of proving the Sublimity of mine: To have it in my power to contribute anything to your Consolation in an Exigence like this, gives me a Transport which Words cannot reveal. (Haywood 1724: 10)

The woman in this example is the opposite of self-centered, so much that she is proclaimed an "Example of Piety" (ibid.). She frugally kept all the money that he had previously given to her and can now prove her own gentle goodness, her own sublimity. She has been moved by his passion, which invoked that sublimity. Here, Haywood is consistent with Longinus who, in the last part of *On Sublimity*, writes: "I would affirm with confidence that there is no tone so lofty as that of genuine passion, in its right place, when it bursts out in a wild gust of mad enthusiasm and as it were fills the speaker's words with frenzy" (Roberts 1899: 59). In order to understand how the passions can invoke sublimity, the passions themselves must be understood from an early eighteenth-century perspective.

---

35 Haywood often describes sublimity by using body-oriented words such as "blood, veins, atoms, hearts, breasts, and eyes" and combining them with the "language of floods, storms, and flames" (Wilputte 2014: 191).

4.2 Desire and Haywood's Contemporaries

> If thou findest any thing wanting, I shall be glad, that what I have writ gives thee any desire, that I should have gone farther. (Locke 1689, *Epistle to the Reader*).

The passions, as used in the eighteenth century, roughly translate to what we today describe as emotions, while the term originally derives from a common Latin translation of the Greek word *pathos*.[36] While the term is prevalent throughout history, it does not necessarily always translate to the same use, or to a fixed, singular understanding as 'the' passions. There is a continuum, however, in the question of how passions can be understood, categorized, in decoding their effects on human beings.

During Haywood's lifetime, the term had gained renewed popularity through the works of seventeenth-century philosophers, who had attempted to classify the passions.[37] They therein referred back to Aristotle's identification of 11 passions. He differentiated between good and bad passions, also called the "concupiscible passions," and the "irascible passions," which only arise "when we face impediment or difficulty" (Schmitter 2023: 199). By writing about the passions, Haywood is thus firmly interwoven with the fabric of early eighteenth-century philosophy, as well as that of the seventeenth century (Schmitter 2023: 199). Robert Burton's *Anatomy of Melancholy* (1628), Descartes' *Passions of the Soul* (1646), John Locke's *Essay Concerning Human Understanding* (1690), Bernard Mandeville's *Fable of the Bees* (1714), Hutcheson's *Essay on the Nature and Conduct of the Passions and Affections* (1742), Hume's *Of the Delicacy of Taste and Passion* (1741, 1777) and, lastly, Adam Smith's *The Theory of Moral Sentiments* (1759) show a heightened interest in the passions. Women philosophers such as Mary Astell used the passions in her *Serious Proposal to the Ladies* (1694) to argue in favor of female education, while writer Madeleine de Scudéry argued in *Célinte* (1661) and *Mathilde d'Aguilar* (1667) "that women as well as men can cultivate the full range of moral virtues" (Conley 2022).

When Haywood writes of the "soft Sublimity of passions," she simultaneously presents herself as an early eighteenth-century adept of the discourse about the concept of sublimity and of the passions. Her reference to "soft Sublimity," for instance, marks the exact opposite of the forceful invocation of certain passions as it instead gently "overawes" (Doran 2015: 4). Here, her approach again resembles

---

[36] For a contemporary study on emotions and passions, see, for instance, Schnell (2021).
[37] Schmitter refers to this process as a taxonomy of passions and explains that for seventeenth-century authors, one of the goals was to list as many passions as possible (2023: 198).

that of Descartes, who argues that, in the list of passions, wonder (or, in Haywood's case, the sublime) has to be the first, as it sparks interest and leads to knowledge. Passions, for Haywood, can be good or bad, not exclusively but primarily depending on how they are being used. If used for good, it can even "bear ... down all the Bars of Bleed and Kin!" (Haywood 1724: 231). At least to a certain extent, she echoes Descartes in his *Passions of the Soul* (1646), in which he argues that almost all passions are in fact good, especially if a person learns to control them. He sets up three conditions according to which this is possible: 1. Make use of your own spirit to know how to act in life; 2. Have a firm and constant resolution to carry out whatever reason recommends without being diverted by passion or appetite; 3. Assure yourself that the good that you do not possess may be beyond your reach. In opposition to his earlier works, in *Passions of the Soul* Descartes no longer considered the passions simple 'perturbations of the soul' but finds them to be useful in creating continuity of thought, but only if they do not exceed reason. While Haywood and Descartes distinguish between good and bad passions, they differ in that the latter finds that "ideal behaviour is that in which the power of the passions is accompanied by a superior strengthening of the I and of rationality" (230), while Haywood believes that the "power of the passions" (Schmitter 2023: 199) unfolds when directed towards community. Here, Haywood is more closely aligned with what Hobbes refers to as "sociable other-directed passions" (ibid.).

What Haywood and Descartes again have in common is that they both agree that the *Terzium* of good passions is that they lead to morally correct behavior. One example of how controlling passions, despite acknowledging "how difficult it is to clearly delineate the passions' influence over us and to assess their merit in making us who we are," can lead to morally correct behavior is carried out in Haywood's preoccupation with desire (Wilputte 2014: 29). Desire is one of the central passions Haywood unravels in *Memoirs of a Certain Island*, very much befitting her reputation as a writer of scandalous fiction.

Desire is one of the oldest classified passions and counts amongst the "four basic passions" as named by Cicero in his *Tusculan Disputations* (ca. 45 BC); it is similarly found among Aristotle's 11 passions. In Locke's *Essay Concerning Human Understanding* (1690), desire is principally something that a person wants or strives towards, so much so that Locke uses "desire" interchangeably with "want" (Locke 1689: d1). Later, at the beginning of the eighteenth century, Hutcheson builds upon Cicero's classifications and adds the following: "[S]uch as pursue some apparent good ... [as] passionate Desire or Cupidity, such as tend to ward off evil ... as Fears or Anger, such as arise upon obtaining what was desired or escaping evil, are turbulent Joys ..." (Hutcheson 2007: 30). Note how the vocabulary in this short excerpt resembles the language used by Haywood, invoking desire, cupidity, and turbulence. Whereas Hutcheson ascribes goodness to the passion of desire, Haywood differentiates between different forms of desire and argues that they are not all, in fact, good.

Her first argument is thus that bad desires lead to bad actions or to no actions at all. In *Memoirs of a Certain Island*, potentially the most evident example of immorality or how bad desire leads to bad actions is Romanus' desire to seize Miranda's finances after he is fatally denounced to the sovereign. Romanus is "possessed of desires" to such an extent he becomes completely subject to their wants and someone who "has not a Soul capable of being touch'd by love" (Haywood 1724: 19). As Miranda, albeit being described as "pure, and untainted, either with the fashionable Vices of the Age, or the common Frailties of her Sex," would probably not have freely given them to him, he "hides his passions" and plans an infiltration of her heart through a pretend friendship (Haywood 1724: 23). He isolates her from her friends and family, writes her love letters and, in one of the bleakest scenes, finally rapes her. Here, rape as a form of "wild desire" or "lust," which draws inspiration from the false demon, is directly linked with financial greed (Diamond 2017: 47f.). Possessive, selfish lust thus consistently goes hand in hand with a critique of financial exploitation. The breach of trust by her supposed friend puts Miranda into a deep melancholy from which she never recovers, while Romanus enriches himself with her finances.[38]

While the people acting according to bad passions are described as inspired by Cupid's demonic impersonator, Lust, the good passions which invoke good actions are exclusively ascribed to Cupid himself. In this, they resemble the "symbolic dichotomy between a heavenly Cupid, seeking divine contemplation, and an earthly one, beholden to sexuality" in Plato's *Symposion* (Grafton 2013: 246). For many ancient poets, Cupid was described as "sweet-bitter," *glukupikros*, unifying both the heavenly and the earthly parts of love (Grafton 2013: 246). In *Memoirs of a Certain Island*, Cupid is split apart between the deity of love and the lustful demon, demonstrating how the passions are as multifaceted as the actions that follow from them.

---

38 While with the example of Romanus the outcome is clearly that of bad actions, no actions at all are also presented negatively. Some of these consequences are illustrated in the example of Duke de Conbree, whose desire was to become rich, but instead lost all his belongings to Lucitario and now has to accept the self-sacrificial savings of a much less well-off woman. Haywood writes that "being rather of a Temper more inclined to Indolence than too much Activity, he forbore any Endeavours either to redress, or revenge those Wrongs, he now, too late, perceiv'd he had sustain'd" (Haywood 1724: 9). De Conbree, being close to Lucitario and the sovereign, had the chance to discover the true nature of the well, but through his inactivity all that remains are "Shame, Disgrace, Remorse, and late Repentance and Despair" from which follows the exploitation (albeit graciously given) of the woman. Instead of "Innocence, Virtue, Constancy," "wild Desires" are thus being followed by "Shame, Disgrace, Remorse, and late Repentance and Despair".

Conversely, the "sweet," good, or noble desires, are those that are "mutual desires," which are simultaneously shared and therein concordant (Haywood 1724: 16). Often, those forms of love are described in terms of what they are not. They are not "selfish" and not full of "ungovernable Heats, Impatiencies, Deceits" (Haywood 1724: 266). In their function, they resemble "sociable other-directed passions" as described by Hobbes (Schmitter 2023, 199). In what follows, I want to look at them a bit closer, as they are directly linked to Haywood's proposed alternative.

What, then, is good desire according to *Memoirs of a Certain Island*? There are two forms of love, which are described as good: 1. love that is constant, and 2. love that is other-directed and charitable.

4.3 Love as a Historical Constant: The Divine Historian

In her employment of the interwoven conceptual tools of sublimity and passion, Haywood demonstrates her familiarity with philosophical discourses of her time, as well as her aptitude at crafting an allegorical social critique[39] that is simultaneously passionate and delicate in its distinctions. Illustrating these first major theoretical and methodical aspects of her work, however, retains a strong relationship to the thematic layer: mores and morals, and their critique. However, in spirit with the professed Hillarian aim of writing impactfully, it is clearly necessary to study how Haywood employs the art of doing exactly that, meaning her use of rhetoric, and to thus examine the rhetorical structure of her work.

While the *narratio* functions as part of the rhetorical frame of *Memoirs of a Certain Island*, it also helps Haywood – on a performative level – to formulate her social critique. "Instead of conveying knowledge," Franklin Ankersmit illustrates, "the historical *narratio* is essentially a proposal to look at the past from a certain point of view" (Ankersmit 1989: 57). The "historical narratio" is significant insofar as both terms, 'history' and 'narratio', are linked by the adaption of the Greek word 'historia' into classical Latin, which has been translated as 'story' or 'narrative'. Therein, "historical narratio" specifically points to a fabricated story of the past, and this is at the core of Haywood's approach. She does not offer, or profess to offer, an 'accurate' retelling of the financial crash that followed the South Sea speculation, but she brings forth a point of view of the crash. She does not try to depict intrigues in a manner that is as close to the truth as possible, but creates fabrications, or deliberately distorted reflections of true events. *Mem-*

---

[39] See, for instance, "The Great and Powerful are never at a loss for Friends to second any Request they shall make" Haywood (1724: 153).

oirs of a Certain Island is an expression of Haywood's time, but it also mirrors it in a manner that is not passively reflective. Instead, that reflection follows and embodies the exact light of her argument. In the words of Tierney-Hynes, Haywood's use of *narratio* "functions as a forum for … explications of philosophical ideas" (Tierney-Hynes 2010: 155), as she not only writes about a certain historical event, but she is performatively, within her text, actively thinking about history. In this way, she herself takes up the role of a historian of philosophy, something that Carnell identifies as a "secret historian," which she defines as "the tendency to reveal the secrets of public figures while concealing the author's own political position and the tendency to muse self-reflectively about the author's own role as a writer of history in relationship to other writers of history" (Carnell 2014: 102).

Haywood's philosophical method thus offers a perspective but remains enclosed in itself. She does not make a claim for truth, but critiques the current situation, reflecting on her own position in it and, in the end, offering an alternative but, by no means, a solution. The draft of her alternative is self-contained, as all possible conclusions drawn from *Memoirs of a Certain Island* remain with the reader, who is personified in the form of the observant – and largely silent – Noble Youth.[40]

In *Memoirs of a Certain Island*, the mantle of the historian is taken up by part-time narrator and outcast deity, Cupid. The god of love and erotic attraction has many other names in the text, one being that of a "Divine Historian" (Haywood 1724: 19). The most obvious reason for this title might be that Cupid is "a Historian" because he tells "tales of amorous intrigue" that, made clear by the use of "tale" are fabrications laced with occasional truth (Diamond 2017: 51). There is another level to Cupid, however, which is that by being this divine historian the deity shows and simultaneously embodies love as a historical constant.

The constancy is shown not by Cupid himself, but by the King of the Isle. He starts by saying that "true is the Suggestion of Humanity, that Love, of all the Gods, once injur'd, is with most difficulty persuaded to forgiveness" (Haywood 1724: 274). What then follows though, is a reminder of love's persistence, historicity, but also her task: "[Y]et was this Isle once thy chief Residence, thy darling Spot of Earth; not thy fair Mother, all-charming Venus, took more delight in the blest Cyprian Shades, than thou hast done in these refreshing Groves." In philosophizing about the role of Cupid in history, Cupid becomes a historian precisely because he thinks of past, present and future together as one. He can philosophize about history only because he simultaneously travels across all three timelines of past, present, future.

---

[40] For example, during the dialogue of Cupid and the King of the Isle, the Noble Youth does not speak a single word and just observes the godly spectacle.

As love is argued as being a reliable constant, and Cupid is love personified, he is shown to be a constant, whereas Lust remains ever temporary, doomed to fade quickly.[41] He takes the Noble Youth back into the past, into a utopia, criticizes the present as filled with people who are possessed with wild desires, and he, together with the King of the Isle, asks what is possible in the future. Concerning the constancy of love, Cupid concludes that love must prevail, but it must also be allowed to prevail.

4.4 Love as an Other-directed Passion: From Self to Community

Haywood's attempted answer to the question of what is possible in the future, of how love can prevail, is informed by her knowledge of the passions and especially desire, the Longinian sublime, and the connections between financial greed and interest. In accordance with the utopian form of *Memoirs of a Certain Island*, Haywood does not bring forward set-in-stone solutions to the problem presented but shows a possible alternative to her present situation. This suggestion is in itself an act of philosophizing about history insofar as she does not ask 'what must happen in the future,' but instead asks, 'what is possible?' She does not ask 'what do we need?' but 'what is it that we do not have?'

While Haywood mentions several paragons from history and the present, there is one that is particularly outstanding. In the dialogue of *Memoirs of a Certain Island*, the King of the Isle provides an alternative to how one could invest in the enchanted well, while still retaining one's dignity and simultaneously benefiting society at large. In order to do so, the King of the Isle tells the redemption story of *Communus*,[42] who is described as someone who is "kind, liberal, hospitable to all" (Haywood 1724: 279). He is portrayed as someone who, despite being rich, invests only a little into the well, only as much as is needed. The King of the Isle explains:

> [H]e revers'd even Fate, and this destructive *Well* (permitted but for the Punishment of those infatuated by it) added to the Power he was before possess'd of, of saving and protecting others, who had neither Vices sufficient to render them of service to *Lucitario's* Party, nor Strength enough of *Virtue* to merit so peculiar a Testimony of the Care of Heaven, as to be unprejudic'd by the Folly of engaging in it. (Haywood 1724: 279)

---

[41] Diamond notes that Haywood also explores the difference between lust and desire in more depth in *Love in Excess* (1719–1720), (2017: 61).

[42] King proposes James Brydges, first Duke of Chandos (1674–1744), as a potential stand-in for Communus, as he had "family and property connections in Herefordshire and Radnorshire where Haywood appears to have had Fowler relations" (2012: 211, fn. 18).

Communus, as the name suggests, is not acting solely on his own interests, he is committed to aiding others who have suffered from blindly trusting the myth of the enchanted well. The King of the Isle goes on to describe him as follows: "*Communus*, rich in the Mind's noblest Virtues, seeks the Distress'd, relieves their Wants with open-hearted Bounty, nor waits to be intreated to do good. The Sick, the Poor, the Captive, the Miserable of all Conditions, feel his tenderest Care …" (Haywood 1724: 279). The wants *Communus* relieves are ambiguous insofar as that they can mean 'want' as in wanting something (neutral), but simultaneously also a plight, or adversity. Haywood's proposed alternative to isolated, individual greed is thus to help others who are suffering, in the form of following a Hobbesian "sociable, other-directed passion." What she seems to call for is thus an altruistic love based on the conservative ideology of the High Church of England and especially the concept of charity (see King 2012: 143).

In order to get closer to the truth of why the citizens of England were so driven by financial greed for something not even graspable, Haywood resorts to a philosophical method highly popular throughout the seventeenth, but also during the eighteenth century. This was the exploration of passion in connection with financial greed/interest. Diamond calls this phenomenon "speculative desire" and therein connects the speculative, the uncertain, with desire, and thus with want.

In *Memoirs of a Certain Island*, not all citizens are described as deserving equal punishment. For instance, those who are good worshippers of Love do not deserve to be punished. Instead, it is specifically those who act according to "Lust and Avarice" who are deserving of retribution. While in *Memoirs of a Certain Island* she is also attacking individuals, the path can already be seen to what Haywood will further develop during her later life. Instead of attempting to appeal to specific party leaders or patrons, she grows more and more weary and ambivalent towards governmental, ministerial, and judicial institutions (King 2012: 186). By the time of the publication of *Evoaii* (1736), she has already grown increasingly critical of Walpole.

Haywood is a philosopher of history insofar as she thinks about the island of England in terms that extend from the past into the future, which is the definition of history. She establishes conceptions of the future, such as those developed in the dialogue between Cupid and the King of the Isle, but these are not fixed conceptions of how the future should be, but how it could be. While doing this, she remains an actress throughout, she plays theatre:

> Some will doubtless take me for a philosopher, – others for a fool; – with some I shall pass for a man of pleasure; – with others for a stoic; – some will look upon me as a courtier; – others as a patriot; – but whether I am any one of these, or whether I am even a man or a woman,

they will find it, after all their conjectures, as difficult to discover as the longitude. (Haywood 1754: 2)

She appears to have been (mostly) right.

5 Brief Outlook

While utopian writing is known for its closed structure, the exploration of Haywood's text is still very much open. This edition is not intended to close the discussion of her philosophy, her economic critique, or her work as a novelist, but rather to offer a beginning. Many further aspects of Haywood's texts are still to be explored, and the study of her philosophy has only just begun.

I thus present to you the first part of *Memoirs of a Certain Island*, which lays the foundation for part two. Part two deals with the aftermath of the South Sea Bubble and the corruptive nature of the Macclesfield Scandal, centering on the relationship between the Sovereign and his or her people. It will be published in 2025.

Bibliography and Further Reading

Anderson, Paul. 1936. "Mistress Delariviere Manley's Biography." *Modern Philology* 33, no. 3: 261–278.

Ankersmit, Franklin. 1989. "The Use of Language in the Writing of History." In *Working with Language: A Multidisciplinary Consideration of Language Use in Work Contexts*, edited by Hywel Coleman, 57–83. Berlin/New York: De Gruyter Mouton.

Ashfield, Andrew, and Peter de Bolla, eds. 1996. "Introduction." In *The Sublime: A Reader in British Eighteenth-Century Aesthetic Theory*, 1–16. Cambridge: Cambridge University Press.

Backscheider, Paula. 1987. "Women Writers and the Chains of Identification." *Studies in the Novel* 19, no. 3: 245–262.

Backscheider, Paula. 2016. "Elizabeth Singer Rowe, and the Development of the English Novel." *Forum for Modern Language Studies* 52, no. 4: 468.

Barbauld, Mrs. Anna Letita. *An essay on the origin and progress of novel-writing: with prefaces, biographical and critical, from the British novelists*. [n.p./n.d.] Pdf. Accessed January 23, 2023. https://www.loc.gov/item/unk82079363/.

Barchas, Janine. 2006. "Apollo, Sappho, and … a Grasshopper?! A Note on the Frontispieces to The Female Spectator." In *Fair Philosopher: Eliza Haywood and The Female Spectator*, edited by Don Newman, and Lynn Wright, 60–71. Lewisburg: Bucknell University Press.

Behn, Aphra. 1684. *Love-letters between a noble-man and his sister, 1640–1689*. London: Randal Taylor.

Blouch, Christine. 1991. "Eliza Haywood and the Romance of Obscurity." *Studies in English Literature* 31, no. 3: 535–552.

Bowers, Toni. 2009. "The Achievement of Scholarly Authority for Women: Trends in the Interpretation of Eighteenth-Century Fiction." *The Eighteenth Century* 50, no. 1: 51–71.
Burke, Edmund. 1791. *An Appeal from the New to the Old Whigs*. London: J. Dodsley, Pall-Mall.
Burton, Antoinette. 2019. "Toward Unsettling Histories of Domesticity." *The American Historical Review* 124, no. 4: 1332–1336.
Carnell, Rachel. 2014. "Eliza Haywood and the Narratological Tropes of Secret History." *Journal for Early Modern Cultural Studies* 14, no. 4: 111.
Cavendish, Margaret. 1994/1666. *The Blazing World and Other Writings*, London: Penguin Classics. [DOI: 10.1017/9781108780780.013]
Clery, Emma. 2013. "'To Dazzle let the Vain Design': Alexander Pope's Portrait Gallery; or, the Impossibility of Brilliant Women." In *Bluestockings Displayed*, edited by Elizabeth Eger, 39–59. Cambridge: Cambridge University Press.
Cole, Megan. 2022. "Fantasy and Education in Eliza Haywood's The Adventures of Eovaai." *Eighteenth-Century Fiction* 34, no. 3: 287–306.
Conley, John. 2022. "Virtue in Madeleine de Scudéry (1607-1701)." *Serie ECC, Encyclopedia of Concise Concepts by Women Philosophers*. Accessed January 23, 2023. https://historyofwomenphilosophers.org/ecc/#hwps.
Creel, Sarah. 2014. "(Re)framing Eliza Haywood: Portraiture, Printer's Ornaments, and the Fashioning of Female Authorship." *Journal for Early Modern Cultural Studies* 14, no. 4: 25–48.
Daniell, Alison. 2023. "Decoding the Bubble: Popular Magic, Financial Deception, and Eliza Haywood's Memoirs of a Certain Island Adjacent to Utopia." In *The Bubble Act*, edited by Helen Paul, Nicholas Di Liberto, and D'Maris Coffman. Cham: Palgrave Macmillan.
Descartes, René. 1989/1649. *Passions of the Soul*. Translated by Stephen Voss. Indianapolis: Hackett Publishing Co.
Diamond, David. 2017. "Eros and Exchange Alley: Speculative Desire in Eliza Haywood's *Memoirs of a Certain Island*." *Eighteenth-Century Fiction* 30, no. 1: 45–64.
Doran, Robert. 2015. *The Theory of the Sublime from Longinius to Kant*. Cambridge: Cambridge University Press.
Dryden, John. 1673. *The Conquest of Granada by the Spaniards*. London: Printed by T.N. for Henry Herringman.
Earle, Peter. 1989. *The Making of the English Middle Class: Business, Society and Family Life in London, 1660–1730*. Berkeley: University of California Press.
Eibach, Joachim, Inken Schmidt-Voges, Simone Derix, Philip Hahn, Elizabeth Harding, Margaeth Lanzinger, and Roman Bonderer, eds. 2015. In *Das Haus in der Geschichte Europas. Ein Handbuch*. Berlin/Boston: de Gruyter Oldenbourg.
Ellis, Markman. 2019. "The tea-table, women, and gossip in early eighteenth-century Britain." In *British Sociability in the Long Eighteenth Century: Challenging the Anglo-French Connection*, edited by Valérie Capdeville, and Alain Kerhervé. Studies in the Eighteenth Century, 69–88. Suffolk: Boydell & Brewer.
Gerrard, Christine. 2003. *Aaron Hill: The Muse's Projector, 1685–1750*. Oxford: Oxford University Press.
Gerrard, Christine. 1994/2011. *The Patriot Opposition to Walpole: Politics, Poetry, and National Myth, 1725–1742*. Oxford: online ed., Oxford Academic. Accessed January 23, 2023. DOI: https://doi.org/10.1093/acprof:oso/9780198129820.001.0001.
Goldgar, Anne. 2008. *Tulipmania. Money, Honor, and Knowledge in the Dutch Golden Age*. Chicago: University of Chicago Press.

Grafton, Anthony, Glenn Most, and Salvatore Settis, eds. 2013. *The Classical Tradition*. Cambridge: The Belknap Press of Harvard University Press.

Hagengruber, Ruth. 2020. "The Stolen History: Retrieving the History of Women Philosophers and its Methodical Implications." In *Methodological Reflections on Women's Contribution and Influence in the History of Philosophy*, edited by Sigridur Thorgeirsdottir, and Ruth Edith Hagengruber. Cham: Springer International Publishing.

Hammond, Brean. 1997. *Professional Imaginative Writing in England, 1670–1740: "Hackney for Bread"*. Oxford: Oxford University Press.

Haywood, Eliza Fowler. 2000/1719–1720. *Love in Excess, or, The Fatal Enquiry*, edited by David Oakleaf. Peterborough/Ontario: Broadview Press Ltd.

Haywood, Eliza Fowler. 1724. *Memoirs of a Certain Island Adjacent to the Kingdom of Utopia*. Part I, Second Edition. Gale Ecco.

Haywood, Eliza Fowler. 2000/1726. "A Pastoral Dialogue, between Alexis and Clorinda; Occasioned by Hillarius's intending a Voyage to America." In *The Tea-Table ... Part the Second*, edited by Alexander Pettit. Selected Works of Eliza Haywood. London: Pickering and Chatto.

Haywood, Eliza Fowler. 2008/1736. *Adventures of Eovaai, princess of Ijaveo. A pre-Adamitical history*, edited by Earla Wilputte. Peterborough: Broadview Press (Broadview literary texts).

Haywood, Eliza. 1742. *Secret histories, novels, and poems*. Vol. II. London: Printed for R. Ware, Amen-Corner.

Haywood, Eliza. 2008/1751. *The History of Miss Betsy Thoughtless*, edited by Christine Blouch. Peterborough: Broadview Press (Broadview literary texts).

Haywood, Eliza Fowler. 2016/1754. *The Invisible Spy*, edited by Carol Stewart. London/New York: Routledge (Chawton House library series. Woman's novels, no. 18).

Hollis, Karen. 1997. "Eliza Haywood and the Gender of Print." *The Eighteenth Century* 38, no. 1: 43–62.

Howard, Genevieve. 2015. "Equal Performances. An Exploration of Eliza Haywood's Depiction of Hillarian Ideals." Master's Thesis. Wellington: Victoria University of Wellington.

Hutcheson, Francis. 2007/1747. *Philosophiae moralis institutio compendiaria*, edited by L. Turco. Indianapolis: Liberty Fund.

Ingrassia, Catherine. 2015. *The Cambridge Companion to Women's Writing in Britain, 1660–1789*. Cambridge: Cambridge University Press.

Johnson, Samuel. 1755. *A Dictionary of the English Language Online*. Accessed January 23, 2023. https://johnsonsdictionaryonline.com/1755/faction_ns.

Jeffares, Alexander. 1993. *Anglo-Irish Literature*. Houndmills: Macmillan.

Keating, Eric. 2015. "In the Bedroom of the King: Affective Politics in the Restoration Secret History." *Journal for Early Modern Cultural Studies* 15, no. 2: 58–82.

King, Kathryn. 2005. "New Contexts for Early Novels by Women." In *A Companion to the Eighteenth-Century English Novel and Culture*, edited by Catherine Ingrassia, and Paula Backscheider. Oxford: Blackwell.

King, Kathryn. 2008. "Eliza Haywood, Savage Love, and Biographical Uncertainty." *The Review of English Studies* 59, no. 242: 722–739.

King, Kathryn. 2012. *A Political Biography of Eliza Haywood*. London: Pickering & Chatto.

Leitch, Vincent. 2001. *The Norton Anthology of Theory and Criticism*. New York: Norton.

Locke, John. 1689. *The Works, vol. 1 An Essay concerning Human Understanding, Part 1*. London: Rivington.

Merriam-Webster.com Dictionary, s.v. "juggle," accessed November 24, 2023. https://www.merriam-webster.com/dictionary/juggle.

Mount, Harry. 2006. "The Monkey with the Magnifying Glass: Constructions of the Connoisseur in Eighteenth-Century Britain." *Oxford Art Journal* 29, no. 2: 167–184.

Paul, Helen, Nicholas Di Liberto, and D'Maris Coffman, eds. 2023. *The Bubble Act: New Perspectives from Passage to Repeal and Beyond*. Cham: Springer International Publishing.

Paul, Helen. 2011. *The South Sea Bubble: An Economic History of its Origins and Consequences*. New York: Routledge.

Pohl, Nicole. 2017. *Women, Space and Utopia 1600–1800*. New York: Ashgate Publishing, Routledge.

Pope, Alexander, 1727/1728. *The Dunciad: With notes variorum, and the prolegomena of Scriblerus*. Book II. London: printed for Lawton Gilliver.

Rapin, de Thoyras. 1732. *Histoire d'Angleterre*. Chez Alexandre de Rogissart, à La Haye.

Roberts, William, trans. 1899. *Longinus on the Sublime*. London: Cambridge University Press.

Sansom, Martha Fowke. 1997. *Clio: The Autobiography of Martha Fowke Sansom, 1689–1736*, edited by Phillis Guskin. Newark/London/Cranbury/NJ: University of Delaware Press.

Savage, Richard. 2013/1726. "Miscellaneous poems and translations. By several hands. Publish'd by Richard Savage, Son of the late Earl Rivers. London." In *Eighteenth Century Collections Online*. Gale. Simon Fraser University.

Savage, Richard. 1896. *A Romance of Real Life*. Edited by Harvey Orrinsmith. London: Richard Bentley.

Schellenberg, Betty. 2015. "The professional female writer." In *The Cambridge Companion to Women's Writing in Britain, 1660–1789*, edited by Catherine Ingrassia, 37–55. Cambridge: Cambridge University Press.

Schmidt-Voges, Inken. 2019. "'Connecting Spheres.' Die Verortung der Geschlechter in 'Haus' und Gesellschaft in Leon Battista Albertis 'Libri della famiglia' (1433/34)." In *Innenräume – Außenräume*, edited by Maria Fritsche, Claudia Opitz-Belakhal, and Inken Schmidt-Voges. Göttingen: Vandenhoeck & Ruprecht.

Schmitter, Amy. 2023. "Managing Mockery: Reason, Passions and the Good Life among Early Modern Women Philosophers." In *The Routledge Handbook of Women and Early Modern European Philosophy*, edited by Karen Detlefsen, and Lisa Shapiro, 240–254. New York: Routledge.

Schnell, Rüdiger. 2021. *Histories of Emotion. Modern - Premodern*. Berlin/Boston: de Gruyter.

Skjönsberg, Max. 2021. *The Persistence of Parties*. Cambridge: Cambridge University Press.

Spedding, Patrick. 2017. "Imagining Eliza Haywood." *Eighteenth-Century Fiction* 29, no. 3: 345–372.

Spedding, Patrick. 2004. "Appendix H." In *A Bibliography of Eliza Haywood*. 763–764. London: Pickering and Chatto.

Spedding, Patrick. 2015. "Wall of Shame." Thursday, February 26, 2015. Accessed November 23, 2023. http://patrickspedding.blogspot.com/2015/02/wall-of-shame.html.

Swift, Jonathan. 1701. *A Discourse of the Contests and Dissensions between the Nobles and the Commons in Athens and Rome*. London: John Nutt.

Swift, Jonathan. [letter dated October 26, 1731]. In *Letters to and from Henrietta, Countess of Suffolk* (1824), 2.29. London: John Nichols and Son.

Tierney-Hynes, Rebecca. 2010. "Fictional Mechanics: Haywood, Reading, and the Passions." *The Eighteenth Century* 51, no. 1: 153–172.

Walpole, Horace Earl of Orford. 1833. *Letters of Horace Walpole, Earl of Orford, to Sir Horace Mann in three volumes*. London: Printed by Samuel Bentley.

Wilputte, Earla. 2014. *Passion and Language in Eighteenth-Century Literature: The Aesthetic Sublime in the Work of Eliza Haywood, Aaron Hill, and Martha Fowke*. Palgrave Macmillan.

Wright, Lynn, and Donald Newman. 2006. *Fair philosopher: Eliza Haywood and The Female Spectator.* Lewisburg: Bucknell University Press.

Wunder, Heide. 2022. "Considering 'Privacy' and Gender in Early Modern German-Speaking Countries." In *Early Modern Privacy*, edited by Michaël Green, Lars Nørgaard, and Mette Bruun, 63–78. Leiden: Brill.

Zorn, Daniel-Pascal. 2018. *Einführung in die Philosophie*. Frankfurt am Main: Vittorio Klostermann GmbH.

Timeline

This timeline shows biographical dates, publications and events that are linked to Haywood in such ways that are presented in this edition. They are by no means exhaustive. For a detailed list of Haywood's publications from 1717 to 1788, see Blouch's edition of *The History of Miss Betsy Thoughtless* (Blouch 2008: 21).

1660 Return of Charles II; Restoration of the Monarchy
1665 Birth of Queen Anne
1670 Birth of Delarivier Manley
1688 Glorious Revolution in England
1693 Birth of Eliza Fowler (Haywood)
1697 Birth of Richard Savage
1701 Jonathan Swift's *Discourse of the Contests and Dissensions* is published
1704 Death of John Locke
1707 Birth of Henry Fielding
1709 Delarivier Manley's *From the New Atalantis* is published
1711 Copyright Act *The Statute of Anne* is implemented;
    Founding of the South Sea Company
1713 Birth of David Hume
    South Sea Company is granted monopoly of trade in South America
1714 Treaty of Utrecht
    Bernard Mandeville's *Fable of the Bees* is published
1715 Death of Queen Anne, succession of George I
    Jacobite Rebellion
1719 Haywood enters the Hillarian Circle and publishes *Love in Excess* (two parts)
1720 The South Sea Bubble bursts, stocks plummet significantly and investors are ruined
1721 Publication of Haywood's first theater play, *The Fair Captive*
1723 Robert Walpole takes up role of Prime Minister
    Publication of *A Wife to be Lett*
    Haywood leaves the Hillarian Circle
1724 in September; Publication of *Memoirs* Vol. 1
1725 in October: Death of Delarivier Manley (b. 1670)
    Publication of *Memoirs* Vol. 2
1726 Publication of *The Tea-Table ... Part the Second*
1726 Richard Savage publishes his 'review poem' of Haywood's *The Rash Resolve*
1728 Alexander Pope's *Dunciad Variorum* is published

1732 Paul de Rapin's *Histoire d'Angleterre* is published
      Samuel Richardson's *Pamela* is published
1741 David Hume writes *Of Parties in General* and *Of the Parties of Great Britain*
      Publication of *Anti-Pamela*
1744 Henry Fielding's *Shamela* is published
      Publication of first version of *The Female Spectator*
1745 Jacobite Rebellion
1749 Publication of *The Goring Letter/Letter to a Friend*
1750 Arrest of Haywood
1751 Haywood publishes *The History of Miss Betsy Thoughtless*
1756 Death of Haywood in Westminster
1759 Birth of Mary Wollstonecraft
1760 John Locke's *An Essay Concerning Human Understanding* is published
1764 Death of George II and succession of George III
      David E. Baker's short biography of Haywood is published

Editorial Notes

This edition is based on the second edition of *Memoirs of a Certain Island* (1724). Original punctuation and spelling have largely been retained. Editorial decisions have always favored the original, while some spellings have been regularized. The page numbers of the original edition, enclosed in curved brackets { } in the text, are integrated into the running text at the relevant point. Page breaks, which are also word divisions, have been standardized so that the page number appears before the divided word. Further changes were limited to those improving readability, such as exchanging em-dashes with the appropriate punctuation marks. Furthermore, the first word of every sentence has been capitalized and the spaces before punctuation marks have been removed. The archaic swash s ſ has been replaced by its contemporary counterpart, s. The capitalization of common nouns has been retained, as well as abbreviations such as "stay'd," as they shape the lyricism of the text and do not impede legibility. The original previews the first word of the following page by doubling it on the previous page. These catchwords were guides for bookbinders to retain the right order of the pages. As this is not necessary for modern typesetting, the first instance of the repeated word has been removed. The original pagination has been retained.

I would like to thank Dr. Ian Copestake for his knowledge and immensely helpful work on the copy-/developmental editing of Haywood's text.[1]

Problems of Haywood Editions

This edition of the first part of Haywood's *Memoirs of a Certain Island* appears exactly 400 years after its initial publication in 1724. While Haywood presumably began the work several years earlier, we have taken this date as an opportunity to celebrate the anniversary of one of Haywood's essential works by making a modernized and faithful edition available that was previously lacking. *Memoirs of a Certain Island* is not alone in this problem, but while other philosophical works, such as *The Adventures of Eovaai, Princess of Ijaveo* (edited by Earla Wilputte) can now be read in connection with Mary Astell's philosophical essays on theories of gender and non-realism, her two-part utopian satire remains isolated,

---

[1] I would also like to thank Ruth Hagengruber for this opportunity, Kathryn King for her trust and encouragement, Christoph Schirmer, Max Weber, and Inga Lassen for their excellent support at De Gruyter. Thanks to John Egle and Jil Muller for their valuable feedback, and David for his time, honest criticism, and love.

available only as a digital replica of the original (Cole 2022). This is one of the reasons why, as Kathryn King rightfully reproves, *Memoirs of a Certain Island* "is more often invoked than actually studied." This is true especially, I and others like Rachel Carnell would add, in terms of its philosophical thinking about history (King 2012: 35). While an attempt has been made to identify the historical likenesses of *Memoirs'* characters whenever useful for the historical or philosophical context, possible mostly thanks to King's impressive detective work, I would advise every Haywood scholar and novice interested in this author's political works to read King's *Political Biography* of Haywood alongside this edition.

This edition has a dual task: It aims to make the text accessible to both Haywood researchers and complete novices alike, and to show how *Memoirs of a Certain Island* connects Haywood's philosophical and historical thinking. As such, it is not meant to be a definitive edition or a last word on Haywood's utopia, but to offer a beginning, a resource for future scholarship.

Memoirs of a Certain Island Adjacent to the Kingdom of Utopia: Volume 1

{1} A Noble Youth, who had ranged o'er almost all the habitable Part of the Globe in search of Pleasure and Improvement, at last arrived at an Island famous for Arts and Sciences, and talked of, by the neighbouring Nations, as a Place where all useful Accomplishments might, in the most elegant manner, be attained. He had no sooner landed, than he was charmed with even the first and rudest Prospect; but when he had entered farther, and could distinctly view the lovely Landscape, he became quite lost, and ravished in Contemplation. Where-e'er he cast his wondering Eyes, all had the Face of Joy! Of everlasting Peace! {2} and soft Repose! no Tumults, no Noise, no stormy Tongues of Faction,[1] nor Elemental Hurricanes seemed ever to have disturbed the Quiet of this happy Shore! Everything was serene and gay! All Nature smiled as at the first Formation! A thousand Breezes fanned the ambient Air, and wanton'd on the ever-blooming Trees! A thousand various kinds of Birds, in warbling Notes, chanted their Maker's Praise, and blest the Paradise they dwelt in! Here yellow Fields confessed indulgent *Ceres!* There verdant Meads rejoiced the brute Creation. At a distance he beheld the tow'ring Mountains rise! Huge Oaks and stately Elms adorned their lofty Summits, and nodding o'er the Verges, spread a delightful Shade o'er all the Vales beneath! The God of Waters too seemed to have made this Isle his choicest Favourite, and from his mighty Source numberless little Streams ran winding thro' the Plains, to glad the Earth, and ease the Tiller's Toil! Ah! *Cry'd the Stranger* (*transported with the rapturous View*) how charming! How glorious! Is all that meets my Sight! How everything is formed for Profit and Delight! The People born under such auspicious Influences must certainly be the *richest* as well as *happiest* Nation in the World! What would I not give to be one of those Darlings of Heaven! With what Tranquility might I pass my Days in these refreshing Groves![2] These cool Retreats! These blissful Bowers! How could I ever wander thro' this enchanting Scene,[3] and still find something new to entertain Reflection! O Land of Joy! Where the extensive Sight at once takes in more than Imagination's slow-paced reach can fathom in an Age! He continued in this extatick Reverie, till, on a purling Rivulet's delightful

---

1 [This and the following dictionary entries are, if not indicated otherwise, taken from *A Dictionary of the English Language* (Johnson 1755): "Faction" could mean both "a party in a state" and "tumult; discord; dissension".]
2 [from *grave*: a walk covered by trees meeting above.]
3 [*enchanter*, French: "enchanted" can refer to both "irresistible influence; overpowering delight" and/or "magical charms; spells; incantation; sorcery".]

Bank, extended at full Length, he spy'd a Being of more than mortal Beauty. It appeared a {3} Boy, not exceeding eight or ten Years of Age; his Complexion seem'd malleable Ivory his polished Limbs and fine-proportioned Body were wholly exposed to View; he was all naked, but where an Azure Scarf fell from his Neck, and served to screen those Parts, which Modesty forbids to be revealed: It was composed of thinnest, purest, Air! bright and clear as an unclouded Sky! His Eyes were Stars, whose Shine outrivalled that which ushers in the Morn, but more benign and soft than those which form the Milky Way! Eternal Youth sat smiling on his Checks! And Graces all Divine play'd round his Ruby Lips! A Wing each Shoulder bore, whose dazzling Pinions[4] were dip'd in liquid Light, and diffused unutterable Day around the Place! In his right Hand he held an unbent Bow, while on the other his heavenly Head leaned pensive and reclined. An Object so new! Astonishing to human Eyes, [it] was very near depriving the Adventurous Gazer of his Senses; but Fate, who had made choice of him to be the Discoverer of Secrets, to which the greater part of the World were wholly Strangers, strengthened him to support all that was. necessary for the mighty Purpose: His Amazement! His Terror! Began by little and little to abate; and at last he! A Mortal, beheld Divinity, without any other Emotions than what proceed from that reverential Awe, which all who but contemplate Incomprehensibility must feel. He doubted not but he was in the presence of a God, and prostrated himself on the Earth in humble Adoration. Rise! (*said the Deity, and as he spoke, Ambrosial Odours issued with his Breath*) Rise, worthy Stranger! For such I am sure thou art, since, uncorrupted by the vile Schism which infects this Isle, thou darest to worship a Power, whom almost all the Natives here renounce. Far be it from me (*reply'd the wondring Youth*) ever {4} to omit that Adoration which is the due of all Celestial Beings—much more to thee! Who, if thy ravishing Form and Bow deceive me not, art the most kind, beneficent, and condescending of them all. Thou judgest right (*resum'd the smiling God*) I am indeed the Deity of *Love!* distinguished Patron of this once happy Isle! The People then were born to Blessings! I interceded with each heavenly Name, and every God combined to make them happy: *Mars* gave them Courage to subdue their foreign Foes! *Minerva* Wisdom, to discover and circumvent home-bred Conspiracies! *Bacchus* enriched their Vintage! *Ceres* bless'd their Harvest! *Venus* gave Beauty to their Nymphs, and my Companion *Honour* influenced their Swains! *Hymen* assisted at their Marriages! Even *Jupiter*, and the Ocean's God heard my Entreaty, and rendered them too great to be withstood; They were formidable to the most distant Nations, their Forces were feared, and their Alliance courted; this Spot of Earth was then the Pride and Envy of the Creation—but,

---

4 [Wings, feathers.]

alas! What is it now? What will it be in time? Divine Justice has already began to inflict the Punishment their Apostacy from all that's good deserves, and they must soon, very soon, be as wretched as they have been bless'd. I can no longer take their part, they no longer vouchsafe to own me, and there is an over-ruling, an Almighty Fate, which prevents even the Immortals themselves from giving unask'd Assistance. No Incense now burns on my neglected Shrine! No Offerings are paid! My Temples are defaced! My Altars broke! And, in my stead, the mistaken Wretches,[5] with sacrilegious Worship, idolize a *Fiend!*'Tis true, the Demon has usurped my Name! My Face! My Voice! They still revere and call on *Cupid*, *Cupid* they still adore. But not a *Cupid* accompany'd with Innocence, {5}Virtue, Constancy, but a *Cupid*, ushered in by wild Desires,[6] Impatiences, Perplexities, and whose ghastly Train are filled with Shame, Disgrace, Remorse, and late Repentance and Despair! Yet this is the Deity to whom they sacrifice this is the God they invoke, and with *Pecunia* drives from their perverted Souls all Sentiments[7] of Honour, Virtue, Truth, or Gratitude. A blind Gratification of unlicens'd Wishes is all they aim at, they endeavour not to *merit*, but *obtain*; and their Designs[8] once compassed, regard not by what means: but soon, tho' too late to repair it, they will perceive their Error. Ruin comes on apace, swift from her horrid Court the Blood-dy'd Monster flies, unnumbered Miseries fill her remorseless Hands, and Plagues on Plagues she brings: Discord and Madness are her Harbingers, and have already begun their Work; a universal Infatuation seems to have seized the Minds of the Inhabitants of yonder proud *Metropolis*; they are in haste to be undone—they hurry to Perdition. But since I see Curiosity and Expectation in thy Eyes, I will once more revisit that ungrateful City, and visible to no sight but thine, show thee the Destruction these Idiots are so fond of, and by what means they are provoking the Vengeance of long-suffering Heaven.

The God no sooner ceased, than, swift as Thought, a radiant Cloud descended, and wrapping itself round them, wasted them in a moment from that blissful Solitude to a Place all Noise, all Hurry, and Confusion! The Stranger found himself in a great Street, where Multitudes of People were passing backwards and forwards; the Press was so thick, just in that part of it where he alighted, that he would have been in some danger of being trod to Death, if not protected by a Deity. There were a vast Number who seemed {6} endeavouring to get through a large Gate-way, which, tho' wide open, was rendred almost inaccessible by the mad Impatience of those, who, jostling for Admittance, were a hindrance to one another:

---

5 [*wrecca*, Saxon: a miserable mortal.]
6 [*desirer*, French; *desiderare*, Latin: to wish; to long for; to covet.]
7 [*sentiment*, French: thought; notion; opinion.]
8 [from the verb: to purpose; to intend any thing.]

but our Knight-Adventurer, accompany'd by his Celestial Guide, made an easy way through the Crowd, and came into a spacious Court, in the middle of which there was a *Well* vastly deep, and of a prodigious Circumference: two stately Figures, opposite to each other, o'erlook'd the liquid Chrystal; one was of *Pecunia*, Goddess of Interest, the other of *Fortune*, mounted on her Wheel's extremest Spoke: a thousand Wretches, in suppliant Postures, invoked the Benevolence of that fickle Deity. The Shrine of *Pecunia* was compassed with her Priests, and round the *Well* unnumbered Crowds stood gazing, as if in expectation of some wonderful Event. Here was to be seen, at once, all the various Sects which make up the whole Sum of Human Kind—all Orders, all Degrees, promiscuously mingled, Nobles and Plebeians, Grandees and Knights of Industry, grave Judges, private Centinels, Priests, Generals, Women of Honour mixed with common Prostitutes, the Prude, Coquette, the Miser, and the Prodigal laying aside all Prejudice of Principle or Education, here met, and joined in Conversation on their common Aim. Nothing ever was more worthy of Observation than the different Looks and Motions of this confused Assembly; some, with Countenance elated, an Air all arrogant, appeared to have arrived at the height of their Wishes, and had nothing to fear either from Gods or Men; others, in all the Postures of the most violent Despair, tearing their Hair, wringing their Hands, beating their Breasts, and filling the regardless Air with Cries and Lamentations; a third sort seemed divided betwixt Hope and Fear, one moment believing they should immediately be {7} possessed of all their Souls were set on, the next that they were undone forever. There were some, tho' but a few, who behaved themselves with Moderation, and would fain have been thought unaffected with their Misfortunes, which yet they could not help discovering, by biting their Lips, hanging down their Heads, and such-like Tokens of sullen, silent Discontent. In fine, in all this numerous Throng,[9] there was scarce a Person who appeared to be in his right Senses, and our Traveller not able to comprehend the meaning of what he saw, took the liberty of entreating his Divine Companion to inform him. The Deity having brought him there for no other purpose, immediately comply'd with his Request, in these or the like words.

The Story of the Enchanted Well

You must know (*said the Celestial Intelligence*) this Spring was first discover'd by a Person called *Lucitario*,[10] a famous Necromancer,[11] who having, by some secret

---

9 [*brang*, Saxon, from thringan, to press: a croud; a multitude pressing against each other.]
10 [James Craggs (King 2012, 36).]

Services, rendered himself dear to the Interest and Favour of the Sovereign of this Island, easily obtain'd his Permission to establish it a Place of Worship. Accordingly he erected those Statues you see placed there, the one of *Fortune*, the other of *Petunia*; and in a little time, by the help of his pernicious Art, wrought so far on the Minds of the deluded Multitude, as to make it almost universally believed, that whoever would be rich, must repair to this miraculous Spring: which tho' in reality never any other than common Water (such as you see it now) he had made appear to the {8} Eye like liquid Gold, flowing in Tides of Wealth to the Receiver's hand. Under pretence of keeping the imaginary Treasure from being plundered, he encompassed it with a Wall, and placed a Guard about it; none therefore were to reap any Advantage from this wonderful and exhaustless Source of Plenty, but those whose Offerings should be acceptable to the Deities, to whom, as he pretended, this *Well* was consecrated. The artful Wretch dress'd up Creatures of his own (O most abominable Profanation!) in those Vestments which Priests are wont to wear when they officiate at the sacred Altars; it was in their Hands the Sacrifices were intrusted, to them all Oblations were paid: and happy did they think themselves, who were most magnificent in their Presents to these pretended holy Men. Some came loaded with Plate, others with Jewels, rich Furniture, Pictures, Beds, every one brought according to his Ability; for their Master *Lucitario* had ordered, that nothing should be refused. 'Tis incredible to what straits three Parts in four of these deluded Islanders reduced themselves, to glut the Avarice of a few, whose Adherence with the Necromancer raised them to a Condition far above what they could have hoped. It was they indeed, who batten'd in the Spoils of the others, the floating *Gold* poured into their Coffers,[12] while *Water* only was the Portion of the rest. Young *Spendthrifts*,[13] who, indulging themselves in the Vices of the Age, had revelled away the greatest part of what their careful Ancestors had saved, were willing to risk the Residue in Offerings to these Shrines, in hope of having twice as much as they had spent restored. Grave *Grandfires*, who had amass'd vast Heaps of Treasure, sufficient to have preserved them and their Posterity for many Generations from Want, gladly plunged it all into this magical *Well*, not {9} doubting in the least but they should have Returns proportionable to the Value of the Sacrifice. The *Rich* were greedy to increase their Store, the *Indigent* eager to know a better State; those who had already made their Fortunes, were ambitious of raising them; those who had not, thought this the only way; all were alike transported, all equally infatuated, and all suffered in the same fatal

---

11 [νεκρὸς and μάντις, Ancient Greek: one who by charms can converse with the ghosts of the dead; a conjurer; an inchanter.]
12 [*cofre*, Saxon: a small chest.]
13 [*spend* and *thrift*: a prodigal; a lavisher.]

Disappointment, except, as I have already taken notice, those who were privy to the Juggle,[14] or whose Interest with *Lucitario* kept him from permitting they should be imposed on. But among all who had the Misfortune of falling into this Snare,[15] none had a greater Loss than the Duke *de Conbree*; he had a plentiful Estate, and sold or mortgaged it all to render himself acceptable to the imaginary Deities of this destructive *Well.* While he had anything to bestow, his Expectation was kept alive by the continual Assurances the counterfeit Priests gave him, that in a very little time he would find his account in what he had done; but when all was gone, when neither Tree nor Acre was left, and Banker would advance no more, he was dismissed from his Attendance at the sacred Spring, with the cool Pity of his base Inveiglers,[16] who told him they were extremely troubled at the Severity of his Fate, but it was not permitted them to pry into the secret Reasons of the Deities displeasure; That *Fortune* seemed averse to his Desires, and he must study Patience and Resignation. Had he not indeed been Master of those Virtues, or had been possessed of a little more Fire in his Constitution, he would at once have demolished the ruinous Structure, and discover'd to the amazed Multitude the secret Passages through which the Wealth they had hoped to gain had been conveyed for other Uses; but being rather of a Temper more inclined to Indolence than too much Activity, he {10} forbore any Endeavours either to redress, or revenge those Wrongs, he now, too late, perceiv'd he had sustain'd. Robb'd of the means of living according to his Quality, and reduced to that uneasy State of a Dependance on his Lady's Jointure for even the common Necessaries of Life, he fell into so excessive a Discontent, that he resolved to shut himself from the View of all who knew him, and retired to the House of a Woman, whom he had formerly been enamour'd with for her fine Voice. She had a very handsome Settlement of some thousand Crowns a year, which he had given her; and O! prodigious Proof of Honour in a Woman of her Profession, she generously relinquish'd it all, nay intreated him on her Knees to resume it, assuring him she gave it back with greater Joy than she receiv'd it: When you bestow'd on me (*said she*) this lavish Testimony of your Love, I accepted it with an infinity of pleasure, because I knew such Offerings come not but from the Heart! by that I found your Passion;[17] but in restoring it, I have an opportunity of proving the Sublimity of mine: To have it in my power to contribute anything to

---

14 [Imposter, deception (Johnson 1755); the act of magic or witchcraft (Merriam Webster).]
15 [*snara*, Swedish and Islandick; *snare*, Danish; *snoor*, Dutch: any thing set to catch an animal; a gin; a net.]
16 [from *inveigle:* seducer; deceiver; allurer to ill.]
17 [*passion*, French; *passio*, Latin: any effect caused by external agency or/and violent commotion of the mind.]

your Consolation in an Exigence[18] like this, gives me a Transport which Words cannot reveal. O that I could also put you in possession of all that cursed *Well* has taken from you! How gladly would I do it, tho' the best part of my Blood were the Exchange. Never did she cease solliciting him in this tender manner, till she had prevail'd on him not only to resume what he had given her, but also to accept of a great deal of ready Money which her Frugality had saved, reserving only so much to herself, as served to initiate her into Holy Orders. She went immediately into a Monastery, and is an Example of *Piety* to those she is now among, as in her late Behaviour she was of *Honour* here. I wish, for the Glory of the {11} Fair Sex, I could produce many more such Instances of Generosity. But, alas! there are but few of a Disposition so Heroick, not but the Avarice and Self-interestedness, which is generally observed in those Women who make Sale of their Beauty, is chiefly owing to Men. When a Courtezan, celebrated for her Charms, receives the Addresses of a Man who, perhaps, to her own knowledge, has been the Undoer of a thousand poor unhappy Creatures, whose artless Innocence required no more than Love for Love; why should she not set a Value on herself, make him bid high for her Possession, revenge her Sex's Injuries, and pay at once for all! Besides Men, when they make choice of a Mistress, seldom regard any thing but her *exterior* Beauties, the *Soul* is the smallest Part of their Aim; and as it very rarely happens that a Woman, who has any Merits *there*, can submit to *bargain* for the Favours she disposes, how can either Love, Gratitude, or Constancy be expected! The *Duke* indeed had the good Fortune to find it otherwise, but such Chances happen not in every Age; I know of none to equal it. The young Count *Marcus*, after having lavished the best part of his Estate on *Mirizaida*, could not be admitted to play at picquet with her, till he produced his Stake; the mercenary Woman perceiving his Ebb of Fortune, fell in league with a Creature of *Lucitario's*, one to whom he left the chief Management of the Affairs of this *Well*; he contrived it so, as to enrich her with the Spoils of the more Worthy; she now keeps her Chariot,[19] a handsome Equipage, passes on those, that know her not, for a Woman of Virtue, and has the assurance to report the *Count* address'd her for Marriage; but that finding him too profuse in his Expences, she had discarded him That is she, the press begins to give way, you may perceive her easily, she stands near the Shrine of *Fortune*; {12} observe with what Disdain she rolls her Eyes around mark, how she laughs, and seems delighted at the melancholy[20] Aspect of a Lady that stands by

---

18 [This word is probably only a corruption of *exigents*, vitiated by an unskilful pronounciation: demand; want; need.]
19 [*car-rhod*, Welch: a wheeled car; for it is known the Britons fought in such; *charriot*, French; *carretta*, Italian.]
20 [Gloom, dismal.]

her. *Venus* has been liberal enough in giving her Attractions Her Face is perfectly lovely her Eyes want not Vivacity nor Sweetness her Features are regular, and what she has not in Complection, is abundantly made up by Art she appears altogether compleat and yet, if you examine her strictly, you will perceive a certain Air about her, which discovers some part of her Character. Of much the same Disposition is that fine Lady on her Right-hand, and owes, with as little desert, much more to the Smiles of Fortune; she has had six several Children by six several Men, without being Wife to any of them has lived from the Age of sixteen to forty-five in the Circumstance of a kept Mistress, but is now married to a Person of the first Quality in the Island. That young blooming Creature who seems talking to her, is her Daughter, she had her by a Gentleman[21] who Is Governour of a foreign Plantation she is extremely agreeable, but inherits too much of her Mother's Humour.[22] But look behold! Where the vain gay *Marthalia*[23] comes see how the Crowd gives back to make room for her what homage does she not now receive from the mean-spirited Multitude; and yet there is scarce one here, that does nor remember her in tatters, and know her for the most dissolute and shameless of her Sex. After a long Scene of continued Lewdness, she at last married an old Servant[24] of the Necromancer's languishes under an incurable Disease, and she has the Management of his Affairs, and is by this means become a Woman of consequence to those unhappy Wretches, who yet have any dependance on this cursed *Well.* Her Change of State has not made the least alteration in her Humour, she was ever {13} proud, inconstant, mercenary, designing, a Contemner of the Gods, and a most zealous Votary to that *Demon,* who, for the Punishment of ill-judging Mortals, is permitted to assume my Name the Advantages of Dress and Grandeur give her Opportunities which before she wanted; she is now caress'd by those, whose Servants once despised her, and the Footman, who could not formerly be prevailed on to take her in his Arms, sees her now in his Master's, and lights him to that Bed, he would not once have ventured to go into himself; so strangely does a little Pomp influence the Minds and Affections of Mankind! But there are some who of late have severely repented trusting themselves in her Embraces, and cursed the artificial Sweets and Perfumes, which hindred them from discovering those Scents, that would have been infallible Warnings of what they might expect in such polluted Sheets. But I can no longer endure to look upon her—the Object is too foul—

---

21 ["Honest gentlemen" describes those unrightfully affected by the immorality of speculation or money in general. "Gentlement were not just superior to tradesmen in social rank, but also in moral stature" (Paul 2011, 12).]
22 [*humeur,* French; *humor,* Latin: general turn or temper of mind.]
23 [Martha Blout(?) (King 2012, 43).]
24 [Sir John Blunt (King 2012, 42).]

for whatever she may appear to you, I, who see into her Soul, and detest the Impurity of it, grow sick at the Reflection; let us take off our Eyes from a Sight so loathed, let us carry them where Pity need not blush. See, where apart from the gazing Crowd, the weeping Graciana[25] sits! how innocent she looks! how lovely in Dejection! How enchanting are her very Tears! How her Glances adorn even the most impairing of all the Passions! What a Sweetness dwells in her Sorrow! One would almost think Joy could not add to the Harmony of her Features! And yet, she is as different from what she once appear'd, her Beauty as much sunk beneath its former Brightness, as it is still superior to most others. But because her History has something particular in it, I will give it you at large.

{14} The History of *Graciana*

Her Father was one of the richest Citizens in the Island, she was his only Child, and it is not to be doubted but that so many Charms as you see in her, join'd to the Reputation of being a very great Fortune, attracted a number of Admirers: the old Gentleman was wearied with the continual Sollicitations of Persons, whose Quality, Estates, and Characters were unexceptionable; but the Tenderness he had for her, finding her Inclinations averse to Marriage, would not suffer him to press her so far, but that he still left it in her power to refuse. In the most happy and undisturb'd Tranquility did she live, till her Intimacy with *Romanus*,[26] a young *Utopian*, who on some disgust had quitted the Place of his Nativity, and was recommended by his Friends to some of the Ministry here, as a Person qualified to serve them in any Employment they should think proper to entrust him with. The Father of *Graciana* being a leading Man in the Senate, was one of those whose Interest he solicited for Promotion; and it was by this means he became acquainted with her, and had opportunity to instill that Poison, which has been the Bane of her Reputation, and her Peace of Mind There was no room for her to suspect his Designs were any other than honourable, the advantage in marrying him being wholly on his side: and this appearance of Security kept her from giving any check to those Emotions which he alone had the power of inspiring In fine, she became entirely my Votary; she loved {15} him with a Tenderness so pure, that it deserv'd my peculiar regard; and as often as I look'd down and consider'd it, I melted into pity for the Woes I knew she was pre-ordain'd to suffer: for *Romanus*, by nature self-interested, ambitious, mercenary, and ungrateful, was little meriting

---

25 [Ms. Child (King 2012, 41).]
26 [Mr. Trenchard (King 2012, 41).]

such a soft Sublimity of Passion. I had not the power to influence a Soul so guarded as was his against my Darts, by Avarice and Pride, those Foes profess'd to Constancy and Love. While he believed a Marriage with *Graciana* would raise his Fortune in the World, so long he intended it; but when once the Scene was chang'd, and she no more could be subservient to his *Interest*, she ceas'd to be of consequence to his *Wishes:* her Beauty, her Virtue, her Good-nature, her Truth and Tenderness, were all too light in his esteem, when poiz'd against the weightier Charms of Grandeur, Noise, and Hurry: a gilt Chariot and splendid Equipage had greater Attractions than the loveliest Eyes; nor would *Apollo*'s Harp have had any Musick in it, comparable to the neighing of half a dozen *Flanders* Mares, and the hoarse Bellowings of a numerous Train, crying, *What's your Honour's Will? Ho, there, my Lord calls!* Her Father dying, left her to the Care of a particular Friend, a very honest Gentleman, but one who had not a Discernment sufficient to prevent him from falling into the Infatuation of *Lucitario's* Magick; he became, like the rest, bigotted to the Enchantments of this *Well*, and sunk in it not only his own Estate, but that of the Orphan entrusted to his Management. When he perceiv'd his Error, Grief for what he had done threw him into a Fever, of which he died. *Romanus*, who had not been consulted in this Affair, was very much concern'd when he was told it he never had an opinion of the *Well*, and knew immediately she was undone, and {16} consequently no Wife for him; the first thing therefore that he thought on, was how to break with her handsomely, for their Loves had already proceeded as far as a Contract, and it was always a Maxim with him never to quarrel with anybody, and when he acted in the most the most inhuman purpose, always to do it with the face of Friendship. He had a vile Passion for the Possession of *Graciana*, which was as yet ungratify'd and to make him entirely at ease, it was necessary first to satiate that, and then find out some means to make the Fault of quitting her wholly on her side.–In order to realise this monstrous Intention, he pretended an Increase of Tenderness, visited her every day, seem'd uneasy whenever he was obliged to take leave of her, writ to her in the most moving Stile, and fashion'd every part of his Behaviour in such a manner as made her think the loss of her Fortune had been far from making any alteration in his Sentiments to her disadvantage. When he found this Stratagem had worked the Effect he aim'd at, and that her Breast was perfectly free from all those but too just Suspicions her Misfortunes had at first created in her, he took his time to make use of the advantage; he then told her, that to his great discontent, he fear'd it would be an Impossibility for them to marry as soon as he had hoped;—the Promises his Friends had given him of making his Fortune were slow in their execution, and till that was compleated, he could not bear to think of suffering her to share an abject State with him, but conjured her, entreated her on his knees with ten thousand well-dissembled Sighs and Tears, and Words all seeming Truth and Ardency of Love, not to bestow on any other that Heart she had made him hope he had an Interest in, and concluded all with telling her, a little time, he doubted not, would make them both happy in their mutual Desires.

{17} He deliver'd this in such a manner, and had so artfully prepar'd her to receive it, that she, wholly free from all Deceit herself, was not the least dubious of what he said, and continu'd to admit his Visits with the same, or more, Freedom than ever. She so stedfastly believ'd she should be one day his Wife, that, by degrees, Intimacy improving Familiarity, she began to consider him as if he were already her Husband; she regarded him with the same Tenderness, the same kind Concern for his Interest, as if the Ceremony of the Church had made her Passion her Duty. Nothing, however, had pass'd but what was consistent with the Rules of Honour, till one unhappy Night, after a thousand repeated Oaths and Protestations of eternal Fidelity, the poor deluded Maid, warm'd with his Fire, and sooth'd by his Vows, yielded to all he ask'd, allay'd the burning Fever in his Breast, and fill'd her own with everlasting Anguish. The Rapture past, and wild Desire appeas'd, all that remain'd now was how to get rid of her: she had Kindred who had the power to revenge her Wrongs, if he should openly affront her, and as all the Acquaintance on both sides were sensible of the Professions he had made her, he must either make it appear publickly she was unworthy of them, or incur a Character he was very unwilling should be given him. To avoid this, he laid a Plot so vile! so horrid! that one would think he must have ransack'd Hell, and chose the blackest Demon there to assist him in the forming it: he told her a long, but plausible, Story, that an Accident had happen'd, which render'd it unsafe for him to be seen in Town; but that not able to quit the sight of his dear *Graciana*, he had taken private Lodgings, and chang'd his Name, and desir'd that she would direct her Letters (as almost every day there pass'd some between them) to the Chevalier[27] d'Eshart.

{18} How might not anyone by such a Tale have been deceiv'd? The unsuspecting Fair condoled his Misfortune, and obey'd his Orders; nothing could be more tender than what she writ, and when he had receiv'd as many as he thought convenient for his purpose, he expos'd them to the Perusal of all those of her Friends, from whose Resentment he had anything to fear. He accompany'd this pretended Discovery of her Falshood, with so many Complaints of the Severity of his Fate in the Injustice she had done him, that everybody was of his side. It was in vain that she protested her Innocence, exclaim'd against the Baseness, the unexampled Barbarity of *Romanus*, swoon'd, almost died to find herself thus cruelly betray'd; not one believ'd, not one pity'd her. He had taken care to make it appear that

---

27 [*chevalier*, French: a knight; a gallant strong man.]

there really was such a Person as the Chevalier *d'Eshart*, who had Lodgings at that very place to which her Letters were directed; and having no date upon them, 'twas easy to pretend they had been sent before that Gentleman left the Island, for he was now gone from it with a design of settling in a distant Nation. In short, everything look'd feasible enough, and he had the Satisfaction of having an unquestionable Pretence never to see her more; the Blame, the Infamy was her's alone, and he is at this day receiv'd and caress'd by the nearest of her Relations, while she is not permitted to own them as such, or to enter their Houses. Cast out and abandon'd by all from whom she could have hoped Support, ruin'd in her Fortune, undone in her Reputation, but more wretched in the Reflection, that she owed all this to her too great Tenderness for the basest of his Sex: she was several times about to lay hands on her Life, but the Gods, to whom she yet is dear for many Virtues, have still averted the intended Blow. She now has pretty well vanquish'd her Despair, {19} but will scarce ever be able to overcome her Melancholy, tho' I dare promise there is something in store for her, which will one day compensate for her past Sufferings.

Here the *Deity* was prevented from saying any more by the Stranger, (who, very much transported with Rage at the Lady's base Treatment) could not forbear crying out, but what is become of *Romanus*, the ingrateful! The perfidious Wretch! Did not such a more than Devil-like Disposition excite the extremest Vengeance of the offended Gods? Did they not make him an instant Example of their Abhorrence of such Crimes? No, *resum'd the Divine Historian*, his time of Punishment is not yet arriv'd; and tho' that which I have related (monstrous as it is) is not the greatest of his Crimes, he is allow'd to continue in them, to perpetrate yet more! Not that Justice sleeps, or is remissive in her Office, but this Traitor to all Honour and Fidelity is permitted to triumph for a while, on purpose to make miserable those unhappy Wretches, who, deviating from the Rules of Virtue, yield themselves a Prey to his Insinuations; he is to them the Minister of avenging Heaven, as the Furies will hereafter be to him. He marry'd soon after the Conclusion of his Affair with *Graciana*, but what avails that sacred Tye! What Benefit has the agreeable *Mariana* of the vast Fortune she brought him! Is she the better used, the more beloved for being one of the best and most tender Wives in the World! No, *Romanus* has not a Soul capable of being touch'd by any of these Virtues; he is too proud to acknowledge an Obligation, and too much an Atheist[28] to yield, even to those Rules the Immortals themselves obey. He had not been a Husband above a Month, before he had a publick Intrigue with the Dutchess *de Cruizalla*, whether it proceeded from Interest or {20} Inclination is uncertain; for the latter has ever been so

---

28 [ἄθεος, Ancient Greek: without God; one that denies the existence of God.]

much govern'd by the former, that it is to be question'd, if ever he thought it worth his while to pursue the one without some View of the other: therefore as this Lady being at that time a very great Favourite with the Sovereign, 'tis highly probable his Passion might arise from a Hope that she would make her Lover's Fortune, either by procuring him a Title, or a Place at Court, both which his subtle-working Wit has long been endeavouring to obtain: but finding his Expectations on that side deceiv'd, he not only broke off his Amour with her, but made it his business to ridicule her in all Companies; his Baseness, and her Indiscretion, made the Affair so known, that her Lord (tho' before that, the most indolent Man in the world as to her Conduct) could not avoid taking notice of it, and ever after kept her in a Restraint no way agreeable to her Humour; but not being very fond of taking that Revenge on *Romanus*, which Husbands in such Cases usually do, he contented himself with doing him what private Mischiefs he could, without calling him to any publick Account. During his Life, *Romanus* found it impossible to succeed in anything, all his Designs were circumvented, all his Artifices subverted, all his Stratagems defeated, but a few Months rid him of this potent Enemy; he died, and left the Stage free for him, whose Cunning and unweary'd Industry could be foiled by none, but where Jealousy made Vengeance equally diligent and watchful. Flattery, of which he is a perfect Master, in a little time after ingratiated him into the favour of some Men in power, who endeavour'd all they could to serve him, assisted his Measures, and had certainly answer'd the Aim of his Ambition, if an unexpected Accident had not happen'd, which put an end at once to their {21} Intentions, and cut him from his Hope forever. He was very near being created a Peer, when the Person, who had been the greatest of his Friends, and most capable of serving him, turn'd his mortal Enemy. The Occasion of it was this: He was entrusted by this Minister with an Intrigue he had with a Woman of Condition; she happen'd to be agreeable to the Taste of *Romanus*, and instead of managing the Affair for his Patron, endeavour'd to supplant him in the Affections of his Mistress. He had the advantage of a much more lovely Person and had Arts of insinuating what he would have believ'd, which were difficult to be withstood. The Lady grew fond of him in a little time, and the Statesman happening to come at an hour when a Visit from him was not expected, catch'd her in Bed with this new Favourite. He took no other Revenge on her than calling her ungrateful and false; but *Romanus* had fallen a Victim that moment to his Rage, had not his Agility been his Protection. He jump'd out of the Window as the other enter'd the Chamber, and the first Gust of Passion being over, he would not expose himself so far, nor the Occasion of his Displeasure, as to send him a Challenge, but took an effectual Method to ruin him another way. He infus'd a Suspicion of his Loyalty in the Sovereign's Breast, and when he came into the Presence, big with the Expectation of approaching Honour, he was dismiss'd with Frowns, and order'd to appear there no more till sent for. He is of too quick an Apprehension not to know immediately from whence this Change proceeded, but there was no Remedy; *he* had now a listing and implacable Enemy. To represent the inward Horrors he felt, or the Curses he vented on himself, and those who had been the Authors of his Disappointment, would ill become the Mouth of a Deity; he rav'd, he tore, blasphem'd the Gods, {22} and call'd all Hell to his assistance to revenge his Cause, but all in vain; his Malice, as his Hope, was fruitless, and enervate Rage recoiled upon himself, preyed on his Vitals, and was very near driving him into Madness; he had certainly sunk into a gloomy Melancholy, if his continual Inventions, his never-ceasing Stratagems had not kept his Mind awake. The perpetual Hurry of his tortur'd Brain, which to another would be the greatest Curse, is to him a Blessing, because it preserves him from falling into a Lethargy of Thought, an Evil of the two more dangerous to the Senses; he is forever studying, for ever contriving, one Scheme is no sooner overthrown, than another is built up. This indeed must be said of him, that he has a very great Genius![29] A prodigious Depth of Thought! An Aptitude of Apprehension! The most agreeable manner of Address, and fine way of delivering his Sentiments, of any Man in the World; and if he had any true Notions of Honour and Virtue, has all the other Requisites to make him as brave and estimable a Man, as his Pride, Ostentation, Avarice, and Hypocrisy have render'd him the contrary.

By what I have told you concerning *Graciana*, the Dutchess *de Cruizalla*, and this other Lady, you may perceive that, with his Ambition, he has the Mixture of a different Passion, tho' 'tis commonly in his power to govern it, whenever it seems to thwart the other more predominant one. His Soul is of too active a Disposition to permit him to leave a moment unimploy'd, and when he has the smallest Cessation[30] from Business, or that the more weighty Cares of his Interest will, give leave for gay Amusements, no Man takes more pleasure in them, or has a greater Relish for that Joy which is in the power of the Fair Sex to bestow. At some unbended Hours that *Cupid*, which these Islanders {23} worship in my room, has so much Influence o'er his Wishes, that he appears as tender, as melting, as assiduous, as if he were form'd for soft Desires alone, and *Love* were the only Business of his Life. It was in one of those ruinous Dispositions (unfortunately for her) he happen'd to be introduc'd to the Acquaintance of the celebrated *Miranda:* vanity, of which he has no small Share, was perhaps not less busy than his other Passion, to induce him to an Attempt of making a Conquest of this Lady's Heart; she was not almost

---

29 [Latin; *genie*, French: mental power or faculties and/or disposition of nature by which any one is qualified for some peculiar employment.]
30 [*cessatio*, Latin: a stop or rest.]

universally admir'd for her *Beauty* alone she had Charms superior far and if a thousand languish'd for the possession of her lovely *Person*, there were ten thousand who would have died to have engross'd her *Mind*. There was something so prodigiously enchanting in the Wonders of her *Wit*, that whenever she open'd her Mouth to speak, her Words seem'd chosen by the God of Eloquence! Nor were her Sentiments less to be admir'd than the manner in which they were express'd; her Soul was all angelick! Pure, and untainted, either with the fashionable Vices of the Age, or the common Frailties of her Sex, and was a *Woman* in nothing but her *Form!* Belov'd by the Gods, ador'd by Men, did the charming, the happy *Miranda* live till this curs'd Interview. O that it had been the Will of *Fate* to have kept forever asunder Souls so opposite to each other! Or permitted her good Genius to have warn'd her of the Danger of such a Meeting! But in her Destiny, Mortals may learn how little they ought to depend on human Wit, and that the most excellent of created Beings is yet widely distant from Perfection. *Romanus*, who had the destructive Art to appear what he pleas'd, and knew how to disguise the Truth so well, that by the most penetrating Eye he might be taken for what he seem'd, put on a Countenance and Behaviour, {24} such as he thought by her's would most engage her to approve of his Conversation. He found she had a Soul perfectly turned for Friendship, all Softness and Tenderness, Constancy and Sincerity, and therefore affected to be so too. All those wild Desires, which, at sight of an Object so enchanting, had invaded his disorder'd Breast, were with undoing Artifice disguised in *Esteem*. He prosess'd only to admire the Beauties of her *Mind*, and but carelesly spoke of the Charms of her *Person*; and tho' he omitted nothing that the most ardent *Lover* would have said, yet he still clos'd his Protestations with some Expression or other, which might assure her that he had no Wishes but what terminated in *Friendship*; He most cautiously avoided giving her any cause to imagine he was possess'd of the Passion he really was; he would often assure her, that he consider'd her not as a *Woman* that in entertaining her, he did not so much as think of the Difference of Sexes, but that he could not help imagining there was something of a Sympathy in their *Souls*, which engaged his tenderest Sentiments. By this way of proceeding he entirely won her to admit his Visits, and to entertain her as often as he had leisure; his Conversation is too engaging, and has, indeed, the Appearance of too many Advantages not to be joyfully accepted by those who apprehend not the Dangers of it. *Miranda* thought herself happy, in having a Friend so qualify'd, the little Foibles[31] and Impertinences of her own Sex took off the pleasure she might else have found in their Society.[32] She had often

---

31 [French: a weak side; a blind side; a failing.]
32 [societé, French; societas, Latin: company; converse.]

wish'd there was such a thing as a Male Friend without Design, and was overjoy'd to have met with one whom she believ'd so perfectly disinterested, and at the same time adorn'd with such a Strength of Judgment, so flowing a Wit, such a Nobleness of Sentiments, and such an elegant manner of uttering what he {25} meant, that in conversing with him the Improvement was equal to the Pleasure. She was extremely desirous of Knowledge, and he, being perfect in the Sciences, would read her Lectures on them for whole days together; bring her the most celebrated Authors, explain those Passages which want of Learning, not Capacity, made not so intelligible to her; in this agreeable, and as yet innocent manner, did a whole Year wear away, in all which time she never had the least reason to suspect he had any Designs to the prejudice of her Virtue; on the contrary, there was not a Person in the World on whom she would have so much depended for a Protector of it: her reserved Temper and Nicety in the choice of her Acquaintance, gave him frequent Opportunities of being alone with her; but his Behaviour was the same, as if the whole World had been present, to witness what he did. Experience of his Modesty, and Confidence in his Honour, made her think herself as safe with him, as with a Brother. By degrees she lov'd him with the same Affection as she would have done so near a Relation, and entertain'd him with as little Caution.

Now mark, by what base, by what, to any other Man, would have been impracticable measures, the artful Traitor pursu'd his Design of ruining this too generous Fair. By Insinuations, too subtle to be inspired but by the most cunning of all the *Fiends*, he wrought so far on her Belief, as to make her break off all Intimacy with her former Friends and Acquaintances; nay, deluded her so far, as to render her nearest Kindred suspected by her. She imagin'd everybody had some Design on her everybody was false—*Romanus* only was to be believ'd, *Romanus* only was to be trusted. So strangely was she infatuated by his Wiles,[33] that she look'd on all other Conversations as {26} dangerous; and as before she kept but little Company, she now admitted of no Visits but from him. Having thus brought her to confess, in all her Actions, she felt for him the tenderest Friendship her Soul was capable of conceiving, he began to prosecute the destructive Stratagem he had long been forming against her Honour. He never saw her now but with a melancholy Gloom on his Countenance, which, on every visit, seem'd to increase: he would, while she was speaking, counterfeit so profound a Reverie, as if he knew not where he was, or how engag'd; and then coming out of it, with a Sigh, beg pardon for his Ill-manners, which immediately he would again fall into. Tears would sometimes fall from his Eyes, which he pretended to endeavour to conceal from her ob-

---

33 [*wile*, Saxon; *wiel*, Islandick: a deceit; a fraud; a trick; a stratagem; a practice artful, sly, and insidious.]

servation; and when she ask'd the reason of so visible a Change, seem confounded that he had so far betray'd himself; assuring her she was mistaken, and that he had no cause for Chagrin, with so awkward an Air, that it might the more confirm her his Mind was overburthen'd[34] with some secret Woe, which, tho' he wou'd conceal, he had not power. The natural Curiosity of her Sex, might, of itself, have made her press him to disclose what had disturb'd him; but the Friendship she had for him (which indeed was of a nature more soft than yet she was sensible of herself) wou'd not suffer her to rest till she was satisfy'd of the Truth; long she intreated, long she conjur'd him to reveal the Cause of his uneasiness; he could not be prevail'd on, and at last told her, That if in reality there was anything that afflicted him, it was not of a nature to be disclos'd till after his Death; but that, said he, will not be long: you will soon, most engaging *Miranda*, be acquainted with the Misfortunes of *Romanus*; what Life denies me to reveal, my Death will in a short time betray; for when I find my latest hour {27} approaching, then, and not till then, can I resolve to make you a Confidant in this Affair. The innocent *Miranda* was so far from suspecting the real Design of these Words, that she rather took it ill that he refus'd to tell her what she so much desir'd to know, imagining his Caution proceeded from his doubt of her Secresy, and testify'd her Resentment in Expressions as severe as the Sweetness of her Disposition wou'd permit; so that at last, seemingly overcome by her Persuasions, and aw'd by her Commands into compliance, he obey'd, but begg'd she wou'd excuse his speaking; and taking up a Pen and Paper, disclos'd the fatal Secret in these Words:

> You press me, Madam, by Adjurations too powerful to be withstood, to let yon know the Cause of that Affliction which my Countenance and Behaviour, in spite of my efforts to the contrary, discover; I dare not disobey, tho' in fulfilling your Commands I render myself the most unhappy of all created Beings. I Love, I Adore, I Languish with the utmost extravagance of Passion for the possession of the incomparable *Miranda*, yet wou'd rather die than prejudice her by the accomplishment of my Desire, had I the means Judge not then too severely of an involuntary Crime, a Crime which is its own punishment, and which never rose even to a single Wish offensive to Virtue. As for my revealing it, I know you have too much Goodness to resent what your own Commands cou'd only have oblig'd me to. I can no more; do not hate my Memory, 'tis all I ask.

The moment he had finish'd these Lines, he rose from the Table with the appearance of a violent Disorder; and by the time he thought she had read them, fell into so admirably well feign'd a Swoon, that had a Physician been present, his Art might have been deceiv'd, and he mistaken it for *real*; But {28} in what Words

---

34 [*byrðen*, Saxon, and therefore properly written *burthen*. It is supposed to come from *burdo*, Latin, a male, as *onus* from ὄνος, an ass.]

shall I make you sensible what 'twas *Miranda* felt in this Surprize? A thousand Passions crowded at once into her Soul; confounded, and asham'd at what she read, she wou'd have spoke, and perhaps, in the first rush of Indignation, have banish'd the Writer from her sight: but then, to behold him thus dejected, thus overcome with grief, thus struggling, as she thought, with the fierce Pangs of desperate, dying Love; repell'd the Dictates of severer Honour, and turn'd her all to Pity and Forgiveness. She ran to him, supported his Head, used all the means she cou'd invent for his Recovery; and when she saw her endeavours had succeeded, and that he open'd his Eyes again, felt a Pleasure, which none but myself, who inspir'd it, can conceive. Both of them, however, remain'd silent for some moments; the tender Maid had too much confusion in her Thoughts to be able to bring forth one Word, and he that had given it her, believ'd it most proper for his Design to persevere in his Dissimulation,[35] and continuing silent, till too plainly reading in her Eyes, the Sentiments of her Soul, at last he broke it in this manner: Ah ! Too divine, too adorable *Miranda! Said he*, why wou'd you extort from my unwilling Lips this long-hid Truth? Why wou'd you enforce a Guilt more shocking than a thousand Deaths? My Passion known, your Honour forbids I e'er shou'd see you more, and my Love will not let me live when banish'd from you: all I have to hope, is, that you will not hate me after Death. Talk not of Death, *(interrupted she, unable to restrain the o'erflowing Tenderness, which, at sight of his Despair, quite drown'd all other Considerations)* I must not, will not let you die, nor can I yield to banish you my Presence; Honour forbids it not, nor can the strictest Rules of Virtue be injur'd by a Friendship such as ours; I have no Friend but you, none on Earth {29} to comfort, to advise, or be the Protector of my artless Innocence, and wou'd you leave me, leave me for ever? 'Twas unkindly urg'd. O, more than Angel *(resum'd be in a Transport)* such heavenly Goodness makes me more undone, but do not, do not suffer me to abuse it. Shou'd I continue to behold you, to be permitted to gaze upon your Charms, to touch your Hand, to grasp that World of Beauty in my Arms, with the allow'd Intimacy of Friendship; who knows how far my Reason might have power to govern wild Desire? How far might I not proceed, transported, hurry'd with my madding Passion! O, rather drive me from your Presence, banish me forever from you, curse me in eternal Absence, my Despair and Death are Woes less dreadful than your loss of Honour. He spoke these Words with such an Emphasis, and accompany'd them with so many marks of Anguish, that if *Miranda* was before resolv'd not to part with him, she wou'd now sooner have forgone her Life; she told him she had a double Security in his and her own Virtue, and had nothing to apprehend from his Passion, but

---

35 [*dissimulatio*, Latin: the act of dissembling; hypocrisy; fallacious appearance; false pretensions.]

what might flow from the Violence he did himself in restraining it; and wish'd, for his sake, that there were a possibility for her to render herself as unlovely in his Eyes as now she appear'd the contrary. Perhaps she was the first of her Sex that ever form'd a Wish like this, and 'tis scarce probable that even she wou'd have been satisfy'd to have had it, in reality, completed. She had Sentiments for him infinitely more tender than she was sensible of herself; and there is something so irresistibly pleasing, even to the most nicely Virtuous, in being thought amiable, by those who appear amiable themselves, that I question if Reason had ever yet the power to fortify a Heart against it. By gentle and unperceptible degrees he had stole on {30} her unguarded Soul, made every Faculty his own, and she was now, e'er she was aware of it, all his. O, let the Fair be warn'd by her Example, nor trust themselves with such dangerous Intimacies! If they must have Male Friends, let it be those who have no other Charms than bare Good-nature to recommend 'em; Wit and Beauty make impressions on the Mind which are not easily eras'd, the unwary Soul insensibly is caught, and when it wou'd, has not the power to get free. Hid beneath the specious show of a disinterested Friendship, the false *Romanus* had opportunity to inspire what Sentiments he pleas'd in the artless Breast of poor *Miranda*; and it was now impossible for her to esteem him less than she had done. But having gone so far as to make a discovery of his Passion, he thought it best to pursue that moment what he had begun; he justly guess'd, that in spite of the Dictates of her tenderness, that scrupulous Modesty, which so long had aw'd him, might, when she had consider'd on what had pass'd, oblige her to recall what she had said, and banish him as an Enemy to her Virtue.

In this surprize therefore, when all her Thoughts were hurry'd and disorder'd when her whole Soul, dissolv'd in soft Commiseration of his Woes, could inspire Words of Consolation only, he took advantage to undo her, and seize that Joy at once, which, 'twas highly probable, should he have given her time for Reflection, would never have been his. With all the Arts of fond seducing Passion, with all the Pomp of ruinous Desire, Impatiencies, Perplexities, melting Languishments, Sighs, Tears, Distractions, feign'd Anguish, real Rapture, did he attack her on the defenceless part; and while he swore to die rather than attempt an injury to her Honour, undermined it, and every moment gaining ground, at last triumph'd o'er all, and revell'd to the height of {31} guilty Transport. 'Twas Absence of Mind, 'twas Surprize, 'twas Inadvertency, 'twas Nature, and Excess of Softness not base Desires, or polluted Wishes, ruin'd this fair Unfortunate! Guilty in *Fact*, but innocent in *Thought!* She yielded, unknowing that she did so. O'erwhelm'd in Pity for the imagin'd Sufferings of a Man who long had been dearer to her than her Life, distracted at his Despair, and panting to relieve him, when laying his burning cheek upon her bosom, he cry'd, *Friendship* allows thus much, nor will *Honour* be offended: she answer'd, or rather her ill Genius spoke thro' her Lips—No, no, my dear, my lov'd *Romanus*, we must never part, our Souls may join their mutual Flame without a Crime. They may indeed, *retorted be, pressing her more closely*, they must, they shall,—and thus—thus—thus! The eternal Blaze shall mingle. These Words were follow'd by Actions only to be guess'd at. I look'd, and saw the lovely Victim, pity'd her Fate, but had not power to avert it. The hurrying Scene of wild Delight once o'er, Reason return'd and Thought again restored, how did the ruin'd Charmer regret what she had done! Her Breast now heav'd with Sighs, her Eyes grew big with Tears and every Look reproach'd the cruel Conquest he had gain'd: her Tongue indeed was silent. Grief and Shame had stopp'd the Utterance of her Words; but her speaking Gestures supply'd the want of Language. *Romanus*, gay and vain on his Success, appeared as much changed from what he lately was, as did *Miranda*, and easily perceiving what her thoughts were, was willing to compleat his Victory, by making her not dissatisfy'd that he had gain'd it, he kiss'd away her Tears, smother'd her Sighs in his still glowing Breast. Vow'd by each God he would be ever true, secret, just and omitted no Argument {32} of fond endearing Love, to prove her Gratitude and Compassion for him, were the highest Effects of her Virtue. There is nothing in the world sooner erased than the Shame which immediately ensues a Condescension such as she had yielded to. The happy Lover easily finds the way to chase the remorseful Confusion from her Soul; and the same Arts which won her to consent, prevail to make her not repent it. *Miranda* forgave him and herself, and placing the ultimate of her Felicity in obliging him, permitted him to indulge in guilty Rapture. But alas! Many Weeks had not pass'd, before, tir'd and grown satiated with the luscious Banquet, he scorn'd and shun'd the too, too liberal Giver—he avoided her, saw her no more, abandon'd her to all the Stings of late Repentance, Despair, and conscious Guilt. In vain she writ, in vain she sent, in vain enquired the Cause of such a sudden Change; he had not Remains enough of Tenderness to make even an excuse for his Behaviour—distracted, wild with such inhuman Treatment, and altogether incapable of revenging it, she fell into Agonies which are not to be conceiv'd. Some base People, who had the Management of her Affairs, perceiving her Inability to look into their Actions with that prudent Care she had been accustom'd, took the advantage of enriching themselves, by rendering her more wretched, in the reducing a very plentiful Fortune to scarce a Competency. The enchanted *Well* was the Pretence, and the Gold they put into their own Pockets, she was made to believe was sunk this way. At last rouzing her Spirits as much as she was able, she began to cast about how she shou'd repair her Losses, and having still the ill-luck to meet with self-interested Advisers, was put into a wrong method of Proceeding; by which, in a little time, she fell into very great Misfortunes. *Romanus*, tho' he {33} knew what had happened, had not the gratitude to offer her either the assistance of his Advice or Purse; she was obliged to leave the Island, and is now gone to seek her Fortune among Strangers. This last event of her hard Fate, touch'd him no more than did the rest. He has at this time an Intrigue with the Wife of the Chevalier *Brisoe*, but the consequence of this Affair is not much to be regarded; she is of a Disposition as wavering as ungrateful, and in everything as base as his own, and whichever of them gets the start in Inconstancy, there is little to be fear'd from the Despair of the other. This is all I have to say of *Romanus*, as to what touches my Prerogative, in his prophaning the name of Love, and calling me to witness the most detested Falshoods. As to his other Crimes, his Deceits, his Treacheries, his Plots, his monstrous Lyes, Hypocrisy, and ruinous Inventions, let the Gods, whom he has injur'd in those points, declare against him, and brand him for what he is—a most consummate Villain.

The God of soft Desires had, perhaps, added somewhat more, to testify the Displeasure he had conceiv'd against this Prophanet of his Name, if the *Stranger*, whose Eyes, for some moments, had been attracted by a Lady lately come into the Assembly, had not taken the liberty of entreating to know who she was. She seem'd to be a Woman of no small consequence to those who were concern'd in the *enchanted Well*; scarce a Person there that she had not acquaintance with: she whisper'd to one, smil'd on another, curt'sy'd to another, was in a moment thro' the Crowd, and appear'd to have vast Business with 'em all. Her Eyes, her Hands, her Tongue, were for ever employ'd in such a manner, that it presently came into his head, that the Searchers after the *perpetual Motion*, might cease from farther enquiry, and find *it here*.

{34} Not the Immutability of the divine Essence cou'd defend the *Deity* from discovering, in his radiant Eyes, a kind of disorder at this Question, pretty near to that which Mortals feel when seiz'd with sudden wonder at some Spectacle which appears a Prodigy. That Woman, *said he*, is a Paradox even to him that created her. Endu'd by Heaven with a thousand Graces, she was sent on Earth to charm and bless the Age she liv'd in; but not content with what she receiv'd from the bounty of the Gods, she enter'd herself a Subject to the *infernal* Potentate,[36] and from his mischief-teaching Court, brought with her all the Venom of the Place; there is in her the Extremes of Good and Evil, there is no Virtue she is not capable of, nor scarce, Vice she does not practise; the greatest Contradictions are center'd in her Humour, she is at once Liberal and Avaricious, Generous and Mercenary, Cunning and Designing, yet unguarded and open-hearted; sometimes cruel and revengeful even for trifling Affronts, at others, and often for the greatest Injuries, too ready to forgive. The Winds are not so uncertain as her Temper, and tho' her Behaviour from fifteen has remark'd her for a zealous Devotee of that *Idol*

---

36 [*potentat*, French: monarch; prince; sovereign.]

for whom I am dethron'd, yet the Objects in whose favour she was possess'd of those Desires, have been so various, so often chang'd, that the World has ever been at a loss on whom to fix the Scandal of her Affections. There is, however, one, and but one Disposition of her Soul, which neither Experience, Misfortunes, nor the Thoughts of approaching Wrinkles, for she is now thirty-seven, can have the power to alter, and that is, an insatiate vanity of being admired for her Beauty; there is nothing so dear, she wou'd not quit for an hour's fulsome Flattery, even from the Man she most despises; nor is there any so contemptible, that {35} she endeavours not to engage, and to that end, will spare no pains, no expense, either of Time, Reputation, Friends, or Money. Among the number of those she spread her Snares for, were two Brothers, both Gentlemen of uncommon Qualifications; the elder, whose Name is *Lauranus*, has scarce his equal in the world, either for the beauties of his Person, or the excellence of his Understanding; 'tis impossible to view him without a mixture of Delight and Reverence, or to hear him without Wonder and Improvement: and to all the Excellencies that bear the Name of Masculine, there is also join'd a sweetness of Disposition, something so very tender, so commiserating, so kind, as exceeds the Gentleness of *Woman*. The younger, who is call'd *Constantius*, if he may be thought possess'd of some of these Accomplishments in a less eminent degree than his Brother, seems in others to excel not only him, but the generality of mankind; he boasts a Faith unshaken! A Constancy which no Temptations have the power to remove, no Provocations can surmount! a Sincerity to all the World, which Interest cannot byass, nor even Complaisance diminish! *Lauranus* has indeed a more penetrating Discernment, he saw immediately into *Flirtillaria*'s Soul, and despised the vain Coquet; but *Constantius*, who, free from all Deceit himself, cou'd not be brought to suspect it in another, much more in one he thought so amiable, was easily deluded by those Pretences which, when she pleases, no Woman can make appear more specious. He was blind to all her Vices, and look'd with favourable Eyes on those Follies which she went not about to conceal: he became her Husband in a short time, and thought himself, by being so, the happiest of his Sex; even Marriage render'd not her Faults conspicuous to his Observation; on the contrary, he imagin'd he every day {36} discover'd some new Beauty in her, and possession but added to the Passion he before had for her—but alas! this heaven of Felicity was but of a short duration, the levity of her Humour cou'd not long restrain itself from breaking out into Extravagancies, such as wou'd scarce gain credit from those not witness of them; and tho', after committing the greatest irregularity, she had Arts to persuade her too believing Husband all her Designs were innocent, yet his Relations were of another mind; and indeed, she sow'd so much Dissension among them, that not one of them cou'd endure her presence, and were continually making him uneasy with the repetition of her Follies.

The first Instance she gave of her propensity to Mischief, was, that *Lauranus* being soon after his Brother marry'd to a Lady every way the reverse of *Flirtillaria*, she made it her business to infuse into her gentle Breast the Poison of Jealousy; the name of *Bride* was hardly exchang'd for that of *Wife*, before she repeated to her all the little Gallantries she had ever heard of *Lauranus*, told her it was a jest for her to expect Constancy from him, whose Inclinations were the most amorous and roving of any Man in the world; and, as well for the gratification of her own Vanity, as to make the other more uneasy, very artfully insinuated, that he had made declarations to herself, which did not become him to the Wife of his Brother. The young Lady entirely unacquainted with the World, too easily believ'd her, and grew extremely melancholy, but conceal'd the Cause of her Chagrin till her Husband, having observ'd the close whispers between her and his Sister, immediately suspected it was by that mischievous Creature she had been told something which had embitter'd the natural Sweetness of her Temper, he never rested till he was Master of the Secret, and when he was so, 'tis not to be doubted but he {37} rid his House of a Guest so disturbing. The two Brothers, who till then had liv'd together in the most perfect Amity, now parted with a good deal of Dissatisfaction on both sides; each had the most tender Affection for the other that ever was known, and this Separation, to both, was worse than Death, tho' neither wou'd seem to regret it. *Lauranus* was griev'd to see his Brother so much infatuated by the wiles of this more than Sorceress, as to defend her in the grossest and most unpardonable Faults; and *Constantius*, who cou'd not think his belov'd Spouse in the wrong, resented the little credit, which he found her denials of what she had done, had gain'd in the Family, and there was an estrangement between them, which nothing before ever had the power to make.

The Father of these Gentlemen had squander'd away a very plentiful Estate; there was but little remaining for the Heir, and scarce any thing for the younger Family. *Constantius* therefore, who had his Fortune to make, cou'd not have pitch'd on a Wife more unfit for his purpose than *Flirtillaria*, who was of a Temper to create him nothing but Enemies; and to add to this, so extravagant in her Expences, that it would have requir'd a Prince's Revenue, to have supply'd her with those Pleasures which were necessary to keep her in good-humour. The little Fortune she brought, was immediately consum'd, and all the Woes of Indigence ensu'd; then it was that the generous *Lauranus* prov'd himself a Brother and a Friend, and forgetting the Provocations she had given him, but suffer'd them just to know what it was to want Relief, and then afforded it in so generous a manner, that they knew no difference between using his Purse and their own; and indeed 'twas hard to say, whether the giver or receiver felt the greatest Pleasure: nor was it only to themselves the noble-minded *Lauranus* {38} confin'd his Generosity, their Children (for the Lady is pretty prolifick) were taken the same tender Care of as his own, their Friends oblig'd. He did not think it enough that his beloved Brother and Family should want no Necessaries of Life, he also put it in his power to confer Favours on others whom, he knew, he could not be happy while they were the contrary. Nor was his Lady in the least chagrin'd at what he did, the Excellence of her Nature, and the Tenderness she had for her Husband, made her regard every thing that belong'd to him with an uncommon Care.

But not all these Obligations had the power to warm the thankless Soul of *Flirtillaria* with the least spark of Gratitude—she secretly hated *Lauranus*, as she did everybody who was not blind to her Faults; and tho' perceiving her incorrigible, he had of late ceas'd to give her any advice, yet she was very well acquainted with his Thoughts of her—she knew he contemn'd her, and would have rejoic'd in an opportunity to have made him been so by the whole World. She envy'd him the Prosperity of his Affairs, tho' it was all which preserv'd herself from falling into the lowest depth of Misery, and while she meanly fawn'd on him, and, much more than he desired, acknowledg'd the Obligations she had to him, curs'd Fortune, in her heart, for giving him the means of conferring them. Ingratitude, however, tho' a Crime as offensive to Heaven as any, was not that which render'd her most despicable to the World, her intolerable Fondness for being admired by the Men, made her take all opportunities of being seen by them; and rather than not oblige them to use her with more respect than any other Woman in Company, would yield to any thing; and rather than not have the Town sensible how much she was admired, would recount all the fine things that were said to her, {39} show what Letters she receiv'd, and make everyone that came to visit her the Confidant of her Amours. To be neglected, she thought, was the worst Scandal could be thrown on her; all her Pride consisted in the Reputation of a number of Adorers, and to those she had in reality, she added in her Report a thousand more. If she knew but the Name of any Gentleman, it was sufficient for her to build a Pretension of an Intimacy with him; and nothing could be more comical, to those that knew it to be Invention, than to hear her run on with all the Volubility in the world for hours together, in the recital of particular Conversations with Persons whom perhaps the never saw in her whole Life. This ridiculous Humour, however, was of some service to her, tho' she did not mean it to be so, for when any Reports reach'd her Husband's ears, of Consequences which he knew were impossible to be true, it serv'd to make those that were so, appear equally fictitious; and whenever he was told that she had been at such a Place, or meeting such a Person, he look'd on all such Accusations as the Effects of Malice, and would say, *Aye, this is as certain as that she was in company the other day with Mr. Such-a-one, a Man who I* knew she has not the least acquaintance with. Thus were all the Remonstrances[37] of his Friends rendred fruitless, and his good Opinion of her still kept up in its first Strength, he could not be brought to believe that she had any Fault greater than that little Vanity, which he perceiv'd too much of in other Women, to think it a Crime unpardonable in her, who in his Judgment had infinitely more cause for it: and while the grave *Sommerius*, the young *Philarchus*, the witty, gay *Burtonius*, the roving, wild *Arthario*, the debonair[38] *Mersus*, and many others, triumph'd in those Joys he believ'd himself the sole Possessor of, was the only Person (excepting those concern'd {40} in it) who pity'd not the Misfortune he labour'd under. In spite of the handsome Allowance they receiv'd from the Generosity of *Lauranus*, the extravagant Expences of the Wife, rendred the Husband one of the most unhappy Men on Earth in almost every Circumstance of Life, which ashamed to reveal, or unwilling to press him farther, to whom already he had been so far oblig'd, all those Woes from which they had been once redeem'd, return'd on this unfortunate Family: it was not now altogether so much in the power of *Lauranus* as it had been, to disburse such a Sum of Money as was requisite to raise his Brother from that Depth of Sorrow, the Profuseness of *Flirtillaria* had plung'd him in; neither did he think it justifiable to take from those little Innocents of his own what was their Due by Birth, to supply the mad Prodigality[39] and lavish Pride of a vile Woman, who, he knew, hated both him and every thing that belong'd to him, and who had not one good Quality to countenance his Favour. Nature, however, and the tender Friendship he had for his Brother, would not suffer him to see him lost; he entreated him to take shelter in his House from the Dangers which threatned him, but *Constantius* could not yet be prevail'd on to leave the Cause of all his Misfortunes, and would not consent to enter those Gates, which were not alike open to his Wife—he rather chose to be Partaker of all the Woes she had brought on herself and him, than live apart from her, she was still his dear Wife, his adorable *Flirtillaria*; nor had anything she had done the power to diminish that unalterable Affection he had begun to love her with. Had their Fortune been drove even to the last degree of Misery, 'tis possible he would have been content to have shared it with her, had she continued to dissemble with him as she had done; but now the Case was alter'd, she wanted to get {41} rid of him, and having lost the advantage of his Brother's Purse, would gladly have been eased of that Impediment a Husband's Presence was, to her procuring the use of others—her Pride must be supported, and her Lovers must now pay for those Favours, they had been accustom'd

---

37 [*remonstrance*, French, from *remonstrate:* show; discovery. Not in use.]
38 [*debonnaire*, French: elegant; civil; well-bred; gentle; complaisant.]
39 [*prodigalité*, French, from *prodigal:* extravagance; profusion; waste; excessive liberality.]

to receive *gratis*. Beside, she had another Contrivance in her head, some of her Kindred were wealthy, but pretty well acquainted with the Extravagance of her Humour, had forbore giving any encouragement to her Follies; she design'd therefore, if she could weary him from living with her, to make her Application to them, form a plausible Story of his Barbarity, and throw the Odium of all on him. The sweetest Disposition may be four'd by continual Provocations, her Behaviour was intolerable, it could not be endur'd even by him, who was willing to bear almost any thing rather than a Separation—he grew uneasy to that degree, that it threw him into a downright Melancholy, and perceiving she took a pleasure in seeing him so, and at last convinc'd that she was far from regarding him with that Tenderness she ought, or that she had once made him hope, he comply'd with the Persuasions of his Friends, retir'd to the House of *Lauranus*, and left her to act as she pleased; there was still remaining a small Annuity, which he was too generous to take from her, and throwing himself wholly on the Good-nature of his Brother, parted from her, but not for ever. Poor unhappy (but still faithful) Gentleman, he flatter'd himself that when left alone, Time and Reflection would work an alteration in her Humour, and she would sue for his Return, and curse those Follies, which, tho' they had not power to estrange, had half broke the Heart of one of the most affectionate Husbands the World ever produc'd. But alas! A little time convinc'd him of his Mistake; she was so far {42} from endeavouring to retrieve her Character, that she exposed herself in such a fashion, that it became scandalous to be seen in her Company: having no longer a dependance on the Friendship of *Lauranus*, nor any remains of awe for the Resentment of *Constantius*, she openly gave loose to those Pleasures she before allow'd herself in something more reserv'd a manner. Her Face was known even in Places the most noted for Debauchery—she made no secret of the Liberties she granted, her Indiscretion, her Madness, in revealing those Crimes any other Woman would have taken all imaginable care to have kept conceal'd, made her justly contemptible to the World; but what rendred her most detestable to the Gods was the monstrous Aspersion she cast on the innocent *Constantius*; she made everybody, not acquainted with the Nobleness of his Nature, or the Baseness of her's, believe he countenanced her Crimes, was the Baud of her Pleasures, and for a little private Interest consented to all she did. In the world's eye, the Unfortunate are always faulty; the unhappy Circumstances to which *Constantius* was reduced, made this Report pass more current than otherwise it would have done; and the little belief he seem'd to give to those who endeavour'd to make him sensible of her Vices, confirm'd them in the opinion he but pretended to be blind to that, in which he found an advantage not to see. The vile Creature had two Children after their Separation, which to most of her Acquaintance she declared were not his; but he acknowledging them to be such, and endeavouring all he could to silence the Clamours[40] of Scandal from being thunder'd against her, drew it all on himself, and became as much the Object of *Blame*, as otherwise he would have been of *Compassion*.

{43} But not all I have recounted of this Woman can excite your wonder half so much as what I've yet to say of her: she has a young Gallant,[41] of whom she is so excessive fond, that she sacrifices her very Pride to oblige him, yet is never happier than when she is inventing something to make him appear ridiculous; she laughs at all Mankind with him, and laughs with all Mankind at him; she makes it her business to expose him in all publick Places, to make him be look'd on as an Ideot, yet in private idolizes him; and both one and the other, without any visible reason, for the young Gentleman is neither Fool enough to create Mirth,[42] nor Wife enough to excite Admiration: she has Sense to know it, but not Solidity to ask herself the question which of the two he is, nor of what advantage it is either to her Interest or Satisfaction to behave to him, and concerning him, as she does. But I am weary of talking of her, the Eyes of the long-deluded *Constantius* at last are open'd, he is convinced of the Injuries he has sustain'd by her; he now thinks of her with the Contempt which is due to her, resolves to see her no more, tho' in bringing himself to that Determination it has cost him many a bitter Pang. Behold another of much the same Character, in everything as ridiculous, in some more vile, that big-bone'd, buxom, brown Woman, who is now talking to her; the Conformity of Manners, join'd to the Fondness both of them have for new Acquaintance, have made them very intimate—her Name is *Gloatitia*, Daughter of the Chevalier *Del Gloatus*. Some say it was from him she learn'd those deluding Arts, she has since practis'd, to the Ruin of as many Women as she could get acquainted with their Lovers or their Husbands. Whether this Report be true, I will not pretend to determine; for my pure and hallow'd Fires would sicken at a sight so {44} horrible, so shocking as an Act of Incest: but this is certain, that they scrupled not to be seen in the same Bed together, and the old Goat would run into luscious Encomiums[43] on the Beauties of her Limbs to all the young *Chevaliers* who came to his Levée.[44] When she was about the Age of Sixteen, he was about to marry her to a young Mechanick, but the Fellow's good Stars directed him to avoid so great an Evil; an intimate Acquaintance of his, one of those to whom already she had been liberal of her Favours, made a timely discovery of her Humour, and to confirm the Veracity of his Words, produc'd some Letters he had received from her,

---

40 [*clamor*, Latin: outcry; noise; exclamation; vociferation.]
41 [from the adjective: a gay, sprightly, airy, splendid man.]
42 [*myrhde*, Saxon: merriment; jollity; gaiety; laughter.]
43 [ἐγκώμιον, Ancient Greek: panegyrick; praise; elogy.]
44 [A dam built to prevent the overflow of a river.]

containing an acknowledgement of all that had pass'd between them. This broke the Match, but she had, however, the good fortune to please a certain Duke, who never was over-nice in his Choice—he had a Son by her, and allow'd her a handsome Subsistence, till happening to come at an hour she did not expect him in, he found the most dirty and disagreeable of all his Footmen in her Arms. 'Tis not to be imagin'd but that the ocular Demonstration of a Falsehood like this, would oblige him to quit her. After this she fell into great Extremities, and, shunn'd by all who had the power to serve her, rang'd the Town for a miserable Maintenance, was common even to the meanest Rank of Men, and at last despis'd by the vilest, and most profligate. Who that sees her now, dress'd in her rich Brocade, Diamonds in her Hair and Breast, and a handsome Equipage to attend her, would believe she had been accustom'd to trudge the Streets with scarce a Shoe, and been transported at the Invitation of a Blue-apron Gallant, who charitably feasted her on the Remnants of those Treats, made for more fortunate Ladies of the same Vocation? Yet all this has been her Case for many Years together, and still would have been so, if *Rutho* had not {45} chang'd the Scene: he was, perhaps, the only Man in the world who wou'd have thought her worth retrieving; but he never had an intrigue with anything but a common Woman, and they say, has suffer'd sufficiently for his Pleasures that way.

He was old and infirm, and had occasion for a Nurse, he therefore took her into Keeping, and allow'd her four hundred Crowns a year; a vast Income for a Creature who had liv'd for a long time withour seeing the thousandth part of such a Sum of her own; but it is not in this Wretch's Nature to be grateful or constant, and she regarded the Man who had preserv'd her from perishing, no otherwise than to make him her Property. The Money she receiv'd from him, served to put her into a habit and manner of living, to draw Company more agreeable to her Taste; she now cou'd dress, make Entertainments, had handsome Lodgings, and it was an advantage to her, that having been known before by few but those of the meaner sort, the extreme vileness of her Character reach'd not the ears of those Persons she was now in a condition to converse with. Everybody knew she had been Mistress to the Duke *Dubarbe*, and believing it was he that debauch'd her, and considering her as an unfortunate Gentlewoman (for *Del Gloatus* was really of a good Family, and had an honourable post in the Army) pity'd a Fault, they believ'd, she had been but ensnar'd to commit. She was visited by several Persons of good Fashion, and some of tolerable Reputation scrupled not to be seen in her Company. *Rutho* had taken Lodgings for her in a Place perfectly pleasant, it was in the Country, but so near the City, that whenever she pleas'd to go to it, she might be there in an hour's time; and indeed it was there she pass'd most of her days and nights, seldom being at home but when she {46} expected her old Gallant, still continuing her former manner of living, tho' with more Privacy, and better Company. The amorous Stealths she took were not, however, so secret, but that *Rutho* at last had intelligence of them, and was about to turn her off, when her Brother, who had been absent from the Island some years, return'd; and being instructed by his Sister, in the Humour and Disposition of *Rutho*, and how to behave, instead of suffering him to do himself Justice, in discarding a Woman who had been so false to him, forced him to marry her: since that, she does what she pleases, goes where she pleases, her Husband is in too much awe of the young *Chevalier*, to dare to discover how much he is dissatisfy'd. Her Actions now plainly demonstrate to the World, it was not *Poverty* alone which had obliged her to those Courses he wou'd have taken her from; her Inclinations now appear bare-faced, and so monstrous impudent is she in pursuing the gratification of them, that she waits not for being address'd, nor thinks it beneath her to make the first application. Two or three indigent Persons, whose Consciences are complaisant enough to yield to any thing for Interest, are maintain'd by her, for no other Service, than to procure her a variety of those Pleasures she most delights in. The best Wine, and Conversation with the handsomest Men, are all the Heaven she wishes, and having an absolute command of the unhappy browbeat *Rutho*'s Purse, is resolv'd to want nothing that she thinks essential to her happiness; from one scene of Debauchery she hurries to another, and scarce a day passes, without being witness of some new Crime as extravagant as shameless. Of all the Gods there is none she acknowledges but *Phœbus*, him she frequently implores for assistance, to charm her Lovers with the Spirit of *Poetry*; but he had receiv'd a Check from *Jupiter*, for inspiring the Genius of a {47} sometime since deceas'd Nobleman, too severe, to dare to aid the Sentiments of this Wanton. She pretends, however, to have an intimate acquaintance with the Muses, has judgment enough to know that *ease* and *please* make a *Rhyme*, and to count ten Syllables on her Fingers. This is the Stock with which she sets up for a Wit, and among some ignorant Wretches passes for such; but with People of true Undestanding, nothing affords more subject of ridicule, than that incoherent Stuff which she calls Verses. She bribed, with all the Favours she is capable of conferring, a Bookseller (famous for publishing soft things) to print some of her Works, on which she is not a little vain: tho' she might very well have spared herself the trouble. Few Men, of any rank whatsoever, but have been honour'd with the receipt of some of her Letters both in Prose and Measure, few Coffee-Houses but have been the Repository of them, she daily hears the upbraidings of one Lover for her discover'd Addresses to another; but she can bear it without blushing, and is not of a humour to make herself uneasy at any thing that is said to her, or of her. The greatest mortification that, perhaps, ever happen'd to her, was, that after having taken the pains to dress herself in the most exact manner she cou'd, in order to charm a young Officer, brought him into her Bed-chamber, dismiss'd her Attendants, and invited him to her Arms with all the tempting languishments of loose Desire, he remain'd insensible! He was not to be provoked! He was not to be mov'd! Cold as a *Greenland* Rock, not all her Fire cou'd melt him! In vain her swimming Eyes declared what 'twas she wish'd; in vain her Robe thrown by, disclos'd her naked heaving Breasts rise swelling to be press'd; in vain her glowing trembling Hands grasp'd his, and gently stole themselves into his Bosom; in vain her {48} longing, her expecting Soul, seem'd to evaporate in Sighs; in vain she fainted, dy'd away before him; all her Blandishments[45] were lost on him, not that his reserve was owing to his Virtue, or to a Frigidity of Nature; in the whole Island, there was not a Man who had less a Notion of the one, nor a greater Warmth of the other; but Favours offer'd in a manner so free, so unsought, so unthought of, instead of gently touching the Passion the endeavour'd to raise, quell'd all the motions of Desire, and shock'd the Soul. In a Scene like this, there was no possibility of a Medium; he must have been extremely *delighted*, if he had not been extremely *disgusted*, and, as he was the latter, pretending a sudden Indisposition, he took his leave before it was consistent with good Manners. Judge with what Confusion a Woman of her Temper must receive such a Baulk, but resolving not to be wholly disappointed, call'd for her Man *Johannes*; he was a tall, well-made young Fellow, of good Features, and a sanguine[46] Complexion, and from that time, was ever ready to afford his Lady consolation. She had not Gratitude, however, long to be sensible of the Obligations she had to him, but for some little negligence of Behaviour, either in publick or private, incens'd his Master against him, and got him turn'd away. In his place there is now another, whom she seems much more to approve of, and has given him a Diamond-Ring, and a Locket of her Hair. But I shou'd wear out the day, to recount the thousandth part of her various Amours, or the unnumber'd Changes of her roving Inclinations; nor does a History, such as hers, become me to relate. I wou'd have pass'd both hers and *Flirtillaria*'s in silence, if the signaliz'd Airs of these Coquets had not oblig'd you to remark them—but by the little I have said concerning them, 'tis easy for you to believe they are Objects of detestation to every {49} heavenly Power, and to me in particular, whose Name they every hour blaspheme, and call to witness of the most abhorr'd Falsities. I shall only add this of *Gloatitia*, that she has lately been deliver'd of a Child which must heir the unhappy *Rutho*'s Estate, tho' to which of her *Enamorato's* the little Compound does with most right belong, even the omnipotent *Jupiter*, who breath'd the Breath of Life into it, can scarce determine.

---

45 [from *blandish; blanditiæ*, Latin: act of fondness; expression of tenderness by gesture.]
46 [*sanguin*, French, *sanguineus*, from *sanguis*, Latin: red; having the colour of blood.]

The Deity of tender Wishes here seem'd to pause, as tho' he were considering which, next to those he had already mentioned, of this numerous Assembly, were most distinguishable for perjur'd Love, and base Ingratitude; and casting round hit sweetly shining Eyes, at last fixed them on a young Lady, whose every Look and Motion spoke perfect Innocence, and heavenly Truth angelick Softness sat on each Feature of her lovely Face, and all the Graces play'd in her modest Smiles. See there! *Resum'd the God, pointing to her, and with a troubled Air shaking his ambrosial Locks*, there is a Form whose Fall all Heaven laments! Not my own *Psyche*'s Loss fill'd me with greater Anguish. Ah! Who that gazes on that world of Beauty, that bright appearance of celestial Virtue could believe it a Repository of loose Desires! Who would imagine, at her years, Deceit grown old! The fair Apostate is scarce nineteen, yet is mistress of more artifice than half her Sex beside. She is the Daughter of a foreign Count, her Name *Clarismonda*, married to a new created Peer of this Island, a Gentleman every way deserving her Person, all charming as it is, tho' it were adorned with a Mind equally lovely; but I was not consulted in the Addresses he made her, nor did *Hymen* smile on their Nuptials. He had been privately contracted to a young Lady of very great merit, whom basely quitting for *Clarismonda*, the immortal Gods thought fit to {50} punish his Infidelity by retaliating it—not all his Accomplishments can inspire him with the Secret to please his Wife. She finds in herself an Aversion to him, and the Marriage-Bed is as loathsome to her as the Grave. Her Husband's Power however, her own seeming Innocence, and untainted Reputation of Virtue, have deter'd any of the Grandees from making an Attempt on her: but she was resolved not to be without a Lover, and made choice of one herself in a manner particular enough. Happening to look out of the Palace Windows one Evening, full of warm Wishes, and amorous Contemplations, she spied a young Soldier, whose Form seem'd very agreeable; the new Desire which that moment invaded her Soul, took from her the power of Consideration; and dressing her immediately in a Suit of her Maid's Clothes, went down into the Court-yard where he was on duty; and conforming her Behaviour, as much as possible, to her Habit, and jigging[47] towards him with the air of an *Abigail*, accosted him with the little Impertinencies of such a Creature. 'Tis very cold, Sir, *said she*, I pity you Soldiers that are confin'd so many hours in all sorts of Weather. Well, you earn your Money very hard, tho' I think a Soldier the most honourable Vocation of any. In this manner did she run on, still observing heedfully his Looks all the time she was speaking; and finding nothing in them, but what promised Success in her Design, she ask'd him how long it would be before he came off Duty; and being told in about half an hour, made an Appointment to

---

47 [A practice of fishing with a jig, a type of fishing lure with an attached weight.]

meet him at a House hard by. He readily comply'd, and she went directly to the place of Assignation to prepare the Woman, who being a Person who work'd for her, was entirely at her devotion, and not a little pleased to be made a Confidant in an Affair such as this. The eager {51} Soldier made all imaginable haste to his pretty Mistress; their meeting was full of Rapture! And 'tis possible with a greater Satisfaction on both sides, as he believ'd her not of a Rank much superior to his own, than if he had been apprized of the real Quality of the Person he possess'd. After passing two or three Hours together in a manner each thought themselves happy in, she cold him it was time to take leave, and putting a piece of Money into his hand, bid him drink her Health, and appointed him to meet her at the same place the next day, and enquire for Mrs. *Molly*. He promised to be punctual, and adjourn'd to a neighbouring House of Entertainment to do as she had ordered, and regale himself with his new Mistress's Bounty. It was in the dark he had receiv'd it: but by the weight imagining it was a Crown-piece, was resolv'd (as Men of his Profession seldom hoard) to indulge himself as far as it would go. After having eat and drank in a plentiful manner, he carelesly threw down the Money, and was walking off; when the People of the House having an Honesty uncommon in this Age, call'd him back, and ask'd if he knew what it was he had given them. The poor Lover was in a terrible apprehension that Mrs. *Molly* had deceiv'd him with false Coin, and was beginning to cast about in his Mind which way he should repair the damage he had done without being oblig'd to pluck off his Regimental Clothes, and leave them for a Pledge; when they told him it was a five-pound piece of Gold, and desired to know if he had no smaller Money, or if he must have it changed. The Extasy with which he heard these words, would be difficult even for me to represent—he jumped about the Room, sung, and cried, my *Molly*, my *Molly*, my *Molly*. Oh, she is a glorious Girl, a dear Girl; never Man had such {52} a generous Wench.[48] Well, I am a lucky Fellow. With a thousand such like Expressions he vented the Rapture he was in, to find himself master of a Sum which to him was a vast one. The People, no doubt, not understanding for what Cause he was so much transported, believ'd him to be mad; but that was none of their Business, they paid themselves for what he had called for, and returning him the rest of the Money, thought no more of him. He had but little Sleep that night, excess of Joy is as great an Enemy to that composer of Senses, as excess of Grief. He counted the fleeting hours, and thought 'em Ages. He rose with *Phœbus*, and watch'd for his setting with the utmost Impatience. The dear expected moment at last arriv'd, and he flew to the rendevouz of Bliss; where enquiring, as he was commanded, for Mrs. *Molly*, all the Surprize, all the Joy, all the Ex-

---

48 [*wencle*, Saxon: a young woman.]

tasy he before had felt, was nothing to that which now seized on each Faculty of his wondering Soul—*Clarismonda* now appeared herself, all her Charms display'd in their full vigour, and illustrated with a Blaze of Jewels; immediately he knew her, and knew also that this most celebrated of all the Court-Beauties and his Mrs. *Molly* were the same. He stood Thunder-struck with Amazement, his tumultuous Thoughts, divided betwixt Joy and Fear took from him the power of Speech. Tho' he had enjoy'd her with all the unlimited Freedom of luxuriant Desire, tho' every naked Charm about her had feasted his impatient Eyes, and his wild Hands travelled o'er all that Field of Beauty; so much was he now aw'd by her discover'd Quality, he scarce dared look upon her. The Confusion she beheld him in, was no more than she expected; but while she pity'd, could not forbear laughing heartily at it: which adding to his {53} Disorder, she was obliged to rise from her Chair; and taking him by the hand, drew him gently to that Couch which had been the Scene of their last night's Pleasures before he could recover himself enough to approach. When she had him there, she easily found means to lessen that Respect, the continuance of which would have been very unserviceable to the purpose she liked him for, and twining her soft snowy Arms about his Waist, and joining close to his, her panting Breast, and warming his trembling Lips with the soft melting Dew of amorous Desire, soon made him know the Passion she was possess'd of, left no distinction of Degrees, and scorn'd the dull Formality of Custom. Nature now play'd its part, the Lover regain'd his Boldness, and the Lady her Satisfaction. When any Cessation from Transports too tumultuous to give leave for Speech, afforded an Interval of Conversation, she told him he should not long remain in the mean station he then was, that she would give him greater Proofs of her Affection than the bestowing of her Person, that she would raise him to a Rank which should countenance his entertaining her in publick. Nor did these Promises deceive him, *Women* are generally more liberal this way than *Men*. She made him tell her where he lodg'd, and the next morning sent him a thousand Crowns. He bought himself with it a Post of Honour in the Army, and is now a Companion for the greatest Men in the Island.

Nature, indeed, has been no less kind to him than *Fortune*; he has, to an agreeable Person, a Capacity which furnishes him with the means of being very entertaining; the change of his Circumstances has made no alteration in his Humour, he is neither Vain nor Proud; and by an affable and pretty Behaviour to all People, escapes the {54} Reflections with which such sudden Elevations are generally accompany'd. He has many Qualifications wonderful to be found in a Man of so narrow an Education; but with those which are truly valuable, he has a Mixture of that which indeed is so incident to the Sex, that 'tis scarce possible to be a Man without being inconstant and ingrateful. Not all the Perfections of the charming *Clarismonda*, not all the Obligations she had conferr'd on him, had the power to fix his Heart, and bind him to her Service. He is excessive fond of a little humble Mistress, without any advantage of Birth, of Education, of Beauty, without any other attraction than Youth; yet, often pretending Business, he avoids the Caresses of the adorable *Clarismonda*, and devotes himself to her. It is with the utmost vigour he flies to the Arms of this Object of his Pleasures, and but with a constrain'd and enforc'd warmth, he receives the Caresses of the other; he has, however, the artifice to disguise it, and to prevent any discovery of his frequent visits there, form'd a Stratagem, which one would not expect from one so little accustom'd to Intrigue. He told *Clarismonda* he had a Sister lately come to Town, whom he was oblig'd to take care of, and maintain in a manner such as might not be a lessening to the Character he then bore; by this means he not only took away all Cause of suspicion, but also had an opportunity of drawing more Money from that Purse he had already been so much oblig'd to. The fond deluded Fair thought herself happy in having it in her power to serve so near a Relation to the Man she lov'd, commanded him to introduce her to her Acquaintance, receiv'd her with the kind familiarity of a long Friendship, is continually making her Presents, and for her suppos'd Brother's sake, endeavours, by all the ways she can invent, to be lov'd by her. How {55} long this Plot will remain undiscover'd, the Book of Fate has not, as yet, disclos'd even to me; but this I am certain of, from the Constitution of *Clarismonda*, and the Companions she has of late made choice of, that it must happen soon, or it will but little alarm her. The Marchioness *Salvida*, and a Society of Ladies that frequent her House, are now about drawing her into a Secret, which will take away all her relish for Intrigue. The abominable Practices of these Women are as offensive to *Nature*, as they are to *Love*. I may hereafter unfold to you some part of the Secrets of this mysterious Cabal. But I am at present too much transported; yonder I see an Object, who while he defies my Power himself, enjoys all the advantages of its Influence on others. I never yet had skill to make any lasting Impression on him; my Darts but slightly graze upon his Heart, prevented from entring by a Shield of Indifference—yet am I ever in his mouth. He so well knows to dress his words in my persuasive Sounds, and imitate my Languishments in his dying Eyes, that few who see and hear him, but wou'd imagine the God of Love inspired his every Motion. *Phœbus* who hates me since his *Daphne*'s Cruelty, in opposition to my Power, has taught him this undoing Art, and by his Example convinc'd the wond'ring Gods, that *Wit* can rival *Love*; and *Artifice* gain more Hearts than *Truth*, tho' utter'd in the softest manner. The lovely Ruiner is call'd *Aristus*, a Name well known to all the Young and Fair, the Amorous and Gay a Name, which carries with it so high a Character of all that's amiable, that it often has gain'd its owner Conquests, without the aid of any other attraction. How often have I heard a Nymph, in words all Rapture, give to her Companion a description of this dangerous Charmer; till the other, touch'd to the Soul, at the delicious Representation, has languish'd to behold {56} him, and long'd to be so ruin'd! How often have I been invok'd, on this account, by those who never saw his Eyes, nor listned to the Temptations of his harmonious Tongue, while the malicious *God* of *Wit* has laugh'd at my inability to relieve them, and still guarded his Favourite from my most watchful Arrows! Not that he is insensible of the Joys which Love affords, never was Mortal more capable of giving or receiving them in the most extatick and luxurious degree. He boldly forces from my Storehouse[49] every Pleasure, and leaves the Pain behind. Assiduity,[50] Impatience, Fears, Doubts, Jealousies, Suspence, is what he never knew—he even Hope disdains—and roving o'er the Plain with Air assur'd, singles the favourite Fair, and but implores and gains. From one Victory he passes to another, enlarges Experience with the different perfections of every kind of Beauty, ravages where-e'er enfranchis'd Inclination calls, and scorns to be confin'd by any particular Charm.

It would be endless to recount the various Amours of this gay Inconstant, or the number of those unhappy Maids, who, bless'd once in his tenderest Vows, now curse his cruel carelessness. He, always easy, always pleas'd, endeavours not to avoid their Complainings, nor gives himself the trouble even to form Excuses for his mutability of liking. *Antoineta* was more oblig'd to him for his Civility this way, than any of his Mistresses; whether he had more Compassion for her than the rest, of whether he imagin'd the violence of her Spirit would transport her to Lengths he did not care to be made the Mark of, is uncertain; but after an Intrigue with her of above fix Moons (a prodigious effect of Constancy from him!) being fully satiated, and wishing to get free from her Embraces, he could not resolve to quit her as he had done the others, but pretending a remorse of {57} Conscience for the Frailties of his Youth, told her, he had made a Vow of an eternal Continency, and made use of all his Artifice, to prevail with her to be easy in a Misfortune which was now irremediable, and in which he suffer'd much more than she. Those that are in the least acquainted with the Humour of that Sex, will readily believe she receiv'd these tidings with but a small degree of Resignation. She was excessively transported at the first, but it wore off; she found means of consolation in the Arms of a new Gallant. She can now hear his Name without being mov'd, and speak of his Amours, without any of that Indignation, which, whenever it appears for an ingrateful Lover, is a never-failing token of some remains, and those not inconsiderable ones, of Tenderness. *Aristus* rejoices to be so easily freed from the Persecution of both her Love and Resentment, and pursues his

---

49 [store and house: magazine; treasury; place in which things are hoarded and reposited against a future time.]
50 [*assiduité*, French, *assiduitas*, Latin: diligence; closeness of application.]

Pleasures as before. He has'a very great concern in the *Enchanted Well*, is one of *Lucitario*'s Party, and consequently a gainer by it. He passes most of his time here, where he finds every day opportunities to advance his Interest with those of either Sex, who can be any way of advantage, either to his Ambition or his Pleasure. He is not less successful in the one than the other, I am the only God whose power he contemns, and all the rest combine to make him happy; I have not Force to combat the united Strength of Heaven's whole Hierarchy; I cannot prejudice him, and it is but in vain the abandon'd Nymphs cry out to me for vengeance and redress. The multitudes he has undone, and those he will yet undo, must bear their wretched Fate, 'till Death, their only Friend, shall give them ease. That tall Man who is now talking to him, is maintain'd by him for the Service of his Amours, and for all his grave Looks, is no better than a Procurer. What a monstrous injury is this to my God-head? But I despair {58} of ever being able to revenge it. Pimps and Bauds usurp my Power, the Women are wholly led by Interest, the Men by Lust, and Love has no part in Enjoyment.

The stinging Reflection, how ill he had been treated in his favourite Island, extracted some Tears of heavenly Dew from the Eyes of this Divinity; he was not able to proceed; he stood mute, bury'd as it were in Thought, and as the Stranger was contemplating on what he had heard, the Cogitations[51] of them both were, on a sudden, disturb'd by several Footmen rushing through the Croud, and crying out, *Stand back there make way for my Lady Dutchess*. Immediately approach'd a Woman of a very graceful Appearance, tho'somewhat in years. Her haughty Port,[52] the Disdain with which she seem'd to look on all the Assembly, and the encourag'd Insolence of her Servants, gave our Adventurer a curiosity of knowing who she was, imagining she had not always appear'd in the Grandeur she then did. The Deity reading in his Eyes the wishes of his Soul, and willing to gratify them, took him by the hand, and drawing him a little distance from the Throng, While, beautiful Stranger, *said he*, you are under my Protection, I must not permit you to gaze on that Woman, who, tho' she was never handsome, and has for many years been past her bloom, yet is mistress of all the seducing Arts the Devil ever taught the most cunning of her Sex; she has been ever a profess'd and open Devotee to that Fiend so many of these wretched Islanders adore, and to satisfy the raging Inspiration, spares no Pains nor Stratagems: she cannot behold a Form so compleat as is yours, without feeling those Desires, which never fail to prompt her to measures the most abhorr'd for the gratification of them. August[53] as now

---

51 [*cogitatio*, Latin: thought; the act of thinking.]
52 [*Portée*, French: carriage; air; mien; manner; bearing; external appearance; demeanour.]
53 [*augustus*, Latin: great; grand; royal; magnificent; awful.]

you see her in all the glare of Pomp and Grandeur, she was once on a {59} level with the meanest of that crowd she now despises. Born of a low Extraction, and of Parents remarkable only for base Actions; she had not arriv'd at the Age of seventeen, before she was a noted Prostitute: nor was this scandalous Profession, the most vile she follow'd; she associated herself with a Gang, who if they had not been more trusty to each other, than Persons of that sort generally are, must have expiated their Crimes with their Deaths, and that in the most shameful manner the Law has the power to inflict; yet, in the midst of all these disadvantages, a young Nobleman, whose Name is Count *Almont*, thought her worthy his Embraces. He maintain'd her in a manner far above her Hopes, really lov'd her, and had that prefect confidence in her Fidelity, that he introduc'd his Friends to her Acquaintance, —made Entertainments for them at her Lodgings, and whenever any Business call'd him out, made no scruple of leaving her alone with any of those he had brought there. Among the number of them, was a certain Duke who takes his Title from a Northern County: from frequent Conversations with him, she had opportunities of practising those Insinuations which seldom failed to gain the point she aim'd at, therefore could not be unsuccessful on a Man whose Credulity seem'd to invite deceit. He became in a little time wholly charm'd with her, thought her the best Woman in the world, ador'd her Humour, and doubted not but that there were uncommon Transports to be found in her Embraces, since he every day saw Instances of the Fondness with which she was regarded by Count *Almont*.

Being become his Rival, he ceased to be his Friend, and was continually labouring to persuade her that he was unworthy of so great a Joy as her Possession. The artful Creature immediately {60} found his design; and one day as he was sitting with her, when word was brought that the Count was coming to visit her, she burst into a flood of well-dissembled Tears; and as tho' she knew not what she said, cry'd out, *Oh Heavens! Now must I be sacrificed !* The believing Duke was in a Rapture at these words, but had not time to express it, because the Count was coming up stairs. But the next time he had an opportunity, he told her that he had long been in love with her that nothing could have given him a Joy adequate to the Knowledge, it was not Inclination which had engaged her to live in that manner with Count *Almont*; and that if she could be prevailed on to quit him, his whole Life and Fortune should be devoted to her. This was all she wanted, she knew there were advantages to be made in being Mistress to the easy-natur'd Duke, which she could not hope for, in a continuance of an Amour with a Man who had possess'd her, and who was not of a Disposition to be too much imposed on. He had of late denied her some Extravagancies she had ask'd of him, and she began to think her power with him on the decline; therefore, stay'd not to be twice entreated to comply with what she so much desired, and believ'd so much to her Interest; and ordering her things to be pack'd up immediately, went away in his Grace's Coach, without giving herself any uneasiness how the Count would take so sudden an Alteration in her Humour; for many Years she reign'd sole and triumphant Empress of his Heart, managed his Fortune, took upon her the government of all his Affairs, and at last, (Oh shame to Nobility!) her Artifice and his mean Notions of true Honour and Greatness, prevail'd on him to marry her! After that, she used him as, indeed, he deserved. The most humble and obliging Mistress was now {61} turn'd the most haughty and imperious Wife; and if his raising her to that Dignity justly subjected him to the ridicule of all Companies abroad, her Behaviour to him made him infinitely more so at home; he became the Jest of his own Servants, he was despised by his Enemies, and pitied by his Friends: seeing, and too late repenting the Folly he had been guilty of, the Grief of it threw him into a lingering Disease, of which he died. The luxurious Dutchess now was at liberty to take the full swing of her Desires; and, accordingly threw out her Lure for all the amorous part of Mankind. Countless were the numbers she found means to attract, but none felt a stronger or more lasting Impression than *Windusius*, a Gentleman, who by his Principles relating to other Affairs, one would not have imagin'd should have been so easily drawn in by one of her's; but there are few young Hearts that are Proof against the Charms of Grandeur. Rich Clothes, a Blaze of Jewels, a splendid Equipage, are apt to dazzle the unwary Gazer, and take the Sense, tho' they cannot reach the Soul. Then she had Arts to supply what Age had taken from her, and make even Wrinkles pleasing; besides, we are not to imagine that the Possession of her antiquated Beauties was his only Aim; he has a good deal of Ambition in his nature, and 'tis not to be doubted but that the hope of raising his Fortune by her means, had at least an equal share in the Inducement. Another Argument also may be alledged in his behalf: he had from his Childhood been absent from the Island, and but just return'd from his Travels, when he was introduc'd to her Acquaintance: therefore, had not the opportunity of being let into the black part of her Character; and as Youth is seldom without some Vanity, was easily flatter'd into a belief that he was the only {62} happy Man; and that those Favours he receiv'd from the Dutchess were the effect's of the most tender Passion. 'Tis true, she took, all imaginable pains to confirm him in this Opinion, and to that end would needs have him with her at a Castle she had situated on a Bank of one of the finest and most delectable Rivers in the whole World. Here it was she used to pass the Summer-Season, and here she now indulg'd herself with this young *Enamorato* in all the riotous Delights of Sense, 'till he, too generous, too sincere, for such a prostituted and polluted Passion, fearing his living with her in that publick manner wou'd be a blot[54] on her Reputation, (which I have already told you, he was ignorant was scandal-proof) begg'd she would reftrain her Raptures from the Eyes of her Servants, and those who visited her, and not with lavish Fondness permit him to remain in the same House with her; but only give him leave to wait on her at proper times, as tho' he came to sollicit some Favour from her, not to receive one. This Request, tho' dictated by the tenderest regard, put the haughty Dutchess into an inconceivable Rage, and he had scarce time to finish what he had to say on that head, before she interrupted him: And are you weary of living with me, *Windusius? Said she:* ungrateful Man! Are you already satiated with my Embraces? Has a Woman of my Quality, my Good-nature, my Sincerity, and Love, no Charms to hold you? Is it, ay, too sure 'tis that, like all your Sex you are fond of Variety! Novelty is the only Charm to please you! You have some other View, some little trifling Creature rivals me in your Esteem, and now you'd leave me, you languish to be happier than 'tis in my power to make you: but go (*continu'd she, pretending to weep*) be gone, be gone for ever from my sight—be gone, and boast you have forsaken a Woman whom your Superiors {63} wou'd die to obtain, and one, who lov'd you with a Fondness which nothing but your Ingratitude can equal. These words, and the moving gestures which accompany'd them, quite dissolv'd the tender Soul of him they were address'd to, and, wholly innocent of her Reproaches, he cou'd not bear the Grief he thought she suffer'd: O forbear, my lovely Dutchess! *Said he,* (kissing and embracing her) forbear to wound me by such unjust suspicions, think not I ever can forget your Goodness, believe me, 'twas out of the extremest regard to your Honour I offer'd this Violence to myself and chose rather to be less frequently happy than I have been in your dear Arms, than endure you should suffer by the malicious Censures of a detracting world. O do not wrong my Love, my endless Gratitude, believe it as it is, the highest proof of tender Passion urg'd me to this proposal, and that I wou'd chuse to die a thousand Deaths to make you happy. These Expressions, and some other Arguments he made use of, a little pacify'd her, and beginning to consider more calmly on what he had said, she cou'd not help acknowledging, that to live together in that manner must render her infamous to all who knew it; yet, not able to resolve to part with him, she bethought her of a Pretence for detaining him, which, to those who were ignorant of the Affair, might seem plausible enough—it was to make him Gentleman of her Horse; but this, tho' a Post no way unbecoming a Gentleman, who had not abundance beside his Birth and Accomplishments to depend on, was not at all agreeable to the Ambition *of Windusius.* He had been

---

54 [from the verb: an obliteration of something written or/and a blur, a spot upon paper, or/and a spot in reputation; a stain; a disgrace; a reproach.]

made to believe that he should have something infinitely superior by the favour of this Lady, and could not descend so far beneath his high-rais'd hopes, as to accept of a Service in her Family. He palliated[55] his refusal however in as {64} handsome a manner as he could, and whatever her Thoughts were, she did not seem to be disgusted at it, but still persisting in her Resolution of detaining him, presently had another Stratagem in her head. She told him she would have him pretend Courtship to some Lady of her Acquaintance, that she would seem to encourage it, and by that means, his continuing in her House and to manage her Affairs as he had done, would be look'd on no other than to engage her to be his Friend in this. He was naturally of a gay Disposition, and was well enough pleased to fool away a Summer in this manner, and reminding her Grace of the promise she had made him, that when they came to Town she would make Interest among her Friends for a Settlement for him, promised never to mention a removal from her. She swore to perform all he desired, but in the mean time, as they had agreed together, she made a Ball, to which all the young Ladies and Gentlemen round the Country were invited. Had his design been to have made love in earnest, he might have been at a loss where to fix among such a number of Beauties; but as his Courtship was to be but a feint, he gave Chance the liberty of determining on whom the Lot should fall. The agreeable *Stanilia*, a young Widow of a great Jointure, and a pretty deal of ready Money in her own possession, happened to be the Woman; she had, to the rest of her Advantages, an unblemish'd Character, and was in every thing a match far above his hopes. He would have been glad to have been her Husband in good earnest, and found his Addresses were receiv'd in such a manner, as he need not despair of one day being so, but he knew the Dutchess's Temper too well, to dare to communicate his Sentiments to her on this occasion. But his endeavouring to conceal it, was in vain; she perceiv'd it, and {65} to make herself yet more valuable in his Esteem, by a proof that his Happiness was dearer to her than her own, told him, that if he could like *Stanilia*, she wou'd advise him to marry her: You may be her Husband (*said she*) and yet remain my *Lover*, and as I have promised to make your Fortune, I know not any way more effectual than by helping you to a Wife such as *Stanilia*. 'Twou'd be impossible to represent with how much satisfaction *Windusius* heard her speak in this manner; she read it in his Countenance, but forbore testifying her displeasure at it; and assuring him she wou'd do every thing in her power to forward his Intentions, withdrew to her Closet to ruminate what course to take, not to do as she had promis'd, but to render his Endeavours fruitless. She now began to hate him heartily, her Pride was shock'd to think he cou'd consent to lie in any other Arms than hers,

---

55 [*pallio*, Latin, from *pallium*, a cloak; *pallier*, French: to cover with excuse.]

but resolv'd not to turn him off, till she had provided herself of another equally qualify'd to please her. It was in a very different manner the open-hearted *Windusius* contemplated on this affair; he was charm'd with the imagin'd generosity of the *Dutchess*, and thought of nothing but continuing her eternal Slave, in spite of those Engagements his Interest made him hope for with the other. He notwithstanding play'd his part so well with *Stanilia*, as to make his counterfeit Passion be believ'd a real one, and she was almost on the point of returning it with more sincerity, than indeed it merited, when the designing *Dutchess* prevented her, by giving her some private hints, that he was not the Man of honour he wou'd seem: I wou'd have you, my dear *Stanilia* (*said she, with an air of the most tender Friendship*) I wou'd have you not to believe too soon, the Hearts of Men are dark; *Windusius* I believe has as much honour as any of that Sex, which takes a pleasure in undoing ours; {66} methinks I wou'd have you make some tryal of his Faith, wou'd have you be more reserv'd in your Behaviour. Or, suppose you countenanced the Addresses of some other; endeavour to pique him some way, and you will soon discover whether his Professions are sincere.

These words had the Effect they aim'd at; *Stanilia*, not imagining the *Dutchess* had any reasons for insincerity in an affair she had brought on herself, and had seem'd so much to encourage, believ'd indeed, char there was cause for doubting the Truth of *Windusius*, and in every thing behav'd to him after, as she had advis'd: she admitted his Visits less frequently than she had been accustom'd; and when she saw him, scarce spoke, or if she did, it was in the coldest manner; and receiv'd a Gentleman, whom he knew had declar'd himself her Lover, with all the gaiety imaginable before his face. This alteration gave him a shock which it wou'd be very difficult to represent; he complain'd of it to the *Dutchess*, and entreated to know what she thought of it, but instead of meeting her Compassion, he excited her Mirth; she fell a laughing, which somewhat surprizing him, How, Madam, (*cry'd he*) is the ruin of those Expectations you had fired me with, of no more consequence to you? Are you pleas'd I lose all hope of ever being master of the Fortune of *Stanilia*? No, *answer'd the dissembling Dutchess*, but I rejoice that you have so good a security of it. I ought, indeed, to ask your pardon for one thing, which is, my suffering you to feel a moment's Pain, for this little Artifice, which I was appriz'd of before it was acted. How, Madam! *interrupted he*, was it then but a feint? For Heaven's sake unfold this Mystery. No more upon my Soul, (*resumed she*) she made me the Confidant of her Designs; she told me that you were dearer to her than her Life, and that nothing {67} should hinder her from giving herself to you; but (added the vain Creature) I will first have the pleasure of tyrannizing a little he must know a little of *Purgatory* before he arrives at *Heaven*; he shall dance Attendance, know Hopes, and Fears, Suspence, Perplexity, Uncertainty, Jealousy and Impatience; tremble at my Frowns, be in an Extasy when I smile, die one day, revive the next, grow lean and pale, and show all the Symptoms of a despairing Lover. In this manner (*continu'd the crafty* Dutchess) did she run on for a whole hour, to all which I made but slight answers; for when once a Woman sets a Resolution to give herself airs of this nature, it is not all that can be said to her will prevent her: I would therefore have you countermine her Stratagems, pretend love to the first Woman that comes in your way, and instead of gratifying her Pride with discovering any uneasiness for her Behaviour, turn the Tables on herself, and let her feel in reality, those disquiets, which the Coquetry of her Humour is preparing for you. But will not that (*cry'd he*) entirely disoblige her? You need not fear it (*answer'd she*) you have her by the Heart, and the apprehensions of losing what she loves,' will make her yield at once, and ease you of the pains of further assiduity. They had a great deal more discourse to the same purpose, the result of which was, his submitting to her reasons, and better judgment in the Caprices of her own Sex.

Aurelia, a young Lady in the Neighbourhood; of a very great Fortune, an agreeable Person, and eminent Extraction, was the Person pitch'd upon to give *Stanilia* cause of jealousy. The *Dutchess* easily found means to bring them acquainted, gave him opportunities of being alone with her, and met with enough to gratify her illnature from the different Complaints of the Persons she {68} impos'd on. *Stanilia*, who was the farthest in the world from any such Designs as she was accus'd of, and truly lov'd *Windusius*, was touch'd to the soul at his Ingratitude. *Aurelia* soon found the Effects of his persuasive Art, and was little less enamour'd than the other; she grew almost mad, when the *Dutchess* (perceiving this last Affair went on more successfully on *Windusius*'s side than she had imagin'd, and that there was a probability he might in time feel the Passion he at present but pretended) told her of his Engagements with *Stanilia*; and *Windusius* was doubly perplex'd, to find so ill an Effect of what the *Dutchess* had suggested on the fair Widow, who resolv'd rather to die, than recede from that strangeness the belief of his inconstancy had oblig'd her to put on; and *Aurelia*, justly suspeding, that he who had been false to one, might probably be so to another, grew also reserv'd and cold. Everyone had their vexations, and the incendiary *Dutchess* had all the Satisfaction she cou'd wish, in triumphing o'er her more lovely Rivals in the Affections of the Man she liked; and at the same time, revenging herself on him, for harbouring a Thought of bestowing any part on another, of that tenderness she desir'd wholly to engross. In this fashion the Mystery was carry'd on for about two Months, and tho' *Windusius* was a Man of a good deal of Penetration, he saw not into the meaning of it. He had so implicit a faith in the *Dutchess*, that he never once suspected she had said any thing but what was extremely to his advantage, and growing weary of (solliciting these Ladies, who both continuing their reserve, sat down contented to indulge his Raptures, with the only Woman, who, as yet, had the power of giving them.

Aurelia, who really lov'd him with a transcendency of Passion, suffer'd it at last to over-rule her {69} Pride; his desisting from visiting her, made her believe she had entirely lost him; but resolving to know her doom, however she might be able to endure the certainty, she sent to desire he wou'd come to her; but he return'd, that some very great Business made it impossible for him to come himself. This cold Indifference confirm'd her in what, she before had too much reason so suspect. She writ to upbraid him with his breach of Faith; he had too much complaisance not to answer her Letter, and not knowing well what excuse to make, evaded any direct reply, and had recourse to an Ænigma taught him by the *Dutchess*, (who, 'tis probable, had herself been formerly put off by the same Stratagem;) That there was an indispensible Necessity for his refraining his visits, but that he ador'd her, and ever shou'd do so, tho' he was oblig'd to leave to *Time* the proof of his Honour and Constancy, and the unfolding a Riddle, which at present seem'd so ambiguous. It wou'd be too tedious to repeat the various disorders which seiz'd the Soul of poor *Aurelia* at receipt of this Letter; she had too good an understanding not to perceive the deceit of it, and the war between her Love and Resentment had like to have been fatal to her. She conceal'd her Grief, as well as she was able, from the observations of all who knew her, but cou'd not forbear writing to him once more. The contents of her Letter being dictated by me, I can very easily repeat—they were these:

Aurelia to the Ingrateful *Windusius*

As easy as you found it to betray a Heart unpractised in Deceit, you will perceive it a Task more difficult to impose a Belief on any Woman of common Understanding, that Love is of a nature to fight against itself. None influenc'd by that Deity, are Masters {70} enough of their Actions to decree any thing to the prejudice of their Passion; nor need I wait the slow result of *Time*, to inform me you are no longer under the subjection of that Power, whose Effects I feel too sensibly in my own Soul, to imagine it can work such contrary ones in yours. I will not occasion you the Guilt of any further Denials of your Apostacy, by asking what it is has influenc'd you to proceed with me in this manner. I can easily guess at it, and shall, I hope, reap this Advantage from your Perjury,[56] never to believe any of your Sex again. I desire no other Revenge for my abused Sincerity, than that you may, some time or other, find a Woman fair enough to create a real Passion in you; and as insensible of it, as you are of mine.

Aurelia.

---

56 [*perjurium*, Latin: false oath.]

There are but a very few, not influenc'd by me, whom such a Letter would have at all affected: but *Windusius*, tho' he knew nothing of those Delicacies I inspire, had a natural Tenderness in his Soul, which would not suffer him to believe another was in pain, without feeling some share of it himself: but, not having it in his power to make her happy (all the Affections his Heart was, as yet, susceptible of, being in favour of the Dutchess) he from this time forbore writing to her, and carefully avoided her Sight; justly supposing, that where there is a real Passion, such a Behaviour was the only way to extinguish it. And indeed, when a Person is incapable of making a return, 'tis infinitely more generous at once to show it, than by a pretended Kindness, endeavour to preserve a fruitless flame, and rack the Heart possess'd of it with the Tortures of Suspence. The soothing *Dutchess* perceiving her Favourite in some little Inquietudes, for those which by her Instigations he had occasion'd in the Breast of *Aurelia*; the sooner {71} to restore him to his former Gaiety, she removed to another fine Seat she had some Leagues farther in the Country, where (as her large Experience of the Temper of Mankind made her not doubt) Variety of Conversation and new Faces would easily obliterate the memory of former ones. A little time confirm'd the Truth of her Suggestions; the unhappy Maid no more had a place in his remembrance; he no longer regretted the Injury he had done her; no longer pity'd the Woes he had reduc'd her to: but it was not consistent with the Justice of the Gods, that he should for ever triumph in his Insensibility; the Hour was now arrived, which should inform him what kind of Torments those are which spring from Tenderness abused, and disappointed Love: But see! he comes! I will oblige him to relate to you the History of his Amours; a History, he has a thousand times in the most bitter Anguish of his Soul repeated to the unanswering Groves and silent Streams. He has been since the truest, most faithful, and zealous of my Devotees; the most religious Observer of my Laws: but alas! it is not in my power to reward his Constancy; Supreme Justice denies me the privilege of blessing him, who has once been false: he must, at least for a time, suffer the same Soul-rending Agonies his Ingratitude inflicted on the unfortunate *Aurelia*. But I will no longer defer the Satisfaction of a Curiosity I have rais'd; he shall himself relate the Particulars of this Affair.

Here the God advancing two or three Paces,[57] made himself known to the disconsolate *Windusius*; who, with down-cast Eyes, folded Arms, and all the signs of a dejected Mind, was approaching the Place they were in: and having signified his Pleasure, by some inward Impulses peculiar to the Deities, led him to the expecting Stranger. The {72} Moments were too precious to be wasted in fruitless Ceremonies;

---

57 [*pas*, French: step; single movement in walking.]

and the first Civilities being pass'd, he began to execute the Commands of his divine Inspirer, in these or the like Words.

The History of the Chevalier *Windusius*, and the fair, false *Wyaria*

I Had not been many Days at *Ponray*, (the Name of that fine Mansion the *Dutchess* had carry'd me to, in order to divert a Melancholy then growing on me) before, among many others who came to bid her welcome to that Place, I distinguish'd the agreeable *Wyaria*, the Daughter of a Country Gentleman, who lived not far from thence: it was from her Eyes I first receiv'd the Darts of Passion; those pleasing Pains, which thrill'd my glowing Veins while gazing on her: the uneasy Languishments I suffer'd in her Absence, the Hopes, the Fears, the soft Anxieties, the thousand nameless, unutterable Perturbations, which every Look and Motion of that sweet Disturber rais'd in my Soul, immediately inform'd me, that I had been mistaken in myself; and that all those Desires I formerly had felt for others, had been no more than light Amusements, the Effects of Youth, Idleness, and the Warmth of Nature ; and far unworthy of the Name of *Love*. Her frequent Visits to the *Dutchess* gave me, in a little time, an Opportunity of declaring my Sentiments; and I had the Blessing, (as I then thought it) to find they were receiv'd in a manner more favourable than I could have {73} hoped. I made her Grace acquainted with my Proceeding, but not with the true state of my Heart; and she encouraged me in this Amour, as she had always done in the beginnings of the others. She told me, that to her knowledge, the Father of *Wyaria* was vastly rich; and had often said before her, That if she marry'd with his Consent, he would give her twenty-thousand Crowns, which was the same he had bestow'd with another on *Batharius*, a Gentleman, who, tho' he had been formerly no better than a Town-Rake,[58] and had spent the best part of his Fortune, had wound himself so far into the old Gentleman's Favour, as to gain his Daughter, and that Dowry[59] with her. All these Circumstances made me not doubt but I should make my Character and Affairs appear in a Light which would not be disagreeable to the Father: I had no Apprehensions but from the young Lady, and those were only such as Love is never unaccompany'd with; and which her obliging Treatment of me, in a short time render'd less and less formidable. The *Dutchess*, who from time to time

---

58 [*Racaille*, French, the low rabble; or *rekel*, Dutch, a worthless cur dog: a loose, disorderly, vicious, wild, gay, thoughtless fellow; a man addicted to pleasure.]
59 [*douaire*, French. It ought to be written *dower:* a portion given with a wife.]

would needs be inform'd of all the Particulars of our Conversations, did not fail to give me Advice how to behave, in a manner, which, if I had not been really in love, would have seem'd the most likely to succeed; but being now too well experienc'd in that Passion, had but little occasion for her Instruction: but while she appear'd so zealous for my Service, was acting in a quite contrary manner, and endeavouring to ruin me in the Opinion of that Lady she had made me believe she was solliciting in my behalf. *Wyaria* was generous enough to tell me of it, and also to give me some Hints of her Grace's Character, which tho' I had lived so long with her, I was utterly a stranger to: the Discovery of her Deceit in this Affair, open'd my Eyes to the Artifice she had made use of in the {74} former ones; and this Knowledge of her Humour, join'd to my Passion for another, made her as odious and detestable to my Soul, as she had once been dear and agreeable: however, by the engaging *Wyaria*'s Advice I concealed my Disgust, continu'd with her as before, and feign'd a Belief of all she said; but whether, not perfect in the Art of Dissimulation, she read in my Eyes the Alteration of my Thoughts; or whether she found, by *Wyaria*'s Behaviour, her Wiles had failed of the Success they aim'd at, is uncertain: but resolving not to be disappointed in every thing, her natural Propensity to Mischief inspir'd her with Measures, to plague those Hearts she now began to imagine were not to be disunited by her Stratagems. Accordingly, all on a sudden, she left *Ponray*, and returned to her Castle on the Riverside, where we had been the beginning of the Summer: it was impossible for me to make any Pretence to stay behind her; and I was obliged to console myself in Absence, with frequent corresponding by Letters with my dear *Wyaria*. Her Father had allow'd of my Visits, and I had no room to doubt but that in a little time I should have his Consent for the compleating my Felicity. Security, therefore, made me more easy, and the tender manner in which she writ to me, and her constant Observance of every Post, assur'd me, that she took no small Satisfaction in this distant Conversation. I also received Letters from her Father, her Sister, and Brother-in-law, with repeated Invitations to come to their House as soon as her Grace's Business would permit me: but alas! That was an Opportunity I vainly languish'd for; and at last, quite weary of Dissimulation, and wild with Impatience, to see my dear, my enchanting *Wyaria*, I forced myself from that Compound of Artifice, Hypocrisy, Avarice, Lust, and every hateful Quality, and flew with the Wings of {75} impatient Affection to my lovely Charmer, to all that I then thought was worthy of my Love. At my Arrival, I found a Reception, such as my utmost Wishes; Doors, Arms, and, as they pretended, Hearts open'd to give me Welcome: the old Gentleman, *Batharius* and his Wife, seem'd to outvy each other in their Love and Fondness of me: but for *Wyaria*, never Man found so endearing a Welcome as I did from her. When Supper was over, the Family retired to their respective Apartments, and only she and I remained: how did the melting Charmer seem to lay open all her Soul! What tender things did she not say! With what sweet Complainings did she not upbraid my tedious Absence! With what an appearance of the sublimest Rapture did she not swear my Presence was the dearest thing on Earth! Oh! Let the God of Love, who heard the perjured Fair, judge my Cause, and punish her in kind! Oh! May she love like me, and be, like me, undone! Let a kind Spring of early Hopes cherish the growing Passion; but e'er the Summer of her Joy arrives, let it be dash'd with sudden Storms and Tempests; let all the Blasts of cold Unkindness, Scorn, and Detestation, nip the gawdy[60] Bloom, and wither it for ever; let her whole future Scene of Life be one continued Horror: and, to add to her Despair, may I be Witness of it. Heaven! With what a Look of Innocence and Sanctity did the Fair Deceiver receive my Transports, and confess her own! The best part of the Night was pass'd before we parted; and, as her Behaviour afterwards inform'd me, it was my fault we stay'd not together the remainder of it. The next day a young Lady, a very great Intimate of hers, came to stay some time with her; she was immediately made acquainted with our Amour, and seem'd extremely to approve of it; and I {76} believe was perfectly sincere in her good Wishes to us both: it happen'd, while she was there, that *Batharius*, whose Agreement on Marriage, was to take some part of his Wife's Fortune in Board, was now to remove with his Family to a House he had taken a few Miles distant from their Father's. The old Gentleman, *Wyaria*, her Companion, and myself, were desired to accompany them: accordingly we did, and tarry'd above a Week; Sports of all sorts abounded, Drinking, Dancing, Hunting, Hawking; nothing was to be seen but Mirth and Jollity: 'till Diversion growing tasteless, for want of Intermission; and *Old Care* beginning to think it time for him to be among his People, we set out for home: he rode a little before, and kept *Smitheria* (that was the Name of the young Lady) in Talk, as we imagin'd, to give me an Opportunity of entertaining his Daughter with more Liberty; and indeed, never did Lover think himself more bless'd than I did at that time: from the Friends of my *Wyaria* I had all the Encouragement imaginable, to assure myself of their Consent to make me happy; and in the kind Eyes of my Charmer, I easily read her Wishes were not inferiour to my own; As we beguil'd the time in Conversation suitable to the Circumstances we were in; on a sudden she changed Colour, and shrieking out, cry'd, *Take me down, take me down, my dear* Windusius! *or I shall fall off my Horse.* You may be sure I immediately obey'd, but frighted, ask'd the Occasion. *Oh! I have the Cramp* (answer'd she) *in the upper part of my Thigh; I cannot bear the Torment; chase it with your warm Hand, for Heaven's sake.* Judge now what I endur'd! Stretch your Imagination to the utmost Extent, and if possible, form ah Idea of the vast Temptation now open'd to me! Think what I felt amidst

---

60 [Showy in a tasteless or vulgar way.]

this Scene of racking {77} Pleasure, what infinite, unutterable, distracting Extasy invaded my whole Soul, while thus employ'd; Fancy[61] you see the lovely Maid extended on the Grass, her shining Eyes swimming in Love, and sparkling with Desire! Her snowy Breasts panting and heaving with impatient Wishes! Her Garments thrown aside, and all the Beauties of her fine-proportioned Limbs expos'd to View! The Legs, the Thighs, the soft, the milk-white Skin! The plump, inviting Flesh, that quiver'd at my Touch! The thousand, thousand nameless Charms which Words cannot express, and Thought alone can paint. But I grow wild at the Remembrance, forget my Wrongs, and almost wish I were again so to be deluded. Never Man, perhaps, endur'd more between Respect and Passion; never did Honour gain a Victory more severe: I resisted all the Dictates of Desire, bore, unappeas'd, the eager Cravings of that tumultuous Momen; and conquer'd *Nature*, to be just to *Virtue*. But Oh! What fierce Convulsions[62] rack'd every throbbing Nerve! What agonizing shootings ran through all my Veins! Cold Sweats, like those of Death, came o'er my Face, while in my burning Breast ten thousand Furies raged. The Pains of Death were mild, to those I felt. *Wyaria* saw, and pity'd my Condition; and telling me she was better, desir'd me to help her to remount. The Command both pleas'd and shock'd me: I obey'd as well as I was able; but alas! The late Conflict discover'd itself in my enfeebled[63] Limbs; my Arms had scarcely Strength to lift her on her Horse, nor my Legs to sustain the weight of my own Body; and it was as much as I could do, for some Moments, to recover myself enough to prosecute our Journey. The Confusion a little over, I endeavour'd to make up the time lost; and it growing late, reminded her we must mend our Pace. But I will not {78} prolong my Narration by a recital of particulars of no great consequence. We got safe to her Father's, who had been come in long before us, and were oblig'd to bear a little Raillery[64] from *Smitheria* for staying behind *Wyaria*, however, seem'd not much concern'd in vindicating the Occasion, and I thought it not my Business. Supper over, the old Man went to Bed, and after a little Chat, young Confidante retired also to hers. When we were alone, the melting Fair, with Love unbounded, began to let loose all her Soul confess'd the Cramp had been but a pretence, only to give me an opportunity of gratifying both our Wishes, avow'd an uneasiness which nothing but possession cou'd abate, and even courted me to ruin her: while I, amaz'd, con-

---

61 [contracted from *phantasy, phantasia*, Latin; φαντασία, Ancient Greek: imagination; the power by which the mind forms to itself images and representations of things, persons, or scenes of being.]
62 [*convulsio*, Latin: a *convulsion* is an involuntary contraction of the fibres and muscles, whereby the body and limbs are preternaturally distorted.]
63 [from *feeble:* to weaken; to enervate; to deprive of strength.]
64 [*raillerie*, French: slight satire; satirical merriment.]

founded, and asham'd to seem insensible of Transport which spoke so plain, cou'd not resolve how to proceed. O Virtue! Wonderful was thy Power, here was a proof of Tenderness, of Truth, of a Sublimity of sincere Affection, which I believe this Age cannot equal; in fine, I bore a second time the tortures of recoiling Nature, deny'd the impatient workings of Desire in my own Breast, and endeavour'd to make hers more temperate. With much persuasion, I at last prevail'd on her to go to Bed; she went, as I thought, to her Friend, and I to the enjoyment of my Thought, which told me, some hovering God, designing good to both, had directed my Actions; and I hoped the same kind Power wou'd also aid me to obtain the Father's approbation on the morrow, and crown both our Wishes.

I cou'd not, however, avoid being somewhat disorder'd on the Reflection of the extraordinary Adventures of this day and night, not all my own Warmth of Constitution, not all my Passion for her, cou'd make me pleas'd to find so much in {79} a Woman who was to be my Wife: but I had not above half an hour's Meditation, before I heard somebody come into my Chamber, I thought it might be one of the Servants, for my Candle was still burning, when, to my great surprize, I saw *Wyaria*. It was she herself, who hastily undrawing my Curtains, threw herself on the Bed by me, and preventing my asking her the meaning of so unexpected a visit, Suspend your wonder, my dear *Windusius, said she*, at this seeming Extravagance, till you know the Cause of my Proceeding in so strange a manner. I am now (*continu'she, bursting into a flood of Tears*) come to make discoveries which will soon cool your *Love*, if ever you had any for me, but in its stead, perhaps, create a greater warmth of *Friendship*. I know what I am going to relate will lose me a *Husband*, but if you are as generous as I believe you are, gain me an eternal *Friend*, and, Oh! I have a dreadful need of one. At these words she sunk, fainting on my Bosom, unable to utter more. Amaz'd at what I saw and heard, I wanted but little of being in the same condition; but recollecting myself as well as I was able, I got out of Bed, and by the help of a little Time and Water recover'd her. As soon as she open'd her Eyes, Great Gods! *cry'd I*, what is all this? From the most tender and passionate Desire, which, but some moments since, took up thy Soul, why art thou thus chang'd, dispirited, dejected, and disorder'd? What can it mean? Or what is to be done? Then, perceiving she answer'd not but with Tears, and such Sighs as gave me apprehensions of a Relapse, I suppress'd all tokens of Astonishment, and began to use Expressions of Consolation My Life! My Angel! *Resum'd I*, my only wish'd for Good! Be comforted, be easy, and whatsoe'er has happen'd to disturb thy gentle Soul, disburthen it on me, proud to sustain thy weight of Anguish; behold in me, {80} thy Friend, thy Lover, thy Husband, or if there be a name which can comprize the Truth, the Tenderness, the Fondness of 'em all, call me by that. Oh! Tell me thy perplexity! I was going on with all the Demonstrations I was capable of, to convince her with how sincere and pure a Passion I regarded her, but laying her Face on my Mouth, to stop any further Speech. Oh forbear (*said she*) forbear this lavish Goodness to an unworthy Wretch, your Love, your Generosity, but racks me more. I cannot bear it; my Crime now shows itself in all its horror, and I grow wild, mad, with the curst Reflection. Here it was as impossible for me to suffer her to proceed, as it had been for her a moment before: Heavens (*cry'd I, loosing myself from her*) What hast thou done? What Crime canst thou be guilty of? Hast thou blasphem'd the Gods? Faintly she answer'd, No. Committed Sacrilege, *said I*, or Murder? Oh no, *return'd she*. Then thou hast lost thy Virtue, *rejoin'd I, with an aking Heart*. Yes, yes, *confess'd the fair Apostate*, and with those words, fell a second time into a Swoon, from which, I found it more difficult to recover her than the former one. It wou'd be very difficult to make you sensible what my afflicted Soul felt at a discovery so alarming; the almighty Power of Love, who inspir'd me with a sublimity of Passion, greater sure than any Mortal ever was before possess'd of, can only represent it. My Grief, my Surprize was equal, but my Resentment too weak, too short-liv'd, for such a monstrous Cause—but alas! What con'd I do? Had any other Tongue inform'd me, with the hazard of my Life I would have clear'd her; but self-accus'd, there was no room for Doubt; and self-condemn'd, none for Indignation. The knowledge of her Crime, and her Repentance for it, came together to me; beside, the one I was {81} but told of, the other I saw. The charming Criminal was almost expiring at my Feet, expiring at the sense of a Wrong she had done me, which but for herself I had not been appriz'd of. There appear'd so much generosity, such a noble open- heartedness in this Behaviour, that, methought, look'd lovely; and she grew, if possible, more dear to my Affections, in guilt thus confess'd, thus atoned, than in the Reputation of perfect Innocence before. At last she was again restor'd to Life, to Sense, and my forgiving Love; but it was hardly in the power of all my fond Endearments to hinder her from doing violence to herself. Oh! S*aid she*, you never, never can pardon such a Fault as mine. I do not, must not hope your Love; but if you e'er committed any secret Sin for which you dread the Vengeance of offended Heaven, as you wou'd wish for Mercy, bestow it now on me; pity and relieve my lost Condition. Cease, cease, my Dear (*interrupted I, touch'd to the Soul at her Complainings*) to wrong a Passion as unalterable as thy own power of charming. Is there an Action I am capable to serve thee in, and canst thou judge so meanly of me, to think I wou'd refuse thee? No, tho' Death, tho' what is infinitely worse than Death, eternal Infamy were sure to ensue, I wou'd for thee endure it; therefore keep me no longer on the Rack—tell me! What is it I must do? Be quick to ease my Anguish, or I shall soon be uncapable of any thing. Oh! 'Tis impossible (*resum'd she, in a dying accent*) that you can forgive me, can love me still. I had not patience to permit her continuance in this Despair, and resolving, if possible, to put an end to it, Correct me instantly, great *Jupiter* (*cry'd I*) if what I say, I mean not. Keep then your Promise, *said she,* remember what you have sworn, for I shall make a fiery tryal of your Truth. Know, *pursu'd she, weeping afresh,* that I {82} am guilty of the Crime I mention'd in its worst shape—Pollution made more black by *Incest!* 'Tis now two Years since my Sister's Husband *Batharius* led me into the detested Secret, which I have still continued in; tho' at each repetition of the horrid Deed, my Soul shrinks in me, and each fond Endearment raises a Fury in my tormented Mind. She could no more, the rising Sighs suppress'd the utterance of her Words, nor if she had spoke, had I the power of listening. The name of *Incest,* like a Thunderbolt, transfixed me! For a while, and lock'd up every Sense in wild Amazement. Never was Confusion equal to what I felt, never was Heart so torn betwixt Love and Rage: and indeed when I consider with what a violence of Passion I regarded her, I wonder that an utter deprivation of Reason did not ensue: I behaved myself (as she afterwards told me) in a manner, which made her fear the sudden shock of the Discovery would entirely take from me the means of doing her the Service she requir'd; which, as soon as she found me in a condition of answering, she inform'd me, was to make her Father acquainted with the Story, and implore his Aid for her retiring to some Place where she might never see the vile *Batharius* more. It would be too tedious to repeat the various and confused Interrogatories I put to her, or the as various Whirls of distracted Passion which seiz'd my tortur'd Brain at her Replies. I was not able for a great while to enter into any settled way of Conversation. But as the most violent Agitations of the Soul cannot always retain their Force, mine began at length to calm; and as Indignation and Grief abated, Curiosity, accompany'd by a Desire, which till then I had never dared to indulge, rose in their stead. Respect, and that Purity of Tenderness with which till now I had ever regarded her, by this Discovery {83} was utterly erased; the humble, the perfect *Lover* was extinct, and I was now all *Man,* resolute, desiring Man! The Advances she had made me, the Adventure of the Cramp, every amorous (to call it no worse) Particular of her Behaviour to me, came now into my head, and I resolv'd to gratify at once my own and her Desires: I found not the least Resistance, and we passed the remainder of the Night in as much Satisfaction, as two Persons possess'd with a Passion (where the Senses only are call'd to counsel, and the Soul has no part) can find in the Enjoyment of each other. When Morning came, she renew'd her Request, that I would make her Father acquainted with the Abuse she had receiv'd from *Batharius,* assuring me it was indifferent to her what became of her, if she was but deliver'd from those Stings of Conscience, which rack'd her Soul in the continuance in her Crime, and which she could no longer sustain: that if he should turn her out of doors, and expose her to all the Miseries of Want and Poverty, she would cheerfully undergo it, and endeavour by the meanest and most servile Offices to get her Bread, rather than feel those innate Torments, which took from her all possibility of ever knowing a Moment's Peace of Mind. With much persuasion I at last consented, and some remains of my former Tenderness still working in me in her behalf, join'd with a little Self-Interest, that if I acted the generous Part, related the whole Affair to the old Man, and told him withal, that my Love to his Daughter made me willing to forgive all Faults, and that I would still make her my Wife; he would double the Portion he design'd for her, and perhaps make me the Heir of all his Wealth. This Imagination was not a little pleasing to me, and after she had retir'd to her own Apartment, I dress'd me, and went about the execution of my Design. I found the old Gentleman walking {84} in his Garden, as was his Custom every Morning; and when the first Salutations were over, telling him, I had an Affair of the greatest consequence in Life to impart to him, we went together into a Grove, where, after some necessary Preparations, such as, desiring him to arm himself with Patience, and giving him some hints, that what I had to say would be a fiery Trial, in Expressions as moderate, and as favourable for her, as the nature of the thing I had to speak of would allow: at last, I made him sensible of the whole horrid Secret. But with what words, noble Stranger! Can I represent to your Imagination the Storm of Rage with which he heard it! He flew out of the Grove like a Man utterly depriv'd of Reason, and drawing his Sword, and calling aloud for *Wyaria*, had certainly in the first Gust of passion plung'd it in her Breast, as she came trembling to know his Commands, if I had not taken care to snatch from him that Instrument of Vengeance. He took her by the shaking Shoulders, and dragging her into the Grove, began to discharge some part of his Rage in Revilings: Thou Scandal of thy Sex, *said he*, thou Blot of thy Family! what is it I have heard of thee! Thou incestuous, thou abandon'd Wretch! What is it thou hast done? Monster, Devil, unnatural Prostitute! With Curses un-number'd did he load her, neither regarding the Condition he beheld her in, for she fainted on the Bank, nor giving me leave to utter the least Word in vindication of her, 'till at length, Compassion for a Woman I had once so dearly lov'd, obliged me to force him from her, and with more gentle Treatment endeavour to call home her wandering Spirits. She was but a few moments before she recover'd, and throwing herself at his Feet, her Eyes streaming with Tears, and wringing her Hands, she implor'd Forgiveness in terms so {85} moving, that the Heart that had been insensible of Pity must have been more than savage, mine quite dissolv'd, and putting myself in the same Posture with her, begg'd him to pardon all; assured him I was so well satisfy'd in her Repentance, that I regarded her with the same Ardency of fond Affection as before, and told him, I was ready to take off the Shame she had brought on herself, by becoming her Husband that very moment, if he would give his Sanction to the Act. An Offer so unexpected seem'd to give a prodigious turn to his Resentment; his Eyes lost immediately great part of their Fierceness; but making no other Answer to it than, Ay, Sir, that is strangely generous indeed! Walk'd a little distance from us, as tho' to consider on what I had said, while I, thinking it best not to suffer him to cool, prosecuted my Intentions in. this manner: the Misfortune, *resum'd I*, is yet a Secret, Sir; the base *Batharius*, for his own sake, never will divulge it, and if I marry *Wyaria*, you may depend on my Care to prevent her from being a second time deluded by his Insinuations: as for the usage she shall receive from me, as I have already told you, I now again confirm it; the true Contrition, and that ingenuous Confession of her Crime to him, from whom of all Mankind, had she not been the sincerest of her Sex, she would most artfully have conceal'd it, will make her ever dear, ever charming to my Soul; I never will reproach, never will hold her in less Esteem, than I should if no such Accident had happen'd. I said a great deal more, to convince him it was not only necessary for the Honour of his family, but also for his Daughter's Happiness, that he should give his Consent to this Match. But, after a long pause, instead of the Gratitude, with which any other Parent would have listen'd to such an Offer; he told me, with an Air of Indifference, that he {86} thought himself obliged to me; but, said he, I suppose you expect something more beside my Blessing. Doubtless, Sir, answer'd I, nor can I think you will deal less generously with me, who am willing to take *Wyaria* with all her Faults, than you have done with *Batharius*, who had with her Sister an untainted Virtue and unblemish'd Reputation. And what then, Sir, (interrupted he briskly) will your Friends do for you? What Jointure will they enable you to make for two thousand Crowns? I am unable to express the Surprize and Indignation I was in at so unexpected a Query. Nothing but to see me in such another, can make you sensible of that Violence of Passion with which I was possess'd at his Behaviour: and not endeavouring to conceal it, How! *Cry'd I*, is a Bargain to be made in an Affair such as this? Do you take me for a Wretch wholly incapable of Reflection? I must unknow what you are sensible of but through my means, if I did not know the Proposition I have made you so much to my Dishonour, that were my Intentions publick, and there be a Man on Earth that loves me, his highest proof of it would be to shoot me thro' the Head: but I will speak no more, (*continu'd I, with a little more Temper*) your Daughter is in presence, let her relate to you the particulars of her Undoing, and with what an uncommon Tenderness I have behav'd in this Affair, then consider whether you ought to treat me in this manner. *Wyaria*, in whose Countenance all the time we were talking one might easily read the Agitations of her Soul, here preventing her Father's Reply, began to unfold the truth of what I had reveal'd. She told him, that it had been more than two years since, deluded by the false *Batharius*, she had yielded to his Desires; that he had, by a great many Arguments which to her seem'd well inforc'd, convinc'd her that Polygamy[65] was no {87} Crime, and that he swore to make

---

65 [*polygamie*, French, πολυγαμία, Ancient Greek: here, plurality of wives.]

her as equal with her Sister, in her Right to him, as she was superiour in his Esteem; that his Love to her was beyond all bounds, and that her Vanity and Inadvertency had render'd her Heart susceptible of the dangerous Impressions his Wit and Assiduity attempted to make; that one day, happening to be alone with him in the House, half by Persuasions, half by Force, he had perpetrated his Design, and had ever since continu'd to abuse her in the same manner; but that, stung with a just sense of what she had done, she could no longer bear the Torment, and fearful herself to reveal the horrid Secret, she had made choice of me as a Person in whose Honour and Good-nature, she was pleased to say, she had the greatest Confidence. She concluded her unhappy Story, with some Expressions how much she was obliged to that uncommon Testimony of my Love of desiring to be her Husband; and intreated by all the Supplications imaginable, that he would grant a Request so much to the advantage of her Peace of Mind, and the Preservation of their House's Honour. I did not fail to second what she had said, and tho' I was a little nettled,[66] as indeed I had good reason, that he should make the least Demur in granting what I might justly have expected he would have been the first in desiring; I conquer'd my Resentment to obey the Dictates of my Love, which, I must confess, as yet pleaded most tenderly in her behalf. But all we could urge was unsuccessful; he said, there were private Reasons, which obliged him to defer giving any direct Reply at that time, but that he would consider of it; assured me, he had the most particular regard for me, that he would very shortly prove how heartily he esteemed me; with a great deal more to the same purpose, which at that time I was weak {88} enough to believe; but withall, desir'd I would for a few days retire from his House, for he was in expectation of a Visit very soon from *Batharius*, whom he was very unwilling to trust me with, after the knowledge of the Injury he had done me in the Person of the Woman I intended for my Wife. I know, (said he) you Young-men, and especially a Chevalier, and a Lover too, are impatient of Indignities; you are not sensible yourself how ill you could brook the Presence of a Wretch, who has offended in the manner he has done; and if a Quarrel, on this occasion, should arise, the whole Affair would become the Talk of the Country; I would have you, therefore, leave us for a while, and you shall hear from me, in a manner, perhaps, more to your advantage than yet you think of. I am asham'd to confess how much I was transported with these words; it presently came into my head, that *Batharius* would be utterly thrown out of the Family, and I declared the Heir of all. Full of these golden Expectations I obey'd, and desiring he would direct for me at my Lady Dutchess's, where I told him I would tarry 'till I receiv'd, his Letter, took an humble Leave of him: my Farewell to *Wyaria* was, you may be

---

66 [from the noun: to sting; to irritate; to provoke.]

sure, a little more prolong'd; for I still lov'd her with a Fondness, which neither Possession, nor the knowedge of her Crime could abate. Oh! Let the God of undissembled Ardors remember mine, when unable to part without a repetition of those Joys we had so lately tasted, the melting Charmer dissolved within my Arms, and pressing me close as her grasp could strain my willing Body to her panting Breast, she cry'd, Oh! That I had never been but yours. Were I Mistress of the Globe, and could dispose of Crowns and Empires at my will, I'd freely quit the boasted Sovereignty but to call back that black detested hour which gave me to {89} *Batharius*. And then again, My *Windusius!* (wou'd she gently murmur out) Judge with how true a Passion I regard thee, when rather than deceive thee, I would accuse myself. Oh! Do not, do not, when cool Reflection overcomes Desire, love me the less for a Generosity so unequall'd. Oh! No, by Heaven, (*interrupted I, rais'd to the highest pitch of Extasy by her imagin'd Tenderness*) thou ever shalt be dearer to my Soul than Wealth, than Life, than even Fame itself, be but hence-forward mine, and only mine. When I am not, (*answer'd she, forcing herself from my Embrace, and kneeling before me with Hands and Eyes lifted up to Heaven*) may the immortal Gods make me an Example of Perfidy, which After-Ages shall with wonder hear of; whenever I, even in Thought, transgress against the firm Affection I now swear to my dear *Windusius*, may I be struck blind and lame; may Diseases of all kinds seize on me, consume my Flesh with un-intermitting Anguish, and rot me to the Bone, 'till my black Soul, driven from this House of Horror, descends to Hell a Prey to endless Torment. She would, if possible, have added to this dreadful Imprecation, if my impatient Love could have permitted it; but free from all Suspicion, from all Fear, I snatch'd her from the Ground, press'd her again to my transported Breast, return'd her Vows, and chased away all her remains of Grief with renewed Endearments, rioting in Pleasures not to be describ'd, we pass'd the hours, and should hardly have had the power to separate ourselves in a much longer time, if the Consideration how much to our mutual Interest it was, not to disoblige the old Gentleman, had not prevail'd on us to do it. With a thousand Vows and Protestations on both sides, of writing to each other often 'till we met again, we at last took leave; {90} she retir'd to her Closet, as she told me, to contemplate on what was pass'd; I to the Stable, where my Man, as I had order'd, waited with my Horse. I was no sooner at the Dutchess's, than I was asked ten thousand Questions concerning my Proceedings; but I related no more, than that the Father of *Wyaria* approved of my Pretensions, and that in a very short time I expected a Summons to be put in possession of every thing I wished; carefully concealing every thing that might redound either to my own Dishonour, or that of my intended Bride. Her Grace did not seem perfectly satisfy'd with what I said, imagining she read something in my Countenance (as indeed she very well might, for Nature never found a Man less capable of Disguises) which spoke past Surprize, and that something extraordinary had happen'd. She did not scruple to tell me what her Thoughts were, and seem'd a little disgusted I did not put the same Confidence in her which I had formerly done: But neither Insinuations nor Resentment had the power to dislodge this Secret from my Breast; and she found herself obliged at length to appear satisfy'd, whether she was so in reality or not: but what her Sentiments were, I had not leisure to examine, having Perturbations of my own which would not suffer me to look into others. Day after Day, Week after Week pass'd away without any Letter, either from *Wyaria*, or her Father: so strange a neglect could not but very much alarm me, and what between Amazement, Indignation, and disappointed Love, I suffer'd infinitely more than is in the power of any words to relate. A whole Month I liv'd in the Tortures of Suspence, than which, those who have known 'em will confess there cannot be severer; and, not able to assign any reason which seem'd so feasible, I imagin'd the Dutchess, to {91} make the more sure Discovery how my Affair stood, had been so wicked as to intercept the Letters directed to me.

This Belief had no sooner got ground in me, than I taxed her with it, and as tho' assured that she had acted in that manner which to me was a Crime unpardonable, reproach'd her in Terms which 'tis probable none, since she had been rais'd to the Title of her Grace, had ever presum'd to do. She heard me however, with a Patience which I have since wonder'd at, and only protesting, by all the Adjurations she was capable of making, that she was innocent, gave my Rage leave to vent itself in what manner it would. But I could not form to myself any other Cause, and continued in my Chagrin 'till I was reliev'd from that by being put into a worse. When I had almost given over all hope, comes a Letter from *Wyaria*, the Contents of which were too remarkable to be forgot; and because no Words but her own can make you sensible of this astonishing Circumstance, I will repeat: they were these.

The undone *Wyaria* to her dear *Windusius*

Condemn me not, my ever-ador'd Windusius, that I have not writ before; both Pen and Paper have been denied me, since you left this Place, and love me with never so violent an Ardor, your Disappointment cannot equal my Affliction. The moment you had taken horse, I was confined to my Chamber, denied the sight of even all of our own Family, but an old grim Wretch who is perfectly my Father's Creature, and to whom it would be but in vain to pour out the load of Anguish my Soul is over-pressed with; 'Tis enough I know my {92} Father has neither the Compassion Nature should oblige him to for his own Child, nor the Gratitude which is due to a Generosity such as yours: he ordains that I shall never see you more, and to that end sends me to the House of *Batharius*, (O horrid, barbarous Usage!) there to remain under the Guardianship of that detested Monster, who will no doubt take care to prevent my making any Elopement. Judge what I must endure in this Confinement, to have my injured Sister, innocent of the Wrongs I have done her, provoking my distracted Conscience by fruitless Attempts of Consolation. My Curst Undoer ever in my Sight, and perhaps when opportunity presents, forced to repeat the Crime, which to have been guilty of, damns me to unceasing Horrors. O save me, save me, I conjure you, if not for Love, for Friendship, for Pity; nay, for the sake of common Humanity defend me from being again subservient to his brutish Will. Invent some Stratagem to take me from him, it matters not what shall hereafter become of the

Forlorn *Wyaria*.

P. S. It was not without great Bribes I furnished myself with the means of sending this. O let not the Supplications of a Woman, who in spite of her Misfortunes loves you more than Life, be altogether unavailing; but as you have sworn yourself my Friend, be just to your own Honour, and shield me from this worst Destruction, and dispose of me hereafter as you please. Once more Adieu. I am this very moment going, therefore be quick in your Relief, if you at all afford it.

It would be wholly impossible, dear Stranger, to make you sensible what 'twas I felt at reading these Lines: I now perceiv'd my hopes of Interest by her Father were utterly abolish'd, I found the old Villain rather than part with his Money would sacrifice his Daughter to all the Miseries of the most abhorred and unnatural Lust, all my pleasing {93} Expectations were now in a moment vanish'd; but I had still Tenderness enough for the unhappy *Wyaria*, to wish to free her from a Life, she had so good cause, and so much seem'd to dread.

With these Cogitations mingled a Reflection that I had wrong'd the Dutchess, in imagining she had intercepted my Letters; and my Remorse for having accused her with it, joined to the Resolution my Rage had inspired me to form, of exposing to the last degree the Father and Brother of *Wyaria*, made me impart the whole Affair to her. I ran immediately to her, related every Circumstance of my ill Usage, and entreated her Advice how to proceed both for Vengeance and Redress. She seem'd (as well she might) prodigiously alarm'd at the account, told me she thought I had a good Escape, and if I would take her Counsel, it would be to trouble myself no farther with any of the Family.

This was, I believe, the only sincere thing she ever said in her Life, at least, to me; and yet this of all she ever said I was the farthest from regarding. Had my Passion for *Wyaria* been extinguished, my Honour could not dispense with the Promise I had made in protecting her, as far as was in my power, from the Abuses of *Batharius:* Friendship, nay, common Humanity, methought, bid me fly to the relief of this poor Penitent, who abandoned by those who ought most to take her part, had no Refuge but myself on Earth. I must have endeavoured her Rescue even for pity sake, but as my Love (if not as violent as it had been) was yet superiour to that with which Men ordinarily are possessed, I thought each Moment I delayed a Crime she might in Justice hate me for.

I passed the Night in Anxieties too great to be described, nor did the Morn bring with it any Tranquillity; for as before my Thoughts were {94} racked with the Apprehensions of her ill Usage, they were now tortur'd with ten thousand various Inventions by what Method I should proceed to give her the Relief she begg'd: and at last, wholly incapable of fixing on any, but resolv'd to attempt every way, I took leave of the Dutchess, much against her Will, and made what haste I could towards the Villa where *Batharius* liv'd.

Her Father's House was in my way, and it came in my head, as I pursued my Journey, to try first what I could do with him; but not knowing well how to contain myself in the Presence of a Wretch, who, for no other Reason than because he would not do me justice, had consented to sacrifice his own Child to the brutish Lust of an incestuous Monster, whom he ought rather to have made an example of; I went into an Inn, which happened to be pretty near the House, and in as civil terms as my Rage would permit me to dissemble with, writ to him, complained of his Breach of his Promise, let him know that I had depended on his Word, look'd on *Wyaria* as my Wife, and was now come to claim her, not taking the least notice that I had received a Letter from her, or that I had the least intimation by any hand whatsoever of her being removed.

This I sent by my Servant, and ordered him to acquaint the old Gentleman where I waited in expectation of his Answer, because I would punctually fulfil the last Command he had given, of not coming to his House, till summoned by him. I did not doubt but that he would be extremely puzzled what excuse to make, and began to sooth Imagination, that as soon as he heard I was there, he would immediately send for *Wyaria*, and make good his Promise to me: but I was soon convinced of the error I had been in, to think there was a possibility for him to repent the Villany he had {95} been guilty of, or that it was in his Nature either to be just, or grateful.

My poor Fellow came back with his Head broke,' and his Arms and Back bruised in a most terrible manner. I needed no more than the sight of him, to inform me what had happened; but when he had recover'd Breath to speak, he told me that the old Fiend had no sooner read my Letter, than he tore it in pieces, and cried, Tell your Master he is a Villain and a Fool, to think to impose upon me and my Family, that I forbid him my House at his peril, and that if he dares to enter my Doors, he shall meet with the same Treatment as his Messenger. With these Words, and many other Scurrilities, he return'd my Civilities: which my Man, unable to endure, retorted on the giver. On which he call'd his Creatures, whether Footmen, Plough-men, Hedgers, or Ditchers, I am not able to say, for 'tis probable they serv'd in all these Capacities, and turn'd him out with the Marks of their Good-Will already mentioned. Had I followed the first Impulses of my Rage, I had certainly gone to the House, and shot him thro' the Heart; but Love interposed for *Wyaria*, and bid my beating Heart inform me I must first deliver her, and then call her Father to an account for the Injury he had done me. It was but a moment before I was determined; Revenge gave way to Tenderness, and I rode on towards *Batharius*'s, hoping there to obtain the most wish'd-for Triumph!

But I had not pursued my Journey above a hundred Paces, before I perceived at a distance two Ladies on horseback, and a Servant with them; both were mask'd, but one of the Horses I knew immediately to be *Wyaria*'s, and that very same she was mounted on, when the Invention of the Cramp had first made me sensible how much I was favour'd in her Inclinations. It will be needless to say I set spurs to my Horse, and would have thought a *Pegasus* too slow to {96} bear me to 'em; by what I have told you of the state of my Heart, you will easily believe I made what speed I could. The foremost of them I presently knew to be the Wife of *Batharius*, whom as not believing of the Confederacy against me, I accosted as civilly as my Impatience to secure the other, who I believed was her Sister, would allow time for. I flew with all the Wings of Joy and fond Desire; but Oh! Immortal Gods! How great was my Surprize how shocking my Disappointment, when laying my hand on the Reins[67] of her Horse, she pluck'd off her Mask, and discovered a Face I had never seen before!

I had not Presence enough of Mind even to ask her Pardon; but returning to the other, who stopt, and seemed amazed at my Proceeding, and preventing the Interrogatories she was about to put to me for what Reason I had done it, desired her to tell me instantly, where *Wyaria* was; told her I look'd on her as my Wife, and would have her produced.

Here this Lady, whom, before I had the greatest esteem for, and who had profess'd the highest regard for me, now show'd herself of a piece with the rest of that accursed Family, and in Expressions, a Gentlewoman should have blush'd to speak, bade me be gone and think not of *Wyaria*, she was not a match for a paultry *Chevalier*, who had no other Jointure to make her, than the precarious dependance of a beggarly Pension; and a Fellow too, (*said she, with all the spite imaginable*) who has render'd himself yet more unworthy the Civilities he has found in our Family, by endeavouring to sow dissension among People, who are too well acquainted with one another's Principles to regard what he has said, any further than to despise and hate the insinuating Reporter. These Words gave me not only to understand she {97} had been inform'd of everything, which at *Wyaria*'s request I had related to her Father, but also, that she believ'd her Husband innocent, and that I had, for some base Interest of my own, been the Inventer of the Story. I wou'd have endeav-

---

67 [*resnes*, French: the part of the bridle, which extends from the horse's head to the driver's or rider's hand.]

our'd to have clear'd myself of an Aspersion so wrongfully cast on me, but she wou'd not give me leave; and continuing her revilings, and assuring me I never should see her Sister any more, who, *she said*, had been too much deceiv'd by my Insinuations, rode away, without suffering me to alledge one word in my Vindication. I did not attempt to stop her, nor give myself any further trouble concerning what Opinion she harbour'd, than what proceeded from my wonder, that a Woman, whom, till then, I had always believ'd had a good deal of discernment, cou'd be so grosly blinded in an Affair, in which most of her Sex are apt to be too quicksighted. My still dear *Wyaria*'s Condition, took up too much of my Thoughts to allow room for any other Consideration to continue; and presently reflecting that her Sister's absence might give the curst *Batharius* an opportunity of abusing her in the manner he had done, I began to renew my pace towards the House, which was now almost in sight; when hearing a Horse gallop after me, I turn'd my head, and saw the Footman, whom I had just before met with the two Ladies, coming with full speed in the very Path I was in. I presently imagin'd he had been sent by them, as no doubt he was, to give notice of my Approach and Intentions, and resolving to stop his Career, I turn'd short upon him, and catching fast hold of the Bridle, Whither in such haste? *Said I*; all your Stratagems to get *Wyaria* out of the way shall be in vain, therefore return to your Mistress, and tell her, that *Windusius* will prove he deserves not the treatment he has met, or perish in the attempt. I said no {98} more, nor indeed had I the power: the Fellow, with an Impudence as great as those to whom he belong'd, giving me a hearty Curse, clap'd Spurs to his Horse, which being a high-mettled one, with a sudden Spring was very near oversetting me and mine. I was so much provok'd at this Insolence from a Servant, that not being at that instant Master of my Passion, I immediately snatch'd one of the Pistols from my Holster, and discharg'd it at him, but good Heaven averted the Mischief, my Rashness else might have been fatal to myself as well as him. He miss'd the Bullets, and receiv'd no other Damage than what his Fright occasion'd, which indeed was violent enough to make him fall from his Horse, and, for some moments, lose the power of Speech; yet the dissembling Villain, too well vers'd in the pernicious Arts of those he serv'd, when I demanded of him, Whether *Wyaria* was at this time in the House of *Batharius*? And offer'd him a handsome reward to reveal the truth of that Affair, had Cunning sufficient to deceive me, and faithful to his horrid Trust, assur'd me she was not; form'd a most plausible Story that she had been sent there, but not believing it a place of Security, imagining I would come in search of her, she was remov'd that very day to an Aunt's she had further in the Country: I, easily betray'd, doubted not of the Truth of what I thought Fear only had extorted from him, gave him what I had promis'd, and dismiss'd him. My Heart methought was something lighter than it had been at this News; I rejoic'd that she was out of the power of *Batharius* for her own sake; however, I still resolv'd not to leave the Country till I had seen her, and therefore knowing very well the way to the Town where this Relation liv'd, I left the Road which led to *Batharius*'s, and took the other; it was but a few Miles, and I reach'd it before dark. At {99} my arrival, the good old Lady was prodigiously alarm'd at my demanding to speak with her Neice, and much more so, when I told her, as I now made no secret of it, the Reasons of my enquiring. She assur'd me I had been misinform'd, for to her certain knowledge *Wyaria* was at her Brother's; and that if I question'd the Truth of what she said, there was a young Lady in the Neighbourhood who cou'd convince me, having been come but that day from the House of *Batharius*, and had seen her there. This Lady was *Smitheria*, who, I told you, had ever been the chief Companion and Considant *Wyaria* had; to her I immediately went, hoping I might now know the certainty of everything; but I found her as much alter'd in her Behaviour to me as the rest had been. She said, indeed, that she had seen *Wyaria*, and din'd with her that day, but she could give no other account of any thing I ask'd; and when I related to her, as I had done to the Aunt, all the particulars of the Affair, she only answer'd, with a good deal of reserve, that she had nothing to do in it, every body was best judge of their own Business; but acknowledg'd, she thought it a little strange things shou'd be carry'd so, after what had past between us. I found there was no farther Satisfaction to be gain'd from her, therefore took my leave, resolving to pursue my Knight-Errantry[68] the next morning, for I was oblig'd to lie in the Town, by reason of its being too late to go that night. *Aurora* had scarcely spread her chearful Dawn, before I was on horseback; but I had gone but a very little way before I was met by the *Chevalier Drusus*, Brother to the Dutchess; he ask'd me, Whither I was going so early? Which I made no hesitation to inform him He then told me he had much to say to me on that Affair, and desired I wou'd alight and go into an Inn hard by. With some unwillingness, to {100} retard even a moment the Execution of my Designs, I was at last prevail'd upon, and he began to endeavour persuading me from so rash an attempt assur'd me that if I went in sight of *Batharius*'s House, I was a dead Man; that there was a Gun plac'd in every Window; that what I had already done to the Servant, had made the whole Country ring; and that there was not the least possibility of getting to the Speech of *Wyaria*; for she was so closely confin'd, that very few of their own Family saw her. All this he protested was true to his knowledge, for he had been there all night, and was come away but when I met him. But it was not in the power of all these Difficulties to deter me, or make me in the least recede from the Resolution of rescuing her, or perishing for her sake; on the contrary, I rather grew more eager to deliver her from a Captivity

---

68 [from *errant:* an errant state; the condition of a wanderer.]

in which I believ'd she suffer'd so much; and I doubt not but I had gone, and really fallen a Sacrifice to their Brutality, if the *Chevalier* had not hit on a Proposal which seem'd rather to facilitate than hinder me from what I wish'd: It was to accompany him first to the old Man's, and by repeating before him the Obligations they had to treat me in a different manner, give him, the *Chevalier*, an opportunity of espousing my Quarrel, which he promis'd faithfully to do, and on the Strength of his own, and his Sister's influence over that Family, prevail on him to go with us to *Batharius*'s, under pretence that he might be able to judge the Truth of the affair, and relate it to the Dutchess. After a good many Arguments on both sides, this was at last agreed on, and away we went to the old Miscr's:[69] we found him at his Gate, and on the first fight of me, he was going so call his Servants, I suppose, to give me a reception I shou'd no way have been pleas'd with; but the *Chevalier* guessing his Intentions, rode up before {101} me, and cry'd, Hold Sir! I bar all outrages; if you offer to insult *Windusius*, I shall take it as done to me; we come to talk to you without heat or passion, —therefore be you as temperate. The old Wretch seem'd a little confus'd at the *Chevalier*'s behaviour; but not being willing to disoblige him: Well then, Sir! *mutter'd he out*, on your account he shall come in, tho' I had sworn solemnly to the contrary: I was about to reply in such a manner, as wou'd certainly have broke all our measures, if my kind Companion had not made a motion to me to be silent. With much ado, I curb'd the struggling Passion, and into the Hall we went; where, on the *Chevalier*'s demanding the reason why he had affronted me in the Person of my Servant, in the manner I had told him; Truly, Sir, *reply'd the grey-beard Villain*, there were sufficient reasons which oblig'd me to act as I did. I had no acquaintance with *Windusius*; I entertain'd him civilly (as he was recommended by her Grace) till he (without any encouragement from me) pretended Love to my Daughter, and after that, forg'd a monstrous Story, which, if we had been so credulous as he hoped we were, might have been the ruin of us all. I have a thousand times since wonder'd at my own patience, that restrain'd me from revenging my wounded Honour with his Life; but remembring the promise I had made to the *Chevalier*, to try first by fair means, I contented myself with proving him a Lyar, by producing those Letters I had received both from him and *Batharius*, while at *Ponray*, entreating me to come down, and that they cou'd not be easy without me. And for the latter Part of the Aspersion he cast on me, of deceiving him with a forg'd Story: Wicked old Man! (*said I, opening a Window which fac'd the Garden, and that Grove where I had made the Discovery to him of* Wyaria's *misfortune*) had those Trees the power of utterance, they wou'd {102} proclaim my Innocence, and your consummate Baseness. Did not your own Daughter attest the

---

69 [*miser*, Latin: a wretched person; one overwhelmed with calamity.]

truth of what I said? Did she not avow her Crime in Terms so piteous, as wou'd have melted any Heart but yours? Did she not kneel, and weep, and beg never to see the curst *Batharius* more? Did she not almost die away before you? Did you then confess me generous? Did you not both confess the Power of unexampl'd Love and Tenderness alone cou'd move me to forgive her Fault, and save her from destruction? Can you deny all this? Can you forget? No, no, *reply'd he*, I do very well remember some of the Pass'ages you mention. But at that time your Behaviour appear'd in a far different light to what it has done since. My Daughter afterwards deny'd it all, and confess'd you had prevail'd on her by your insinuations to join with you in this deceit, only to get my Consent to marry her, which, otherwise you both knew wou'd be impossible. But she is now of another mind, she never desires to see you more. 'Tis false, (*interrupted I, fiercely*) and to prove it so, read this. In speaking these Words, I drew out the Letter she had writ, conjuring me to come to her Assistance.

Never did I see so much confusion in any Face, as appeal'd in his at sight of these Lines. He cou'd not, for some time, utter one Word, but recollecting himself a little, at last; Well, *said he*, if she knows her own mind no better than this, I have done with her. The *Chevalier* here thought it a proper time for what we had agreed on, and preventing me from speaking; Come, Sir, (*rejoin'd he*) for the Satisfaction of us all, let them come Face to Face, I'll answer for my Friend, that if the young Lady declares before us she designs not to see him, he never will attempt it more. Never by Heaven, (*added I*). At this proposition the old Man paus'd, loth he was to grant {103} it, yet lother to disoblige the *Chevalier*. In fine, after a long pause, he told us he would comply with this, provided that I would be content with her Company, and not endeavour to enter the House, which he said *Batharius* had sworn I never shou'd. I told him I was far from designing it; all I wanted was to be satisfy'd from *Wyaria's* own Mouth, that she expected no Assistance from me. Every body being settl'd, he order'd his Horse to be got ready, which being perform'd, we all set forward toward the decisive Scene. When we came to the Court-Yard, he took the *Chevalier* with him, leaving me to attend their return. In about half an hour the latter came to me, told me he found them wavering, that the Father and *Batharius* were in consultation, but had not seen *Wyaria*; and that believing I shou'd be out of patience, he came to bear me company, till we saw what wou'd be done. And in truth, we stay'd a considerable Time, and no body appearing, the *Chevalier* went in again, but came back without knowing the result of any thing; at least as he told me. He went a third time, return'd again alone, 'till I imagining they design'd to fool me, grew quite outrageous, swore I wou'd fire the House, and burn them out, but I wou'd see her, with a thousand more Extravagancies of the like nature; which he, I doubt not, (being, as I have since been inform'd, more a Friend to them than me) repeated to them at his next going in. After that, the mighty Business was concluded. *Wyaria*, all undress'd, Her Hair hanging loose upon her Shoulders, her Eyes swell'd with Tears, a moving Spectacle of Grief and Horror appear'd before my sight. She was supported as she approach'd me, by her Father on one side, and a young Priest, Brother to *Batharius*, on the other, and indeed the trembling Condition she was in, made her stand in need of them. Well, Madam! Said *I*, I am {104} come, in obedience to your Commands, to offer you what assistance is in my power. Say you will be mine, and it shall not be Human Force shall keep you from me. I never will, *answer'd she*, (with an Assurance sure, which none of her Sex beside, after what had pass'd between us, could have spoke with, and which seem'd very much to contradict that good Opinion her Looks had inspir'd). How! (*resum'd I, scarce able to contain myself*). Can *Wyaria* so far forget herself, or what she owes to *Windusius*, or her own Honour? I had proceeded, but she prevented me, by saying, 'Tis no matter what I owe; I conjure you for the love of Heaven to trouble me no more. With these Words she sunk fainting in the Arms of those that held her, and cut off those upbraidings she must else have expected from me. They carry'd her into the House, and the *Chevalier* telling me, I now had all I cou'd demand, and that it wou'd neither be wise, nor good-natur'd to force myself upon her after what she had declar'd, took an abrupt leave of me, and follow'd them. My amazement had so far stupefy'd my Senses, that for a good while I had not power to leave the Place; and I know not when I should have remov'd, if my Man had not taken the liberty to remind me, that if I were seen by any of the Family, they might imagine I tarry'd[70] on some design contrary to my promise. Yes, (*said I, waking from my Lethargy*) I will go forever from her sight, and if possible, avoid the very hearing of her, false, ingrateful, perjur'd as she is. I continu'd to upbraid her in my Thoughts, for a considerable time, and when the first Tempest of that Passion, which her astonishing Behaviour had rais'd, was a little calm'd, and more sedate Reflection had room to play its part, even then my former Tenderness return'd not: reason indeed suggested, that she had been forc'd to what she did, but then it also told me, no Woman, {105} who by any threats cou'd be prevail'd on to join with her Undoers (for such in this respect were all her Family) against the Man who was ready to give her the highest Testimony of his Love, cou'd be worthy of a sincere Affection. The more I consider'd on all the particulars of this Affair, the more I thought I had occasion to rejoice, that she had behav'd in a manner so effectual to cure me of that Passion I otherwise should have retain'd for her; and since it was an Impossibility to marry her with her Father's Consent, and have a Portion with her, it much better agreed with my Circumstances, that I ceas'd wishing her such, than to have suffer'd

---

70 [To wait for.]

my ungovern'd Fondness to transport me so far, as to have taken her without. But alas! Tho' I from that moment left off to love her as I had done, by the unceasing anguish which has never since forsaken me, I find, that when once a true and ardent Flame has kindled up the Heart, tho' it may seem extinguished, there will remain some Embers, which with inward consumings destroy the very Vitals, and are never, never to be put out. All I could do to forget her was in vain, and tho' I thought of her, as a Creature far unworthy of my Love, yet! Could not help a secret desire that she had not been so. But I was not enough acquainted with my own Heart to know this of myself, till the old Man happening to die about a Year after, leaving her, and her Fortune entirely at her own disposal; I began to hope she wou'd at last shew herself the Woman of Honour, I once believ'd her to be; expected every Post, that I shou'd hear from her, and receive a full Account in what manner she had been forc'd to seem so ungenerous, and so false. But no Letter coming, I had no longer Patience, and writ a long Epistle full of Upbraidings and Complaints; receiving no Answer, I sent another, but to no more purpose than the former. Then my Resentment again exerted itself {106} in me, and assur'd me what she had done was not so much by Constraint, as thro' the Changeableness of her own Temper. Now I endeavour'd as much as was in my power to hate her heartily, and for a time, perhaps, did so; till one unlucky Day, happening to be passing thro' the Streets, a Chariot and fix, with two Ladies in it, came swiftly by me: I immediately knew one of them to be *Wyaria*, and not all the Rage I had conceiv'd against her, cou'd defend my Heart from feeling something, even in this transient View, like what I had formerly done whenever she appear'd. A Flood of Tenderness overflow'd all other Considerations, and pleaded in her behalf, that my Letters had been intercepted, or by some other accident miscarry'd; and that not receiving them, she might perhaps have been ignorant where to direct for me in Town: but resolving to be ascertain'd, and once again from herself receive my doom, I made it my business to find where she lodg'd, and by diligent enquiries, in a few days heard she was at the House of a Lady, whose Name was *Deveres*, and there directed another Mandate, sent it by my Servant, that I might be certain. She receiv'd it, and order'd him not to return without an Answer. To go about to describe the Hopes, the Fears, the swift Vicissitudes[71] of various Tumults which swell'd my throbbing Heart while he was gone, wou'd be as vain, as to endeavour to make you sensible what it was I felt; when being come back, he told me, that he had seen her at the Window, but that having gain'd sight of him, would not suffer him to be admitted any further than the Door, therefore he was blig'd to send in the Letter by a Footman who belong'd to the House, to whom he heard her say, as

---

71 [*vicissitudo*, Latin: regular change; return of the same things in the same succession.]

soon as she had read it: Take this Packet of incoherent Nonsense back to him thar brought it, and bid him tell the Person that sent it, that he is an impudent Fellow to pretend to write {107} to one he knows not. I never saw him, nor heard of him in my Life. I must have been strangely stupefy'd, if I cou'd have harbour'd the least kind thought of her after this; but what I endur'd in this fatal certainty of her unexampled baseness and perfidy, can only be conceiv'd. No words can do it Justice— 'tis unutterable as the monstrous Cause.

Here the Remembrance of what he had suffered for the sake of this vile Woman, adding to the present Anguish of his Soul, made the poor *Windusius* unable to proceed. He paused, to vent some Sighs, and wipe away some Tears, which, in spite of his Endeavours to restrain them, ran from his manly Eyes; and that Truce of Speech gave the Stranger an opportunity to let him know the part he took in his Sorrows, and to testify the Amazement he was in at so strange an instance of Levity in that Sex, which, to do them Justice, are by Nature infinitely more constant than the other. Pity is a vast Alleviator of Grief: the abandoned Lover found so much Ease in the Commiseration of this generous Youth, that he immediately recover'd himself enough to pursue his Story.

I am ashamed (resum'd he) of the Weakness I yet am guilty of, for this worthless Woman; and tho' by what I have already related, you must acknowledge I ought not to think of her but with the utmost Detestation, yet that which still remains to be told of her, will make me seem less than Man, not to abhor her very Name, and for her sake, the whole Race of Womankind. Though too much confirm'd of her Perfidiousness by the Account my Servant brought, I was willing to be more so, must make more Trials yet; and to that end obtained the Favour of a Lady of my Acquaintance to go to her (for I had often been there, and she was always denied) and in my Name intreat an Interview; which, if she {108} refused, and still persisted in the Denial of knowing me, that she should produce that Letter I have already had occasion to make mention of, (and which stood me in good stead, when her Father would have palmed the Odium of Deceit on me) and several others which, before that, I had received from her. The Lady was perfectly sincere in her Endeavours to serve me, and had the Address to get herself admitted to her. Madam *Deveres* and she were in a Room together, and my Friend, after she had taken her aside, finding she gave her the same Answer she had done my Servant, and absolutely deny'd all Knowledge of me, with a thousand Imprecations, was so provoked at it, that she thought she ought to be expos'd to the World; and plucking the Letters out of her Pocket, shewed them to Madam *Deveres*, and related all the Intrigue as she had it from me. The perjured Creature was, it seems, in some Confusion at the sight of her own Hand, which was very well known to Madam *Deveres*, and not having Presence enough of Mind to invent any way to come off, nor Generosity enough to own the Truth, fell a railing at the Person by whom she was convicted, and endeavoured by her Clamours to silence what the other had to say, 'till Madam *Deveres*, ashamed of her Behaviour, taking up the Letters, See Madam! Said she, you ought rather to be dumb, these Monitors, methinks, should strike you so; is not here your own Hand, your Manner of Writing, nay, your very Seal? (for tho' broke, 'tis easy to see on it the Impression of your Arms.) Are not these Evidences too plain against you? These Remonstrances were answered by *Wyaria* with a good deal of Warmth, which occasioned more severe Reflections from the other, it ended in a mortal Quarrel: and I hear, for I have since had a personal Acquaintance with this good Lady, that they parted that Day, and {109} have never seen each other since. But now the Foulness of *Wyaria*'s Soul appeared in all its Deformity to me, and to all who knew her History; the vile *Batharius*, that Betrayer of her Honour, that Ruiner of her Virtue, that Debaucher of her Principles, that Wretch, whom to avoid, a thousand times she has sworn she would hazard more than Life, is now the only Person she makes choice of for a Friend: she has committed the Management of her Fortune wholly to his Care, lives in his House, scarce sees any-body but himself, admits no Visitors, nor will receive any Overtures of Marriage, tho' her Beauty and Estate have drawn the richest and most worthy Gentlemen of the Country to make them. What Judgment then can we form of her, but that, grown fond of the Crime for which the once appeared so penitent, the quits all other Considerations to indulge it? Oh ! May the horrid Truth be known to all! May the quick Ears of busy *Fame* catch from my Lips the Secret, and all her hundred Tongues speak nothing else but *Incest*, and *Wyaria*.

The broken-hearted *Windusius* had, perhaps, continued longer in these Exclamations, if the God of Love, who knew he had finished his Narration, and was desirous to entertain the Stranger with some other Theme, had not, on a sudden, shewed himself between them, and vouchsafing some words of divine Consolation to his dejected Votary, dismiss'd him; having Intelligences to communicate to the other, which Fate permitted not to be revealed to any but himself.

When they were alone, (*said the heavenly Disposer of the supremest Joy*) I am very well pleased that my unhappy Votary has concluded the little History I influenced him to give you; because, tho' there was enough in it to excite the wonder of a Person unacquainted with the Vices of these Islanders, yet {110} you will find all he has been able to inform you of, Hypocrisy, Artifice, and every other Crime, but small, in competition with what you are still to be made sensible of. Let us return to the promiscuous Throng, which watch the expected Flow of the Enchanted *Well*; there are two Ladies just mingled with them, whose Amours afford more Variety of Incidents, and are greater Examples of Perjury and Inconstancy, than the Annals of a thousand Ages can produce. The Stranger, tho' almost buried in Reflection, on what he had been told by *Windusius*, was yet Master of Presence of Mind enough to know what was owing to the Deity who descended to favour me so far, and bowed down to the Earth in token of Obedience, and Readiness to follow wheresoever he led.

By the Aid of a supernatural Conveyance, they were again, immediately, in sight of that Assembly from which they had so lately parted; but, at the Appearance of a Man of very good Figure, and who, by many Marks, might be known a Person of Condition, tho' somewhat dejected in his Air, the Deity stopped short, and turning to our Traveller, I cannot proceed, *said he*, without desiring you to take notice of that Gentleman; He is the Duke *de Ulto*, he passes in the World for one of the greatest Favourites of Heaven; his splendid Fortune is the Envy of many of his Equals, and the Homage of his Inferiors: he is in the prime of his Years, has a most healthy and vigorous Constitution; has a much greater share of Friends than Enemies; and, as he wants no Favours from the one, he has no occasion to stand in fear of the Malice of the other; yet cannot all these Advantages make him happy: he nourishes a Canker[72] in his Bosom, which renders all these Blessings unavailing, destroys his Peace, and fills his Nights and Days with galling Anguish. He was married very {111} young to the Daughter of the late Prince *del Carnel*, a Family remarkable for the Extremes of Virtue and of Vice; the Bride, who owed her being so only to Constraint, having the most strong Aversion that could be to the Duke, soon made him know how little Satisfaction there is to be found in a Match where Love has no part. They had not been married three Days before she gave publick Testimonies how much she hated her Husband. The agreeable Count *Hermio* was the Man she adored, and she had either too little the Power of disguising her Inclinations, or too much Pride, to give herself the Trouble. The whole Town was sensible of the Affair, and the Duke sufficiently ridiculed for marrying into a Family famous for Intrigue. He made a Complaint of it to the Princess, but she only laughed at the little Knowledge he seemed to have of the Behaviour of the *Beau Monde*; and was so far from checking her Daughter, that she rather encouraged a Disposition, which (*she said*) discover'd so much Vivacity and Gallantry. Whether it was owing to his want of Spirit, that he did not endeavour to revenge his Injuries on him, through whose Insinuations he had sustain'd them, or to his Prudence, that he would not do anything which he thought might make his Disgrace become more publick; or through Tenderness for her who had occasion'd it; has been the Cause of many Disputes among those, who were the most acquainted with him of his own Specie: but I, who saw into the deepest Recesses of his Heart, and pitied the Conflicts there, knew his Patience proceeded only from the

---

72 [*cancer*, Latin: it seems to have the same meaning and original with *cancer*, but to be accidentally written with a *k*, when it denotes bad qualities in a less degree; or, *canker* might come from *chancre*, French, and *cancer* from the Latin.]

latter of those Reasons I mentioned. He passionately lov'd the unthinking Dutchess, and could not bear to do a Justice which should occasion her an anxious Moment; he rather chose, by all the soft Endearments imaginable, to out-vye his Rival in Assiduity and Fondness, than to render himself yet more {112} disagreeable by Admonitions; a Proof of Love, which few of that Sex, especially those of her haughty Temper, can brook to be troubled with. In fine, he laid by all the Authority of a Husband, and resum'd the Obsequiousness of the beseeching Lover: but to what purpose? When once the Heart is truly possessed with a Passion, 'tis only in the power of the beloved Object's self to erase it. In spite of all he could do, Count *Hermio* still triumph'd over him, all he did was graceful, all he said enchanting; every Action, every Word of his was a Charm: and nothing in the good-natur'd, too submissive Duke, had the power to please her. The amorous Pair continued to indulge themselves in all the riotous Delights of loose Desire, for so long a time, that their Constancy made the Passion they were possessed of be believ'd was influenc'd by me: so exactly, sometimes, does that Demon, *Lust*, resemble me, that, 'till the fatal Consequences of his Inspiration convince the mistaken Judger of his Error, the difference between us is not to be distinguish'd; 'tis by my *Unchangeableness* alone I am proved the *God:* those other Flames may burn as fierce, may seem as bright, but soon the Blaze goes out, leaves not a Glow to warm the Heart which lately was all on fire, and is no more remembered but by the Smoke of Infamy's black Vapour. Nature never formed a Face more exquisitely lovely, a Shape more delicate, an Air and Mein more enchanting than that of the Dutchess; and, to add to the Beauties of her Person, she has a Wit the most poinant that ever was, there is something so irresistibly striking, so intelligible in her Eyes, that discovers to all who look upon her, without the Aid of Words, she has a Soul full of a thousand Excellencies: yet not all these Attractions, not all these unequall'd Charms had the power to fix *Hermio* her's for ever; he grew satiated {113} at last, her Sweets grew tasteless and insipid, and to obtain in Marriage the Daughter of a petty Citizen, without Birth, without Beauty, without any other Qualification than her Wealth to recommend her, swore never to see the lovely Dutchess more. The Vanity of the other did not fail to blaze abroad a Vow which she thought would give so much Reputation to the force of her own Charms: she was presently inform'd of it; and Rage o'ercoming disappointed Softness, resolv'd he should keep it in a stricter manner, than her Pride would give her leave to imagine he design'd, and from that moment carefully avoided him. That she might the better do so, and ar the same time have liberty to indulge her Spleen for a Treatment she so little expected, she pretended an Indisposition, and retir'd to a place the Duke had in the Country. It had been a Maxim with her Mother, that there was no Remedy so effectual to erase the Memory of an *old* Lover, as throwing herself into the Arms of a *new* one: She was willing however to make trial of it a Lady so young and beautiful could not fail of Opportunities, and she soon had it in her power to write under the Recipe, *Probatum est*. The *Count* was in a little while forgot, and by entering into a *Plurality* of Amours, knew none of those enslaving Fondnesses she before had felt in the Enjoyment of a *single* one. The whole time of her being in the Country was one continual Scene of Gallantry, the Duke was not insensible of it; and half distracted that he could not go to her by reason of his Attendance on the *Sovereign*, and not daring to command what he desir'd, obtained the favour of a Royal Mandate to oblige her immediate Appearance at Court.

Thus were the Country Ladies happily deliver'd from an Enemy too potent for their more feeble {114} Charms to cope with, and everyone now triumph'd in the Restoration of a Husband, or a Lover, whose Hearts had for a time been captiv'd by this universal Rival. She was so much vexed that there was any thing on Earth which had the power to rule her Actions, that the grew sullen and lost very much of that Briskness of Deportment,[73] which had been the Encouragement of many who else would not have presum'd to have discoursed her on the score of Gallantry; and this Appearance of Reserve, gave the Duke some hope that she might by degrees be prevail'd on to think it the most becoming manner of Behaviour for a Woman in her Circumstances, who was not only a Wife, but a Mother of several Children, and whose Quality and Character in the World made her Actions more conspicuous than those of a less distinguish'd Rank. But this consolatory Expectation lasted not long, the Freedom of her Temper again return'd, she relapsed into her former Inadvertencies, and he no more had hope his Condition would ever alter. She was not for some Years, however, after this, fam'd for any particular Intrigue; and tho' there was room enough to imagine she countenanced the Addresses of several young Noblemen about the Palace, yet none could prove she held a criminal Correspondence with any one of them; besides, whatever her Behaviour was to him in *private*, she treated the Duke, her Husband, in *publick*, with much more Civility than she had been accustom'd to do, and his Patience became everyday less and less the Subject of Ridicule.

She continued her Imprudence, but did nothing new, which could be prov'd dishonourable; and there being no present Theme for Scandal, the Town grew weary of talking of the past. 'Tis possible their Affairs might still have been in this Position, {115} if the Duke, (who is certainly of a Humour the most easily impos'd on in every Circumstance of Life, of any Man in the World) had not been drawn into the Infatuation of the *enchanted Well*; and to farther the Hope which *Lucitario* had given him of being an immense gainer by it; brought to his House a Dependant and Creature of the *Necromancer's*.

---

73 [*deportement*, French: conduct; management; manner of acting.]

His Name was *Melanthus*, and bore the Title of a *Chevalier*, tho' the Gods never inspir'd any of his Family to do an Action which could deserve an *Escutcheon*:[74] but as it is neither Virtue nor Bravery which are requisite for Preferment in this Island, his Father and himself found means to wind themselves so far into the favour of the Nobility, as to get Posts, and those not inconsiderable ones at Court. The younger had Arts which render'd him extremely acceptable to the Ladies he danc'd well, sung very agreeably, and was always furnish'd with one Story or another for their Entertainment. The Dutchess was immediately charm'd; and he had not the liberty of visiting there above a Month, before the Duke perceiv'd he had sufficient Reasons to repent his having brought him there. Her Passion for Count *Hermio* had not been more visible to his Observation; he grew almost distracted at the daily Instances of it; he reproach'd her in secret, but she as little regarded his Resentment as she had ever done his Tenderness.

Never was Vexation greater than what he endur'd; his Concern in the *enchanted Well*, oblig'd him to entertain this Destroyer of his Peace, this Violater of his Honour, with all the Respect imaginable, and 'tis probable to know the Constraints he put on himself, and the Pain he underwent in stifling his too just Indignation, gave the Pride of this Upstart as great a Satisfaction, as the {116} Enjoyment of the loveliest Woman in the World did a contrary Passion. For more than two Years was this Intrigue carried on, in all which time Interest and Fear of *Lucitario*'s Displeasure kept the injur'd Husband from discovering any part of his Chagrin to him who had occasion'd it; how long he would have been able to have retain'd this Government of himself, is only known to *Jupiter*, for *Melanthus* was taken with a loathsome Disease of which he died, pitied by few, by none lamented but the Dutchess; tho' had every one that knew him join'd in one common Cry of Lamentation, all had been drown'd! All had been hush'd by those of her Despair! The Duke was with her in her Dressing-Room, when word was brought that he had breath'd his last. Is he then dead? *Said she, starting up, and looking wildly on the Person who had given the Account; which on her asking, he again repeated, and added also some Circumstances of the Manner of his Death.* Then I will not live, *rejoin'd she, tearing her Hair and Garment,* Heaven has done its worst, since *Melanthus*, my dear, ador'd *Melanthus* is no more! This World has nothing left that is worthy of me. She run on so fast in these distracted kind of Exclamations, that it was but in vain that the Duke both threaten'd and entreated her Silence. She heard him not, regarded him not, 'till taking her in his Arms, and forcing her from the Floor where she had thrown herself. You shall not thus, *said he, with a loud and menacing Voice*, expose yourself and me; if you are mad, I will have Persons

---

74 [A shield or emblem showing a coat of arms.]

proper for the Occasion to attend you; nor shall you for the future be trusted with yourself; there are dark Rooms, and Beds of Straw, and other Requisites for Ladies in your Condition, to be found, such Usage, may, perhaps, bring you to a just Sense of what you owe my Character and your own, which {117} too mild a Treatment has made you utterly forget.

'Tis probable she listen'd to part of these Words, for struggling with her might, and loosing herself from him, Villain! *cry'd she*, Fool! Always the Object of my Hate, now of my Scorn, know 'tis my only Pride, my only Glory, to have been lov'd by the adorable *Melanthus*, and to gall thee more, I will avow it too, avow it to the whole World, and think it greater Honour, as it is greater Pleasure, to die with him, than 'tis to live with thee!

She had scarce finish'd this Declaration before she was out of the Room; she flew down Stairs, and thro' a great Court-Yard into the Street with such precipitation, that it would have been impossible for any one, not agitated with the same Vehemence of Passion, to have overtaken her, had the Surprize at the Extravagance of such a Behaviour, not taken from them the power of attempting it. The Duke remain'd with part of her Robes in his hands, which were torn in struggling to get from him, like one whom a Bolt of Thunder had riveted to the Earth; her Women, and Pages who were attending in the Ante[75]-Chamber, and had heard all that pass'd, seem'd little less astonish'd. None had the power of Utterance, for a time; but when they regain'd it, 'tis easy to believe the Discourse which such an Adventure occasion'd, was not soon at an end.

In the mean while, the Dutchess, wholly bereft of Reason, wild with impatient Sorrow, with Garments ruffled, and dishevell'd Hair, ran through the Streets, regardless of the gaping Croud, which her distracted Looks and Dishabillée[76] had drawn about her, nor stop'd till at the Gate of that dear House, in which she had pass'd so many happy Hours with her Soul's Darling *Melanthus*. {118} Demanding to see his Body, she was admitted by the wondering Servant. But it would take more time than I can spare, to recount to you the various Turns of Frenzy which possess'd her at sight of an Object at once so shocking to Nature and to Love; she clung about the cold and breathless Corse, bath'd it with her Tears, press'd the clammy Lips with hers, and seem'd to strive to breathe her Soul between them, as tho' she had hope to re-animate the still-lov'd Heart, which had been used to dictate the tender Words they spoke; it was not without the utmost Force, that some Persons sent by her Mother (whom the Duke had by this time inform'd of

---

75 [A Latin particle signifying *before*, which is frequently used in compositions; as, *antediluvian*, before the flood; *antechamber*, a chamber leading into another apartment.]
76 [Undressed.]

her Behaviour) tore her from this Scene of Horror; nor was it any thing but the most watchful Diligence that prevented her from destroying herself, after she was remov'd.

She remain'd for some time in the Duke her Husband's House, in the most piteous Condition imaginable, nor when she was, in all appearance, perfectly recover'd of that Violence of Passion which might very well bear the Denomination of Madness, would the consent to eat, or sleep with him; nay, not even to speak to him. Neither did he seem desirous of it, therefore the Building being extremely large, their Apartments were as distant from each other, as they could be order'd; if they met, it was by chance, and they pass'd each other but as Strangers.

In this uneasy and discontented State both languish'd away some Months, 'till the Duke, still loving her with a Tenderness, which not all her Ingratitude could erase, yet asham'd to acknowledge what he thought so great a Weakness, bethought him of a Method, which, 'till then, never came into his Mind: he remembred to have been told by some that knew the Sex, that many Women, who have {119} little or no sense of Gratitude, have a very quick one of Jealousy; and rather than not undo a Rival, would yield to that which no other Motive could induce them to accept: that Vanity which had, in her days of Gaiety, been a very conspicuous part of the Dutchess's Character, inclin'd him to believe that if he counterfeited a Passion for another, it might give her some Alarms, the Consequence of which could not but be favourable to him. Full of this hope, he made his Addresses to a Creature of almost the most indifferent Figure he could chuse out, on purpose that she might receive the more poinant Shock, when she reflected that the Man who had possessed her, could after feel a Passion for one so every way the reverse. He entertain'd her in so publick and so splendid a manner, that the whole Town rang of it. Everybody was surpriz'd at the Alteration, some blam'd his Choice, others commended his Resentment, which they imagin'd it proceeded from; but few saw into the true Reason of it. Perceiving all he yet had done, work'd not the Effect he aim'd at, he went farther, made her a Settlement of five thousand Crowns a Year and at last took her into the House, and lodg'd her in an Apartment next to the Dutchess's. As regardless as she really was of all he had done before, this last Action piqu'd her to the Soul; she could not bear so near a Neighbourhood of a Woman whom she and all the World believ'd her Husband's Mistress, tho' a Husband she had never lov'd, and resolv'd never to bed with more: but knowing herself too guilty, and too publickly so, to complain, she disguised the Chagrin she conceiv'd at it while she tarried in the House, which indeed was no longer than her Equipage could be got ready. She took Shipping in a very little time, and left the Island.

{120} The Duke either ashamed to descend so far, after her Usage, or because he knew it would be in vain, did not endeavour to stay her; and what the Consequence of this Separation will be, the mysterious Book of Fate can only say: but if one may form a guess by the Place she has made choice of for her Retirement, it is not with a design to lead the Life of a *Recluse* that she is gone.

The Stranger had not time to testify any part of that Compassion which he conceiv'd for the Duke of *Ulto*'s Misfortunes: his celestial Informer had no sooner ended the Account he had given of him, than they were in sight of the *Well*, and the Deity, impatient to reveal the Histories of the two Ladies he had mention'd, after having pointed them out, pursued his Design in this manner;

I would have you, O Youth, most worthy of my Advice! *Said he*, take a particular care how you commence an Acquaintance with either of those Women. You may think there is no danger in a Conversation with them, because you see that neither of them is young nor beautiful; but it is not always with the least lovely, that the Heart is most secure; there are Methods of ensnaring which the truly Worthy disdain the use of, but by those conscious of their own Defects are studied with the greatest Zeal; you will find the Examples of this Truth in the Recitals I am about to make: *Cesaria* is about a Year the elder of the two, and for that Reason her Character and Circumstances shall be the first which shall astonish you.

{121} The History of *Cesaria*, Marchioness del Keisar

By no Desert, by no good Quality, but the Recommendation of a great Sum of Money to her Dowry, was she rais'd to the Title she is now possess'd of. The young Marquiss at his coming to his Estate, found it very much involv'd, Money therefore was what he wanted to pay off the Mortgages; and *Cesaria* being possess'd of that, he requir'd not the Addition of any other Charm. His Marriage with her did indeed set free his Patrimony, but entail'd a Load of Anguish on his Heart, which all the Wealth in the Universe could not buy off: it must be confess'd that at first he gave her some little Occasion for Chagrin, by giving into those Debaucheries which among the Nobility of this Island are become too fashionable; he gamed, drank hard, had his Amours, but none of these to a scandalous Excess, nor could he be ever tax'd, even in his loosest Hours, of doing an ill-natur'd or dishonourable Action. Had he been bless'd with a Wife who knew how to use proper Methods to reclaim him, he had doubtless much sooner been brought to quit those Extravagancies which at worst could be call'd no other than the Sallies of Youth, and which Custom, and the Company he kept, made seem more excusable to his Reflection, than in reality they were. But *Cesaria*, of a perverse and peevish Disposition, took not the least care to make Home pleasing to him; on the contrary, she was for ever upbraiding him with the vast Fortune she had brought him, {122} telling him she wish'd she had never seen his Face, that he was an unworthy Man;

and all this she utter'd in the rudest manner, for she had neither a natural Genius, nor the Improvements of Education to render her polite, or obliging. How little such a Behaviour was likely to succeed, any one may judge the Provocations on both sides increased daily, 'till at last their manner of living together was intolerable; I had never been by either of them consulted in the Nuptials, neither had seen in the other any thing to create a tender Wish: he had married her meerly for the sake of Interest and Convenience; she, him, for Title and Precedence: and both thinking the Remedy a greater Evil than the Disease, join'd to curse the Tye they had not power to break. The continual Disagreement between them, was too publick not to occasion such kind of Conversation as commonly fills the Town when such Eruptions happen; and when once 'tis known that a Husband and Wife are at enmity with each other, it lays the Woman open to all manner of Temptations. As few Attractions as *Cesaria* was Mistress of, she was not without those who swore she had more than any of her Sex, nor did she want a good share of that Foible which most of them are possess'd of, the Vanity of believing all that was said in her Praise. This Love of Flattery, join'd to the Insinuations of some Women-Acquaintance, led her into Secrets to which before she was altogether a Stranger; she fell, as it were, insensibly into Intrigue; but when once enter'd, the greatest *Machiavellian* of her Sex that way, could never out-do her in Stratagem and Artifices.

That Lady with whom she is now talking, (and whose History I shall anon relate) and a third who is since dead, form'd a Cabal, swore to maintain the Secrets of each other with an inviolable {123} Fidelity, and to do their utmost to expose and render odious all Womankind besides they used frequently to go out upon Parties, as they term'd it, that is, pretend a Jaunt[77] into the Country, which in reality was no farther than a *Bagnio*:[78] each had her Gallant, tho' not always the same; for this *Triumvirate* had concluded it impolitick that each should have no more than one String to her Bow. It would be too tedious to recount their various Amours, no Degree, no Rank, no Complexion, but they made trial of, till by a long Continuance in these vicious Practices, *Cesaria* grew bold in Infamy, and seem'd to glory in her Shamelessness. She gave a Proof of it, which I question if the most abandon'd trading Prostitute would not have blush'd to have done; she would have her Favourite Woman *Juditha* lie on a Pallet[79] by her, whenever she receiv'd a new Gallant in Bed, saying, she would make her judge which of them appear'd

---

77 [from the verb: ramble; flight; excursion. It is commonly used ludicrously, but solemnly by *Milton*.]
78 [*bagno*, Italian, a bath: a house for bathing, sweating, and otherwise cleansing the body.]
79 [*paillet*, in *Chaucer*, which was probably the French word from *paille*, straw, and secondarily, a bed.]

to have the greatest Passion for her, and was most worthy of her Embraces. 'Tis certain, however, that among the Multiplicity of her Enamoratoes, young *Damias* was for a great while the reigning Monarch of her Soul; insomuch, that when he was obliged to take a long Voyage, whence he did not return so soon as was expected, she had recourse to Sigils[80], Charms, Talismans, and Hell only knows what Arts to bring him back. She went to a Pretender in the Diabolical Science (of which there are a great Number in this Island) and told him if he could give her this Proof of his Skill, she would spare no Cost to gratify him. He assured her, 'twas in his power, but that the Expence would be great, and to defray it, she must lay down at least two hundred Crowns. She made no scruple of giving what he demanded, and desired he would be as expeditious in the Affair as possible.

{124} A Day was set for this Trial of his Capacity, and she coming according to Appointment, a Circle was made, in the middle of which she was placed, with a strict Charge neither to move, nor speak, whatever happen'd. This she assur'd him she had Courage enough to obey and all things ready, he began his Incantations. An Image was made in Wax, resembling *Damias*, which, with other magical Preparations, were thrown into a Pot, under which flood a Chafing-Dish,[81] with Ingredients for Fire, when the Conjurer should find a lucky Moment to kindle it. He tumbled over a great Number of Leaves of a Book he held in his Hand, then muttering a long unintelligible Invocation, with a great deal of Solemnity lighted the fatal Fuel. The Fumigation immediately grew so strong, and the Stench so horridly suffocating, that *Cesaria* was unable to endure it; and starting up, cry'd: What have you done? O *Jupiter!* I am poison'd. The Fellow feign'd to be in a prodigious Rage, threw down his Book, and told her she had ruin'd all; and if she would have the Design go on, and *Damias* recall'd, she must produce the same Sum she had given him before, for he must now begin all again. She had too much Sense not to see into the meaning of the Trick he had put upon her, and would not be cheated twice; nay, she was so angry at the Imposition, that she would have sued him openly by form of Law, to oblige him to return the Money he had taken, if a certain Lady, to whom she told the Affair, and who had more Concern for her Reputation than she had herself, had not with a great many Persuasions prevail'd on her to let it die.

None of her Spells having any Effect, and *Damias* not returning, she at length grew weary of wishing for him, and sought her Consolation in Embraces less difficult to be obtain'd. In the meantime, the {125} Marquiss perfectly acquainted with

---

80 [*sigillum*, Latin: seal.]
81 [A type of serving pan.]

her monstrous Actions, was endeavouring a Divorce, not doubting but that it would be easy to prove her Behaviour had highly justified his Proceeding in that manner against her. She was secretly inform'd of it; and before he could get any Process out, found means to give something in his Meat, which for a time wholly depriv'd him of the Use of Reason—he was for three Years like a Man infatuated. This she kept close from the Eye of the World, and pretending he was only a little indispos'd, in his Delirium made him assign the entire Management of his Estate to her: she had been made to believe by those that prepared them for her, that the pernicious Drugs she had given him, would not cease their Effect 'till Death, but she found the Deceit at a time she least expected it; all on a sudden he recover'd as from a long Sleep; and hastily leaving the Place she had conceal'd him in, applied to Officers proper for the purpose; and bringing them with him, broke into his House, surpriz'd her in the midst of her Riots; and seizing on everything that belong'd to her, turn'd her and those of the Family, which he had reason to suspect had been her Adherents, out of doors. He now pursued his Intention of being divorced, with all imaginable Vigour; and had not been unsuccessful in his Endeavours, if Death had not put an end to his Prosecution.

He left behind him two Sons and a Daughter, a young Lady of an uncommon Beauty; her Fate is justly deserving Commiseration, since her too great Tenderness for a Mother, tho' an unworthy one, would not suffer her to leave her in her Affliction, tho' commanded by the Marquiss to do so; which incensed him so far, as to make him forget he was a Father, and cut her off at once from his Favour and Fortune. She is doubly undone in her {126} Interest and Reputation by this Division between her Parents; for 'tis to be hoped her Brother may repair the *one*, the other 'tis impossible should ever be retrieved, at least while she continues to reside with the Marchioness. As for that Wanton, she is so far from having any Remorse for the Crimes she has been guilty of, that she adds daily to the Number of them; and tho' her own Sons avoid her Presence, and have obliged her to commence a Suit in Law against them for her Dower,[82] tho' the whole World contemns her, and all the Vertuous hate her, tho' she finds herself a Companion for none but the most abandon'd and profligate part of the Creation, yet she regards it not, but perseveres in those Vices which have justly render'd her so detestable both to the Gods, and all good Men.

---

82 [*douaire*, French: that which the wife bringeth to her husband in marriage.]

The History of *Hortensia*

That other Lady, much the most agreeable as to her Person, as I have already told you, was Partaker of all the Vices of the Marchioness, always one of her Party, and Partner in most of the same Scenes of Debauchery. She is full as loose in her Inclinations, but more avaricious in her Humour; and 'tis not to be wonder'd at, that such a Composition should be capable of every kind of Evil. She began to intrigue at a very early Age, and grew immediately a Proficient in the Art; that Modesty, which is, or ought to be the Characteristick of Womanhood, was thrown off with her Bib[83] and Apron, and she so soon forgot what 'twas to blush, and was so careless in concealing her Amours, that {127} at Fourteen she was surprized even in the very Act of Shame with the young Chevalier *Brunett*, by two of his Companions; she only laugh'd, and told them they wish'd themselves in his place. Even Incest was not capable of shocking her; having in a few Years run thro' a handsome Fortune, she receiv'd a Maintenance from two Brothers, who by turns caress'd her, and by consent contributed to her Support. After submitting to the Circumstance of a kept Mistress, she became the most mercenary, and self-interested of all that ever follow'd the Profession, the most despicable of Mankind, if they had Wealth, were welcome to her Arms; but without that Charm, not the most lovely could be receiv'd. Till her Acquaintance with *Cesaria*, and the Wife of a certain great Man, since dead, she preserv'd this Principle, but those Ladies soon convinced her of the Possibility of indulging herself in Pleasures without prejudice to her Interest; and being once brought into the Party, confessed she found her Account in it. This Triumvirate had a League among themselves, never to interfere with each other's Property, and to be aiding and assisting to each other as much as possible in the procuring new Conquests, and securing former ones. She now gave loose to Desires of a far different nature than the Love of Gold, but had the Address to divide herself between the two Passions, so as to prevent the one from being any way prejudicial to the other. One Hour of Love was succeeded by another of Interest. She was so exact an Oeconomist, and made so good use of her Time, that she had always an Opportunity of being happy with the Man she liked, and never miss'd one with the Man whose Purse was at her devotion.

It was in this detestable manner she liv'd, till the Baron *de Chevreron* grew infatuated by her destructive Charms, and, contrary, to all Advice, {128} took her to his honourable Embraces. He married her without any other Portion than a Load of Infamy, and behav'd himself to her in a manner very different from that with

---

83 [A small piece of linen put upon the breasts of children, over their cloaths.]

which he had treated his former Wife, tho' she had been a most accomplish'd Lady, was descended from one of the best Families among the Gentry in the Island, and had ever deservedly bore the Character of a Woman of nice Honour and Virtue. But 'tis this that drives me from any longer Residence among these ingrateful People; if they love at all, it is always an Object undeserving Affection; the favourite and most conspicuous Attributes of my God-head, Constancy and Sincerity, are despis'd, ill-treated, and a little superficial Beauty, or the Reputation of a trifling flashy Wit, triumphs over the most excellent Qualifications of the Soul.

The Baron doted on his unenvy'd Happiness; and tho' she prosecuted her former Pleasures with little less Privacy than before, he was blind to her Faults, continued his Fondness to her, and by his last Testament left her possess'd of the greatest part of his Wealth, tho' to the entire Disappointment and Ruin of one of the finest Youths in the World, his Nephew, and whom he had the Charge of from his Infancy, with his Promise to make a Provision for him proportionable to his Birth. This vile Woman, his Uncle yet unburied, turn'd him out of Doors, and he has been since oblig'd to Law to give him even that small Pittance the Baron left him.

Notwithstanding the Riches she was possess'd of by the Dotage[84] and Death of her Husband, she thought it not beneath her to add to them, by making Sale of her Favours to those whose Inclinations led them to become Customers, and has by those shameful Measures amass'd together a vast heap of Money. She is now past her Prime; but still finds some {129} who think her very desirable. She is oblig'd indeed to make Advances, and softens her Charms much more than she was accustom'd; the severe and haughty Air in *Youth* commanded Admiration; but in her *Declension*,[85] would be far from answering her Aim. Her Voice now wears a tender Accent, her Eyes persuasive Glances. See with what Kindness in her Deportment she is accosting that grave old Person, mark how she presses his Hand, and looks fondly in his Face while she is talking to him. She knows him to be of an amorous Disposition; and tho' the most avaricious Man on Earth in other Affairs, grudges nor to pay largely for his Pleasures this way. His Name is *Serpentius*, descended from a Family little distinguish'd for any extraordinary Qualification, none of them have done any thing worthy of bearing Arms, nor is he any more than a Trading *Citizen*, tho' a much more eminent one than any of his Ancestors. His natural Capacity and Cunning, and Readiness to conform to any Principles which would be of advantage towards his getting Money, render'd him a fit Engine for the great Mover of this Machine. *Lucitario* soon found him out, entrusted him

---

84 [from *dote:* loss of understanding; imbecillity of mind; deliriousness.]
85 [*declinatio*, Latin: tendency from a greater to a less degree of excellence.]

with the whole Secret, and making it prodigiously to his own Interest to be faithful to his, obliged him to be so, who 'till that time had never given any Demonstration that he could be so: but here indeed, he had sufficient Opportunity to exercise his Talent; to be a just Servant to the *Necromancer*, there was a Necessity he must be a Villain to all Mankind beside, and long Custom had made the Art of deceiving so habitual to him, that to have been employ'd in any Concern where Honesty and fair Dealing were requisite to make him a Gainer, he would have found it difficult to render himself capable; but in a Business where both Profit and Inclination join'd to make him diligent, 'tis almost {130} incredible what vast Advantages he has made by it. Numberless are the Wretches he has drawn in to put Faith in the Enchantment of this fatal *Well!* And scarce to be counted the Hundreds of shining Gods, which bless his crouded Coffers, and reward his Zeal; but as avaricious as he is in every other Affair of Life, none can be more profusely lavish than he is in the Gratification of his brutal Inclination: the most profligate of Womenkind have been taken and supported by him, in a Fashion which has made those of Quality look on the fine Presents with which he adorn'd them, with as much Envy, as they did with Contempt on the means by which they had acquir'd them; 'Tis the Knowledge of this which makes *Hortensia* so willing to engage him; and 'tis not to be doubted but she will find all those Advantages she expects in an Intimacy with him.—But see where the young gay *Bellario* comes, observe his Air, his Mien,[86] his Shape, his Face, and tell me if you can find those Perfections in him, which might justly entitle him to the Character of agreeable, and excuse the Foible of the Fair Sex, whose darling Favourite he is.

Here paused the God, expecting a Reply to what he ask'd; but the Stranger, surpriz'd to be told there were any who could discover such Charms in a Person who to him appear'd very far from handsome, (for *Bellario* had neither Stature, Proportion, nor Features, to be distinguish'd from the most indifferent of Mankind) only said, that if that Gentleman were possess'd of no greater Excellencies of Mind, than Body, those who were pleased with him had occasion for an uncommon share of Wit to defend their Choice from being prodigiously the Subject of Satyr. I did not doubt, *resum'd the Deity*, but you would be of this Opinion; but when I shall inform you, that of the two his Soul is less {131} worthy of Esteem, than even his Form, unlovely as it is, you will not wonder I have determined to withdraw my Influence from a People whose Affections are so ill directed.

This *Bellario* has not one good Quality to recommend him, unless Vanity, Ostentation, Pride, and Ill-nature may be allow'd to be of the Number; but that which has won him the Ladies Favour, is that he is always the first in the fashion as to his

---

86 [*mine*, French: air; look; manner.]

Dress, can instruct them in the modelling theirs, and has an unweary'd Propensity to Scandal; he is one that never speaks ill of any to their Faces, nor well behind their Backs: he has all the News of the Tow; and what he wants in Intelligence, he makes up with Invention, so is never at a loss for Conversation.

With these Materials, and a vast stock of Assurance, he sets up for a Wit, and values himself as much on the Reputation of being one, as he does in the Reversion of an Estate, at present in the possession of an Uncle, who has a greater regard for Merit, than to suffer any part of it to descend where there is so visible a Deficiency, if he can any way avoid it. He is taking all possible Measures to cut off the Entail; and 'tis highly probable this Fop may in the end find himself as much mistaken in his hope of being rich, as those who have been weak enough to confide in what he has told them, have done of his Veracity and good Sense.

He drop'd, in a publick Coffee-House, the other day, a Packet of Letters, written to him by several Ladies, with a design to expose them, and make known the force of his own Charm; but a *Silph*, who happened to have a particular regard for one of the fair Scriblers, prevented his Intention, and snatch'd it from the Ground unseen by any body: swift as an Arrow from the twanging Bow, he cut the yielding Air, and reach'd *Olympus*, where at that {132} time a general Assembly of the Gods commanded my Attendance. The charitable Spirit reveal'd the intended Evil, and begg'd I would no more trust with my Darts a Wretch so incapable of using them either to my Honour, or that of the Fair Sex, who felt their Power. Nothing could be more tender than some of those Letters—but you shall judge of them —the kind Emissary who brought them to me, whether on Earth he wanders, skims thro' the Air, or glides on the smooth Surface of some delightful Stream, Millions of Furlongs[87] distant, will hear, and obey my Call.

The Deity of pleasing Languishments now turn'd his radiant Eyes to that part of the *Hemisphere* where the bright God of Day mounts his refulgent Car, to glad the waking World with Light restor'd; and uttering some Words too mysterious for the Comprehension of a mortal Capacity, surpriz'd the gazing Stranger with an instant Performance of his Promise. The Papers from a Height unfathomable to fleshly Eyes, flew down like Atoms in the Sun's Beams; and without any visible Direction darted themselves into the Divine Hands which open'd to receive them, and in a moment deliver'd the whole Packet to the wondring Youth, who, as he was commanded, began to inspect the Contents, and in the first found these Lines:

---

87 [*farlang*, Saxon: a measure of length; the eighth part of a mile.]

To the most Agreeable of his Sex, the Charming and Accomplish'd *Bellario*

If Love were a Passion that would admit of Argument, how many could I raise in Opposition to the Tenderness I feel for you. Not but when I consider the numberless Perfections you are master of, even Reason tells me you are worthy of all a Woman can bestow; but {133} then your Inconstancy, that cruel Mutability of Temper which renders it impossible to have any Dependance on your Words or Oaths, makes you the most dangerous of all created Beings; 'tis unsafe to hear you, sure Destruction attends the unwary Nymph, who listens to your deceiving Accents. I know I am lost, I see my Ruin, yet have not power to shun the dear Deceit. In pity come no more near me, avoid my Presence, tell me you hate me; do anything rather than undo me by a pretended Softness which I well know your Heart is incapable of feeling—but Oh! The mad Request! How could I support the Grant of it? How bear the Pangs of an eternal Absence? I live but in your Love; false tho' I know your Vows, they yet are all that my fond Soul can cherish as a Blessing; haste then to repeat them, to charm me to an Extasy; regard not the wild Extravagances of a Passion which knows not what to wish, to hope or fear. Do you instruct me, inform my wandering Sense, convert the less pleasing Agitations all into Desire, and raise to Immortality the whole Soul of

The Distractedly Enamour'd *Amabella*.

P. S. I shall expect you this Evening; fail not to come if you esteem my Love, or think me worthy of yours.

This Billet, *said the divine Relater of these Wonders*, was written by the Daughter of a certain Marquiss, who refusing the honourable Pretensions of one of the finest young Noblemen in the Island, listen'd to the undoing Addresses of this *Bellario*. He has since that debauch'd her; she had a Child by him, of which she was deliver'd at a Midwife's House, privately as she thought; but the Affair took wind, {134} and her Father has sent her to an Aunt's in the Country, where she still lives in a Retirement and Restraint far unsuitable to her Inclinations. But this Adventure is not the most remarkable that has happen'd to *Bellario*, as you will perceive when you have proceeded a little farther in the Packet. The Stranger by this time had opened another Letter, and read in it as follows:

To the Angel of my Wishes, my dear, dear *Bellario*

I Long'd for an Opportunity to let you know what pass'd since last Night; dearly had I like to have purchas'd those few happy Moments in which I had you in my Arms. My Husband, unknown to me, was in an Arbour all the while, and cross'd the Garden just as you passed through it to the Back-gate: he heard the Door unlock; and believing it to be Thieves, rais'd the House immediately: all the Servants were dispatch'd, some one way, some another, with Lights and a strict Charge to be careful in their Search; but they returning without being able to bring any Intelligence, which was rather owing to my good Fortune than your Caution, he grew sullen on a sudden, and put me into a terrible Apprehension that he was suspicious of the Truth. I was so much alarm'd at it, knowing how violent he is in all his Passions, that I believe it would have gone nigh to have thrown me into a Swoon, if he had not as soon as we were alone, told me that he was strangely uneasy: for he certainly had seen the Appearance of a Man, and that he believ'd it was a Spirit. He then made me acquainted with a long Story, which 'till then I had never heard, that having in his Youth fought a Duel with a young *Chevalier*, he had the Misfortune of wounding him mortally. This Suggestion has taken so deep a {135} Root in him, that all I could say was ineffectual to remove it: he stedfastly believes you were the Spirit of that departed Gentleman, and expects no other than that he shall be haunted by this perturb'd Apparition. I could not forbear being surpriz'd at first, that a Man of his good Sense in other things should so unaccountably be possessed of a Whimsey like this; but on second Thoughts was well enough pleased at it; for I fancy it may be of no small Service to the promoting our Conversation. If he should happen to surprize us, it is but my counterfeiting a prodigious Terror, and crying out, a Ghost! A Ghost! And he will scarce come near enough to distinguish the Flesh from the Spirit. I confess I have had no little Diversion in my Thoughts since this Knowledge of his Prepossession, I wish it may afford you as much, and that I were Conjurer enough set a Spell to keep the dear charming Apparition for ever in the Circle of my Arms. I am, with all imaginable Transport,

My Lovely *Bellario's*
Eternally devoted
Clione.

P. S. I had forgot to let you know my Spouse will be abroad all the Afternoon, and you may venture to come, without danger of Exorcism: Farewell. The little Sleep I had after you left me, was taken up in dreaming of you.

The Stranger had no sooner finish'd, than the Deity preventing the Exclamations be perceiv'd the other about to make, told him that *Clione* was a Woman who had the most doating Husband on Earth; that he study'd nothing so much as how to {136} please her, and had settled a Jointure on her, vastly beyond the Expectations of her Friends: but she sold the Reversion of it, made an Elopement from her Husband, and having squander'd away the best part of her Money, and being in a little time abandoned by *Bellario*, lives now at large contemn'd by all who know her. But, *continued the Heavenly Inspirer of Desire*, neither this nor the former Letter can afford you half that matter of Reflection as will the next you shall peruse. These Words added to the impatient Curiosity of him they were address'd to; and hastily unfolding that Paper which promised to discover something so surprising, found it contain'd this Declaration.

To my Soul's Joy, and Care, the most Adorable *Bellario*

I receiv'd your last, if possible, with greater Transport than any of your former ones, because it gives me an Opportunity of proving the Sincerity of my Affection, but am amazed my dear *Bellario* should make any Apology for his Request to one that loves him as I do. I send you enclosed the trifling Sum you writ for; and be assured, that to serve you, I would not refuse a much greater, were it in my power. I only wish I had the means to put you past those Dangers you fear. If I had been bless'd with your Affection sooner, it had been better for us both; I then should have given you Instances of my Love worth your receiving. My Daughter should have been yet unmarried, if Money was the Requisite to get her a Husband, and my Son have had an Education less expensive; but as I have reduced myself by a too fond maternal Care, I am ashamed to think how little I am able to show the Fervency of my Zeal for the dear Interest of the charming *Bellario*. However, I beg {137} you will always command me; and when you no longer reap any Benefit from my good Wishes, believe it as it is, that you suffer only through my Inability. There yet remains some Timber on the Land which I have power to cut down, and some Plate in my Bureau which I am not tied from the disposal of; and if another Accident of this kind or any other should happen, I beg you will make the same use of my Friendship as now. To the last Guinea all is yours, and you may easily believe it when you are already convinc'd that you are the entire Possessor of my Soul, and that there is nothing on Earth so dear and valuable as *Bellario*, to his

Most Passionate and
Ever Faithful
Luina.

This Woman, *said the God*, is the Jest of all who know her, and even despis'd by that Demon, whose Influence obliges her to act in a manner so contradictory to Reason, and indeed to Nature: it is not above five Moons since she buried her third Husband, for whose Sake she had almost given up all the Frugality her two former ones had amass'd; yet is she now equally infatuated by *Bellario*. The Sum mention'd in the Letter was no less than two thousand Crowns; but that was but the beginning of the Favours he requir'd: Whenever he lost at play, or saw a fine Jewel he had a mind to purchase, it was to *Luina* he had recourse; 'till she has now little left to bestow, but the Continuance of those amorous Fondnesses, which were scarce supportable, even when he was a gainer by the Frenzy which inspir'd her to treat him with them, but are now no longer worth the pains of {138} Dissimulation. Age therefore has its Follies as well as Youth; and the Inhabitants of this Isle are so degenerated from these noble Principles they once boasted to excel all other Nations in, that they are now Objects of Pity to those Nations who envied them before. Nature is so much inverted, that that Sex whose Right 'tis to attract and command, are the first who sue for what they ought to fly, and court Undoing as a Favour. How many Men are there who have no other Dependance, and owe their whole Support to the lavish and unbecoming Fondness of Womankind! 'Tis grown a kind of Trade, and neither Sex blush to be obliged this way. Oh! Why do these detested Bargainmakers blaspheme my Name, and call these purchas'd, these polluted Joys, the Rewards of Love! Base, mean, abandoned, mercenary Prostitutes; how dare they impute that to my Influence, which *Interest* only, sordid *Interest* excites, and where, as one of their own Poets says,

—Cou'd the Experiment be try'd,
A Dog with Two-Pence would not be deny'd!

Reflection at this moment had so great a Force on the offended Deity, that he had power to proceed no farther. The utterance of his Words was stop'd with inward Agonies, his Cheeks sweated ambrosial Dew, and from his shining Eyes big chrystal Drops descended; which falling on the Earth, rose in a new Creation of Flowers more beautiful and sweet than e'er yet bless'd the Sense of the admiring Stranger: but cautious how to proceed, believing it the highest Presumption to attempt any Condolance of a Power so much above him;. and having nothing to offer in Vindication of a Race so unworthy of the heavenly Care, stood silent in awful Contemplation, 'till the {139} Divinity laying his Hand on the Packet, by that Sign giving to understand he would have him examine what farther it contain'd, again permitted him to satisfy his Curiosity; which he continued to do, by opening the next Billet, which contain'd these Words:

To the Everlasting Charmer of my Nights, and Joy of my Days, my lovely *Bellario*

I Have been in all the Confusion imaginable since you left me; what could you mean by going away so abruptly? I expected to have been bless'd with your dear Society the whole Night, I should easily have made a Pretence to have got rid of those troublesome Impertinents, that came to visit me: but I fear, you were glad of an Excuse to leave me; nor are my Suspicions without Cause. *Clarina* hurried after you immediately, and *Cimene*, who knows all her Secrets, assured me you had made an Assignation with her by your Eyes: she told me also, that this was not the first time you had been together, and that she had seen Letters from you, containing the most tender Declarations of Love imaginable. If this be true, how truely miserable is *Melantha*? To have you mine, and wholly mine, I would with pleasure forgo all other Considerations; but dear as you are, I cannot consent to share you with another. No, whenever the cruel Certainty of that arrives, I never will consent to see you more, I'll tear myself from all those Joys, those nameless, numberless, inconceivable Felicities your Presence gives, tho' in executing this Resolution, I must endure Agonies such as they tell us are the Portion of the Damn'd. Oh! *Bellario*, what do I feel in but the bare Imagination that thou canst be false! Lovely Undoer of my Peace, be quick to prove *Cimene* in the wrong. What we wish, we easily believe, my fond Soul would give the Lye to a Person {140} of more Veracity than she, if you profess'd your Innocence Haste then to bless me with your Vows, those soft, those tender, those prevailing Vows, which have had the power to render those I made to Heaven, and my too cautious Friends, of no effect: In thy dear Arms let me lose all my Fears, and with renew'd Endearments drive from my tormented Breast this Devil, Jealousy. Stay not to write, there is nothing but your Presence can give me ease; if all I heard be not Truth, if indeed I am not the most unhappy, the most accurs'd of all my easy yielding Sex, come with the Bearer, and meet with equal Ardors, equal Extasies, the

Impatient, the Adoring,
The Heart-tortur'd
Melantha.

The next Billet which presented itself, seeming to be writ by the same Hand, he waited not for any Intelligence from his divine Informer, but proceeded to examine what it contain'd, which was in this manner.

> To the most Ungrateful of Mankind, the Perjur'd, but still Dear *Bellario*
>
> It is then true that I am lost, betray'd, abandoned; your Silence, and your Absence confess your Inconstancy, and show me what a wretched Fool I have been, to trust a Man who I knew had been false to others. Oh! I could curse myself, and tear out my own fond credulous Heart. It is not in your power to be just, or good: ingratitude is ingrafted in your very Nature, 'tis a part of your Being, and you cannot shake it off without {141} parting at the same time with Life. Blind and stupid that I was, to imagine there could be a Reformation in him whose whole Soul is made up of Hypocrisy and Deceit, and whose every Action, since he could write Man, has shew'd the *Villain*. Oh! I am mad! Pardon the harsh Expressions of my jealous Frenzy. I mean not as I say. I love you still, nor scarce repent the Ruin I have yielded to; all Men are false, all Men are Hypocrites in Love, and you but as the rest, only more lovely, more endearing far; and if you have the Vices incident to your Sex, you have, to excuse the Woman they undo, Perfections which not one besides yourself can boast. Never were Eyes so form'd to charm, as yours. Never had any Tongue persuasive Force like yours. The Gods of Love and Wit, conspire to aid you. Thou more than Angel! Thou God of my Desires! Thou something more than Words can speak! Oh! I grow wild again, Remembrance of those extatick Joys your Kindness has bestow'd, is as dangerous to Sense, as those Heart-rending Agonies your Falshood now inflicts. Neither are to be borne, each is enough to overthrow Reflection; how is my divided Soul then rent 'twixt both! Pity me, ease me, see me once more, and tell me if Clarina must engross you all; give me but the Satisfaction of knowing whether I ought to love or hate you. Oh! That I had never known a Cause to doubt which Choice to make. Curse on the vain officious Tongue that rais'd this jealous Fury. Curse on my Readiness to listen to such destructive Tales. But doubly curs'd be my own want of Charms, which had not power to hold you, yet flatter'd me they had. Torture, Distraction, Hell, what will become of me, I cannot, I will not survive the Knowledge that you are mine no more. Yet this Suspence is worse than all yet ever bore the Name of Horror. Let me not linger in it, if you have Humanity; declare my Doom at once; be kind in Cruelty at least, and let one {142} Death conclude the thousand, thousand Deaths which every Minute of Uncertainty brings with it, to
>
> The Miserable, but
Still Adoring
Melantha.
>
> P. S. I have order'd the Messenger to bring an Answer; if he comes without, depend I will murder him, and then myself.

The Deity perceiving the Amazement which these distracted Epistles created in the Mind of him who read them, related the History of the Lady in these or the like Terms:

Melantha, said he, was the only Daughter of a Country Gentleman of a plentiful Estate; some Business happening to call *Bellario* to the Village where they liv'd, he presently cast his Eyes on the Heiress, with a design of making his Fortune by marrying her. He made his Addresses with such Success, that he soon found himself enough in the favour of the young Lady, to encourage him to hope he should have her Consent; but the Father's was not so easy to be obtain'd; he look'd on him with other Eyes; and finding his Daughter too much prepossessed with a good Opinion of him, forbad him his House, and threaten'd her with his eternal Displeasure, if she continu'd any Correspondence with him.

Bellario, who never had Tenderness enough of Nature to feel my Influence, regarded it no farther than as this Disappointment was a Prejudice to his Interest; and Vain, Ostentatious, and Self-sufficient, to give himself an Air of not valuing {143} *Melantha*, or her Fortune, immediately made court to a young Lady in the Neighbourhood: her Name was *Lucilla*, pretty enough to excuse the violent Passion he pretended to her, and of a Birth superior to *Melantha*, tho' much below her in point of the World's Idol, Wealth. The poor young artless Maid, unskill'd in Deceit, and unacquainted with those Artifices, which those who call themselves the *Beau Monde* make use of in Conversation, thought *Bellario* the finest thing she had ever seen, admir'd his Wit, his Manner of Address, his Notions, his Knowledge seem'd to her, who never had experienc'd better, to be prodigious: and she believ'd him so worthy of her Affections, that she could not without being guilty of sinning against Reason, deny him the utmost Proof of them. In fine, he won so far upon her, as to obtain the last Favour a Woman has to bestow: she grew with Child by him, and an Aunt of her's, with whom she was educated, perceiving it, was not a little confounded what she should do to repair the Disgrace her Niece was like to fall into. She talk'd to *Bellario* on the Affair, and press'd him to marry her, as the unhappy young Lady had told her he had promis'd, but he had been too wary, to give any such Testimony under his Hand, and had little Regard to a verbal Contract. He denied he had made her any such Promise; and tho' he refus'd what she desired with the most courtly Air imaginable, 'twas easy for her to see there was nothing to be expected from him; she thereon fell to catechising her Niece with all Severity, who asham'd of her Weakness, and half distracted at the discover'd Coldness and Perjury of *Bellario*, attempted to put an end at once to her Life, and the Misery which attended it. She swallow'd Poison; but being discover'd before it had time to work the pernicious Effect it was design'd for, proper Medicines {144} were applied to expel it, and she liv'd; and what was more to be admir'd, the Child within her suffer'd not by what she had taken, and she was in due time deliver'd of a Daughter.

Bellario all this while was paying his Devoirs to a Widow Lady of a great Jointure, and had certainly obtained his Point, but for the sudden arrival of her Brother; who perfectly acquainted with *Bellario*'s Character, gave her a reasonable warning, and wrought so far upon her, as to prevail on her to dismiss him.

These Amours could not but make a prodigious *Eclat* in the Country; *Melantha* soon heard of them, and tho' she had lost all hope of marrying him herself, could not be told of his addressing another Woman so near her, without feeling an inexpressible Chagrin. She writ to upbraid him with the little Tenderness she now perceiv'd he ever had for her, since he could so soon carry it elsewhere—but alas! She knew not what she did in renewing this Correspondence with him, tho' she design'd no more than to express her Resentment. That very Resentment show'd so much of Love, that it embolden'd him to imagine he might prevail on her to believe any thing. He answer'd her Letter with all the seeming Affection imaginable, fill'd it with Protestations that he never did, nor never could love any but herself that his Passion for *Lucilla*, and the other Lady, had been but counterfeited, only to discover what Impression the News of such a Behaviour would make on her; and concluded with an entreaty that she would vouchsafe him a Meeting in private, when he told her he doubted not but he should convince her, that he was and would be eternally her Slave. The credulous Maid, who in spite of all she had been inform'd of, ceas'd not to love him with an unbated Fondness, receiv'd his fictitious Promises with a Transport beyond what {145} even his Vanity had made him hope; she consented to see him, and made the Appointment at an old Woman's House, who formerly had been a Servant in the Family, and now liv'd but a small distance off. His Behaviour seconding what his Letter had begun, she was now, more than ever, all his own; and if he did not at that time entirely compleat his Triumph over her Virtue, it was only because the old Woman, at whose House they met, fearing the Consequence, took care they should not have any Opportunity; but he made so good use of the little Time he had to talk to her alone, that he obtained her Promise to follow him to Town, which she soon after did; and the Effect of that Condescension was such as may easily be guess'd at. He enjoy'd, forsook, and despis'd her, in less time than it took in persuading her. She is now undone in every Circumstance, and pity'd by all but him who occasion'd her Misfortunes. Her Sufferings are of a nature which would oblige me to dwell longer in the Commiseration of them; but that I see your Curiosity impatient for the Contents of the yet remaining Billets. Make haste therefore to gratify it, for the day is far spent, and before the close of it I have much to say. Here ceas'd the *Deity*, and the Stranger pleased to obey the Command he had received, went on to the next Letter, in which he found these Lines.

> To the Deceitful *Bellario*
>
> If my Actions had not too plainly testify'd the guilty Passion you have inspir'd me with, I should rather have chose to suffer in Silence, than by making you this Complaint, run the Risque of being more exposed. I am told it is a common Thing with you to betray, and after to ridicule the Wretch who gives Credit to your Insinuations; nor can you blame me for believing a Report {146} which brings with it its own Confirmation. I have heard my own Words repeated, those foolish, fond Expressions which my ungovern'd Tenderness

taught my unwary Tongue, when in your Arms I laugh'd at Honour, and thought your Love sufficient recompence for loss of Virtue, Fame and Grandure; are made the Jest of your loose Companions. They criticize on all my soft Endearments, and construe each unguarded Sentence as they please. This cannot be Suggestion. No, 'tis too true, and you are the most base as well as most inconstant of Mankind. Monster! Is it not enough that you have ruin'd me, that your cursed Artifices have drawn me from the best of Husbands, seduced me from all which ought to be dear or valuable to a Woman's Soul? But you must also make a Sport of my Misfortune. What have I done, that you should use me thus? Or, how dare you affront me in this manner? Believe me, I have a Mind as capable of *Revenge* as Love, and since deny'd the one, will have recourse to the *other*. I expect your immediate Answer. 1 wish 'twere in your power to make Atonement for the Wrongs you have done me; there is nothing I so passionately wish, as that there were a possibility of renewing the Esteem I once had for you. Write me your real Sentiments, that I may be assured what it is you deserve from

Bellimante.

You perceive, *resum'd the God*, that this is a Lady whose Complaisance for *Bellario* render'd, not only the Nuptial Tye, but all other Considerations also fruitless; nor need I tell you what after ensued, the next will inform you, and save me the pains of relating Circumstances so detectable to the Deity of Truth and Tenderness. These Words giving the Stranger to understand the Catastrophe of her History was to be explain'd in this manner, hastily open'd another Letter, which he found written in the same Character, and read as follows.

{147} To the most Wicked of his Sex, the Unjust, Ingrateful and Perjur'd *Bellario*

Dare you then defy my Rage? Do you believe there is nothing to be feared from the just Indignation of a Woman wrong'd as I have been; or if I should consent to be passive under the Indignities you have offer'd, do you not think high Heaven would revenge my Cause, and strike you dead with Lightning? Villain, as you are, how have you Impudence to breathe the same Air with me, and persist in a Behaviour so different from what you have sworn! But Oh, well may you despise and ridicule my enervate Resentment—you know, alas! I must depart the Island, and you will soon lose every thing of me, but the Memory. Yet, cruel Man, is not that enough? Will not your Conscience be a worse Tormentor than all the Fiends my Rage would muster up? Will it not perpetually upbraid you with the Miseries you have brought on an unhappy Woman, who lov'd you more than Life? Is it not for you that I am undone in my Reputation, in the Esteem of my Friends, in the World's Friendship? Have I not for you, lost for ever the endearing Fondness of a Husband, whose every Grain was worth the Mass of your whole Family? Have I not disgrac'd myself for ever? Has not the extravagant Profusion of my Love for you, deprived me of every Support of Life. Am I not obliged to fly my Native Country, and seek a wretched and uncertain Dependance in a Foreign Clime.[88] But what of all this! Have I not hazarded my eternal State, incurr'd the Sentence of everlasting Woe, and plung'd my Soul as well as Body in the deep Chasm of unceasing Horror? And do you, you, for whose

---

88 [contracted from *clime*, and therefore properly poetical: climate; region; tract of earth.]

sake I am so cursed, despise me? I cannot bear it; the Thought will bring Distraction. If Wishes have the power to blast you, depend you shall not long triumph in the Ruin of Bellimante.

{148} P. S. I embark this Night, and should wish the Ship that bears me hence might sink, and I go to the Bottom, if I were certain my injur'd Ghost would have the power to haunt you, and curse your Days and Nights, as you have mine; but whatever is denied to me, may Hell and its worst Furies do, and not one Hour of future Peace attend you; Restlessness, Distraction be your Portion in this Life, and everlasting Horrors in the next.

No Interruption being given by the Celestial Historian, the Stranger found in the next that offered itself to his perusal, these Lines.

To the Unkind, but Ever-charming, *Bellario*

There is something so strangely cruel, as well as unjust in your late Behaviour, that I can't imagine how you can answer it to your own Good-Nature. If I entreated to see you on any mercenary score, or had any other Design in that Request, than merely for the Pleasure I should receive in such an Interview, I should not wonder a Man who knows the World so well as *Bellario*, should refuse me. But you are perfectly sensible I ask no other Return, than Love for Love; and not to grant me that, nor give me any reason why you will not, is ungenerous and ingrateful to the last degree. To avoid a Woman, whose Presence you so lately coveted, without even the Shadow of a Cause for such a Change of Treatment, is what in my Opinion can't be accounted for by Reason, Honour, or indeed even common Complaisance; but I will trouble you no farther at this time, than to assure you I will not be condemn'd unknowing of the Crime for which I am so, and if you delay to write or come, I will bring to your own House my too just Complaint, will upbraid you in the Face of the whole World, will do everything my Tenderness will permit, to revenge the {149} Injury you have done me. Haste then, my Dear, my sweet Disturber, to vindicate your own Honour and Generosity, and save from Despair,

Your most passionately devoted
Alma.

The enquiring Youth expecting some farther Information of this Lady, paus'd on concluding her Epistle; but the Deity being silent, he pass'd to the next, which contain'd these Words.

To the Lovely *Bellario*

I Know not if you are enough acquainted with your own Perfections, to be sensible of the Impression they have made on me. Nor might I perhaps appear considerable enough in your Eyes, for you to take notice of what else you must have certainly read in mine. The Passion therefore which you have inspir'd, being not of a nature to endure Restraint, this comes to reveal it, and to tell you this Evening in the Palace-Garden about Ten you may find a farther Explanation of the Meaning of her, who wishes no greater Blessing than to be Yours.

Clio.

As the Stranger was beginning to open another *Billet*, the God prevented him, by saying, there remains no more of any consequence; beside, too much Time has been already spent on a Subject so trifling as *Bellario*. Let us now turn our Eyes again on that numerous Assembly: see where, conspicuous by his Port and Grandeur, the Prince *Del Ponto* stands; Observe his Air, his Mien, his Shape, you will find few who equal him in the Graces of his Person. *Nature* has been as liberal of her {150} Gifts as *Fortune*, both have done their utmost to make him appear great and lovely; yet if you regard him heedfully, you will read something in his yes which discovers he has a Soul far unworthy of the Case in which it is inshrin'd. The meanest of the *Plebeian* Crowd who court his Favour, or implore his Bounty, has not a Disposition more sordid and avaricious; there is none so vile, whom, for Interest, he will not basely fawn on; nor any so much below him, whom, to make instrumental to his Gains, he will not treat as his Superiors. He married a Lady of Birth equal to his own, but denies that unhappy Princess every thing befitting her Quality; and on her refusing to come into some Measures to which her Spirit render'd her averse, obliges her to live in a lonely Country-House, a great distance from all her Friends and Relations, scarce allowing her an Equipage fit for the Wife of a private Gentleman. But notwithstanding his Neglect of her he ought to love, he is not insensible of Beauty, he is accounted one of the most amorous of the Nobility; and 'tis certain, to gratify his Inclinations that way, will make no scruple of sacrificing everything but Money. The Wives and Daughters of his nearest Friends, or even Kindred, are not secure from his Sollicitations; and numberless are the Families, whose Honour has been stain'd by his seducing Arts. But the most remarkable, and worthy Commiseration, was, that of *Bellengar*; he was bred with the Prince, had been his Companion from Childhood, came to this Island with him, for both are Foreigners. They were almost inseparable, and never had any one Man a greater Regard, a more true Respect, and disinterested Zeal to serve another, than he had for this Prince: knowing his Temper, he always took care never to ask any other Favours of him, than such as it would cost him nothing to bellow, and {151} by this means preserved the Reputation of being lov'd by him; which Honour, 'tis probable, he still might have maintain'd, if his Inclinations had not led him to marry a young Lady of an extraordinary Beauty. The Prince visited him on this occasion, and no sooner saw the Bride, than he languish'd for her. Insolent, on his Quality, he made her an immediate Declaration of his Sentiments; which if she listen'd not to with that Pleasure which his Vanity had made him to expect, yet it was not with that Austerity which becomes a Woman of true Virtue: he perceiv'd he should find some difficulty in obtaining her, but had no great cause to despair he should gain his Point in the end. Knowing Opportunity and Importunity to be the two great Ruiners of the Sex, he gave not over the *one*, till he had found the *other:* hapning to come one Evening when her Husband was abroad, no Company with her, she in a languishing Posture lying on a Couch, all undress'd, and full of those destructive Softnesses which ordinarily inhabit the Breasts of the Young and Gay, he let not slip the lucky Moment; but pressing her with all the Force of vigorous Desire, with strenuous Embraces rendring the Efforts she made to rise of no effect, and stopping with Kisses the Breath she would have made use of in Reproaches for the Liberties he took, in a short time compleated his Design, and finish'd her Undoing. The Transport over, he wanted not enough to say in excuse of the Violence he had been guilty of. Never was my Name more prophan'd than in this Scene of Perjury and Deceit, and so much Regard the Fair Sex still pay me, that few of them but are willing to pardon all the Faults they think occasion'd by my Influence. Madam *de Bellengar* forgave his Crime, and was, without much difficulty, prevail'd on to permit he should repeat the sweet Offence. This fine Woman had {152} more Beauty than Discretion, and though she was not a Fool, suffer'd her Vanity so much to overcome her considerative Faculty, that the Pleasure of being belov'd by a Man of the Prince *Del Ponto*'s Quality and Figure, seem'd of greater Value than her Reputation: this Humour, join'd with the little Regard he had for the Honour of any Woman he had deluded, made them not so cautious as they ought to have been; the Affair was soon made publick, and *Bellengar* was not the last who perceived it. The Grief which seiz'd his Soul at this Discovery, cannot very easily be conceiv'd; had any other Man injur'd him in this manner, he would have endeavour'd to repair it by the Blood of the Offender; but the Obligations he had receiv'd from the *Prince*, tied his Hand: he contented himself therefore for some time with secretly reproaching his Wife; but finding all his Admonitions vain, that she continu'd her Assignations with the injurious Destroyer of the Honour of them both; and that in so publick a manner, that his Patience grew the Jest of all who knew him; the abus'd Gratitude and Tenderness which had so long with-held him, now gave way to just Resentment and Desire of Vengeance. He made it his business to find out the exact Place and Time of their Meeting; and as soon as his Emissary, employ'd for that purpose, brought an Account they were together, flew to the Rendezvous, and forcibly entring the Chamber they were in, accosted them with Language befitting the Wrong they had done him; and, too furious to attend the Ceremony of a formal Challenge, told the Prince, he must prepare that Moment to defend the Indignity he had offer'd, or expect to fall a Sacrifice to the Honour he had violated. This Threat was accompany'd by an Attempt to execute what it meant; and the *Prince*, who at sight of him guess'd the Intent of his {153} coming, had his Sword our almost as soon as the other: they made several Passes at each other, in one of which, the Prince, having more good Fortune than Justice on his side, disarm'd his Adversary, before the Cries of Madam *de Bellengar* had drawn the People of the House, to prevent what Mischief the Fury of both seem'd to threaten. They came in, however, in good time for the defenceless

Husband, who was on the point of being stabb'd by the *Prince*, after he had dropt his Sword: the Presence of so many Witnesses, who, perhaps, might not all of them be of a Principle, to be brib'd to Secresy in a Case so detestable as Murder, was all that preserv'd him from the Rage of the detected Prince: but as a late happily inspir'd Poet says,

> Forgiveness to the Injur'd does belong,
> But they ne'er pardon who have done the Wrong.[89]

He had gone too far in his ill Treatment of *de Bellengar*, to hope he ever could be reconcil'd. He knew it was impossible for him to be any other than an implacable Ill-wisher, and resolv'd to put it out of his power to do him any further Mischief than that of enervate Railing. He went immediately to the *Sovereign*, and made a Complaint, that being retir'd in pursuit of his private Pleasures, *Bellengar* had broke in upon him, assaulted his Life, and had wanted but very little of sacrificing him to his Malice. The Great and Powerful are never at a loss for Friends to second any Request they shall make; the Prince *Del Ponto* had Interest enough to be the Ruin of the little Fortune of this unhappy Gentleman, as he before had been of his Tranquillity. He was tried by Judges wholly devoted to the Service of his Enemy, and being convicted of an Assault against a Prince, his Superior and Patron, his Estate was seiz'd on as a Forfeit {154} for his Crime, and himself condemn'd to languish the Remainder of his Days in Banishment. The ill-fated and unfaithful Wife, during the whole Proceeding, remain'd wholly passive, nor mov'd, nor spoke in vindication of a Husband, undone by her Perfidy and Ingratitude. So much had the Artifices of the Prince won her to his side, that she wish'd for nothing more than to be eternally freed from the Sight of a Man, who, she was sensible, could not look on her but with Horror ; not doubting but she should find from her protesting Lover a Support as magnificent as her Pride and Vanity could ask: but, alas! how was she deceived, how in a Moment did all her gilded Expectations vanish? *Bellengar* gone, her Evidence no longer fear'd, and her Charms, by repeated Enjoyments, no longer desirable, she found herself immediately the most wretched Creature on Earth: not only all the Friends of *Bellengar*, but those also who had formerly been her own, too well acquainted with her Behaviour in this Affair, shunn'd her Society, refus'd her all Assistance; and despis'd by him who had ruin'd her, and justly hated by all the World beside, she fell into Miseries, such as even the Crime which brought them on, could not render unpitiable. Retaining still too much of her former Pride, to submit to a less mean way of Life than she had been accustom'd, she run excessively in debt, was thrown into

---

89 [Reference to Dryden (1673, Part ii. Act i. Sc. 2).]

Prison; where receiving no Relief, she was near perishing for want of common Necessaries, when a Fellow-sufferer, who had long been in the same Place, and was at last deliver'd by the Kindness of his Friends, hapned to feel the Influence of her Beauty, which even in this Distress had some Remains of its once attractive Force; he pretended his own Debts to be much greater than they were, and by that means paid part of her's, and got her Discharge at the {155} same time his own was sign'd: she could do no less than make him all the Retributions he desir'd for so unexpected a Redemption. She lived some time with him as a Mistress, but he marrying, she was again driven to seek a way of Subsistence; and fearing to fall into the same Condition from which his Passion had releas'd her, she threw off all Notions of Honour, and grew a common Prostitute: in that wretched and abhorr'd State, she now drags on an odious Life, which in all probability must soon be finish'd by a Disease as loathsome as the Crime, whose Punishment it is. Yet so impossible is it for the Great and Rich to have any Faults, that notwithstanding the Pain this unhappy Lady sustains, through the Delusions of this Prince: notwithstanding the Contempt he since has had for the Sufferings he occasion'd; that very Gentleman, who you now see courting his Favour, and bowing to him with the Appearance of the highest Regard, is her near Relation: but, indeed, it is not much to be wonder'd at, that he should worship any thing for Interest, when he can consent to throw one of the most lovely Women in the World, and one whom, till he debauch'd her Principles, was the best of Wives, into the Arms of an old Court-Leacher, who in exchange bestow'd a Place on him of about two thousand Crowns a Year. What will not these wretched Islanders do for Interest! What Sense have they of present Shame, or future Punishments! Does not one of the first of their Nobility, neglecting the Embraces of his almost Virgin-Bride, live in Pollution with his own Sister? Has not another prostituted his Daughter?

Adultery and Incest are grown common Crimes, and scarce wear any other Name than that of venial Transgressions. And well indeed may these appear less monstrous, when there's a reigning Sin yet more unnatural, more horrid, than Hell, or any {156} Fiend but *Man*, has power to invent. Both Sexes, as not content to mingle with each other in unlawful Blendings, turn to their own, perverting Nature, and defiling their own Specie: and *Man* with *Man*, *Woman* with *Woman* sins! But this Vice is of a kind too monstrous for any but the Damn'd, by whose Accusation they must hereafter be sentenc'd by the infernal Judges, to describe. If you make any long Abode[90] in this Place, you will see and hear too much of it, for there are but few, except those whose Trade is Religion, who seem not to glory in their Crimes, nor even among the most hypocritical Part of them, is

---

90 [from *abide*: habitation, dwelling, place of residence.]

there so great a Caution, but that a Penetration such as yours will easily discover the false Gloss. I see a Lady yonder, whose Variety of Adventures makes her History more entertaining than any I have yet related; nor would I omit giving you a Detail of her Life, if it were only to prove how weak human Judgment is, when it pretends to a more than ordinary Excellence; and that even *Penitence*, one of the most beautiful Virtues in the eye of Heaven, when stretch'd too far, may degenerate into Vice. What I mean by too far, is, when, to testify an Excess of it, the Professor goes beyond the Bounds of Nature; and to be impartially just to one good Quality, injures another equally valuable. *Tenderness*, the peculiar Characteristick of the softer Sex, this Lady seems to have thrown off. But to make you sensible of her Fault, without being guilty of an Injustice equal to her own, you must also be acquainted with the pretended Reasons which induc'd her to commit it; therefore I shall inform you of some few of the Particulars of a Life which has not many Parallels.

{157} The History of *Masonia*, Count *Marville*, and Count *Riverius*

She was the only Daughter of a Gentleman of a distinguish'd Family, had a liberal Education, and a vast Fortune. As to her personal Charms, you may believe a Woman so agreeable, when turn'd of Forty, cou'd not be wanting in the attractive Power when in her Bloom. Among a number of Admirers was Count *Marville*, who, more for his Quality and Estate, than any other Endowment of Mind or Body, was the Person pitch'd on by her Father, to be her Husband. She was married to him very young, and tho' her Inclination was not consulted in the Match, might probably have afterwards been well enough satisfy'd with her Fate, had he behaved in any tolerable manner; but nothing was ever more gross, and more unbecoming a Man of his Figure, than the Treatment she received from him. The Name of *Bride* was scarcely exchanged for that of *Wife*, before he avow'd a publick Dislike of her, and while all the young Gallants of the Court seemed to envy the Happiness he enjoy'd, expressed a Contempt of it, which could not but be stinging to a Woman who had the least share of Pride. Frequently has he brought into his own House the most shameless and abandon'd Prostitutes, caress'd and entertain'd them in her hearing, almost in her fight ; left her to mourn his barbarous Neglect, while he pass'd the Night in all the Riots and study'd Debauchery his lewd Companions cou'd invent.

'Tis impossible to know any thing of the World, without knowing also, that such Conduct in a {158} *Husband* must be a prodigious Encouragement to draw loose Addresses on the *Wife*, and as *Masonia* was a Woman generally lik'd, there were not a few who rejoic'd in the Hope, that her ill Usage at *Home*, might induce her to accept of better Entertainment *Abroad*; and grew bold enough to make Declarations to her, of a nature which, had the *Count* been less notorious in his Behaviour, they never wou'd have presum'd to have done: but never were the Seeds of Virtue more deeply rooted, than in the Heart of this abused Lady, and as she had been taught to abhor Unchastity, as a Vice the most pernicious to a Woman's Character, so she also found not in herself the least Propensity, to wish it were not so. The falling Snow, or Air new rarefy'd by *Phœbus*'s Beams, is not more pure, more free from Stain than was her spotless Mind; she sinn'd not even in Thought that way, nor was her Soul less guarded against Anger and Revenge; she endeavour'd, rather by Patience and Resignation to baffle the Malice of her Fate, than by returning Infidelity for Infidelity, deserve it. Thus for a long time did she continue an eminent Example of suffering Virtue; *Marville*, tho'he hated her enough to wish it, had it not in his power to tax her with one Word or Action unbecoming her Character or Circumstances: it was only by the most meek and gentle means she attempted to reclaim him, and it was in as austere a manner, as the Mildness of her Disposition wou'd permit, that she repell'd the Addresses of those who offer'd any thing to the prejudice of her Honour. Continued Repulses, and the Appearance of the most fix'd Resolution never to swerve from the Paths of Virtue, in time freed her from those unpleasing Sollicitations, and she was beginning to hope her Character so well establish'd, that none for the future wou'd make any Pretences of that nature, when she found herself deceiv'd, and {159} that she had still a Lover so much the more dangerous than the former ones, by being less assured. There was not a Day in which she did not receive a Letter from this passionate *Incognito*; it wou'd be impossible for me to inspire Expressions more soft and tender, or more full of Respect, than those in which he declared his Sentiments. He profess'd a Regard for her, so pure, that he even wish'd not to receive a Condescension to the disadvantage of her Fame or Virtue; vow'd, that, tho' he found it impossible to live unpity'd by her, he wou'd prefer Death, to the attempting any Action, which might cause a Blush in her: but all the while artfully insinuating, that if Honour oblig'd her to think of no other Man, while the Wife of Count *Marville*; to continue in that Station, after such known ill Treatment, call'd her Judgment very much in question, since she might lawfully sue for a Divorce. It was impossible for her to hinder the Receipt of these *Billets*; the Character in which the Superscription was writ, was so often chang'd, that till she open'd them she knew not they came from the same Person; nor was it only at home she found herself oblig'd to take them; whether she went to the Drawing-Room, to Church, or to the Garden of the Royal-Palace, the dextrous Writer found some way to convey, what he wou'd have her read, either into her Pocket, or the Sleeves of her Gown, and seldom it was, that they brought not something inclosed, which testify'd the Passion of him that gave it, more than all the Asseverations they contained beside. A fine Ring, Locket, or a Jewel for her Hair, were the daily Presents of this lavish *Enamorato*. By the Richness of these Presents, she knew he must be a Man of a very considerable Fortune, and by the Places where she received them, that he was of Quality, and of her particular Acquaintance, or cou'd not have had the Opportunity of coming {160} near enough to convey them; but not all her Penetration, tho' no Woman is Mistress of more, could find out who he was. There were many who look'd on her with the Eyes of Desire, and sometimes she imagin'd she saw in one, marks of this respectful Lover; sometimes in another, the Caution which the real Person observ'd in all his Words and Actions, took from her all Possibility of being certain. The young Count *De Riverius*, by frequenting all Places where she went, distinguishing her with a particular regard from all the Ladies in Company, being on her side in whatever Argument she was pleased to hold, and a thousand other such like Demonstrations of the highest Esteem, had often made her fancy him the Person; but then the known Wildness of his Temper (for he was accounted one of the most loose and debauch'd of all the young Noblemen about the Court check'd that Opinion; and she thought it impossible for a Man of his gay roving Disposition, and who had revell'd thro' all the selected Beauties of a whole Nation, to confine himself to that Reserve, and humble Awe, where he had a Design. The Behaviour of this unknown Lover, however, fill'd her with Sentiments, not at all to the advantage of her Peace; and her Husband persisting in his barbarous Usage of her, she compar'd the one with the other, and began to reflect how happy she might have been, if it had been her Lot to have married a Man who had the Love or the Respect of this *Incognito*; and at last, without reflecting on the Danger of such a Knowledge, wish'd to know, to whom she was so much oblig'd, that she might pay him back in *Friendship* some part of what she ow'd to his *Love*. All his Letters expressing only the most pure Affection, without the least mixture of loose Desire, made her imagine she might safely trust the Conversation of so disinterested a Tenderness, and began to think it wou'd be a {161} prodigious Alleviation of her Misfortunes to have such a Friend to condole them, and advise her what Method she should take to make them less. It was not long after this Inclination had taken possession of her Soul, that an Accident happened to give her the Gratification of it: one day, as she was at her Cabinet[91] looking over her Jewels, among which were those she had receiv'd from her conceal'd Admirer, Count *Riverius* came to make her a

---

91 [*cabinet*, French: a set of boxes or drawers for curiosities; a private box and/or any place in which things of value are hidden.]

Visit; and being told she was in her Closet, ran directly thither[92] with a Freedom which his Intimacy in the Family render'd not unpardonable: perceiving how she was employ'd, he took the occasion of praising her Fancy in the choice of her Ornaments, and among the rest, laid his Hand on a fine Locket, the middle of which was an entire Ruby made in the shape of a Heart, and set round with *Diamonds*, and Saphirs, telling her he thought it perfectly handsome, but did not remember he had ever seen her wear it, as indeed he had not; for this being one of those Presents, she had forbore the use of them, lest it might serve as an Encouragement to him who sent them. Viewing it more nearly, as seeming to admire the Workmanship, he told her he was assured this had been the Offering of some unhappy Adorer, the Design of it in the Colours of the Stones plainly denoting a bleeding Heart, but in the midst of Tortures encompassed with Sincerity and Honour.

These Words touching a little too nearly the Soul of her they were address'd to, she endeavour'd to snatch it from him, crying, No more of your Raillery; you witty Men make the most unaccountable Constructions. In the Struggle it happened to fall to the ground; and flying suddenly open, discover'd there was something in the inside, which by looking on it, or handling when shut, could not be discover'd by the nicest Eye; {162} *Masonia* hastily taking it up, curious to see what it contain'd, to her great Surprize found it the Picture of *Riverius*, drawn so exactly to the Life, that on the first Glimpse she was no longer to seek for her so long unknown Adorer. The Presence of Mind she show'd on this Occasion, was very wonderful: Had she taken any Notice of the Discovery she had made, she presently consider'd it would be a sufficient Handle for him to make a Declaration to her, which his Respect had hitherto prevented him from doing, and that she must then be obliged either to banish him her Presence, which she could not yet resolve to do, or by continuing to admit his Visits, give him leave to hope. Therefore shutting hastily the Case, put it into her Pocket; and turning to her Cabinet, with admirable Artifice, immediately began a Discourse of something vastly foreign to what they had been talking of; never was Confusion greater than than that of *Riverius*, who, tho' he had certainly an Aim in all he had done, and had behav'd in this humble manner only to inspire her with so much Tenderness for her unknown Admirer, that it should be out of her power to be very much incensed, when he should declare himself her Lover; yet he thought it not yet time, he was fearful she was not yet enough prepared, and dreaded an Eclaircissement,[93] which 'twas probable might ruin him for ever in her good Opinion; he expected nothing less than that she would have return'd those Presents and Letters to the Sender of them, with all

---

92 [*þiðer*, Saxon: to that place: it is opposed to *hither.*]
93 [French: explanation; the act of clearing up an affair by verbal expostulation.]

the Indignation of offended Virtue, and was about to throw himself on his Knees before her, to consess his Crime, and to intreat her Pity and Forgiveness, when so contrary to what his Fears suggested, she evaded taking any notice of what she had discovered.

{163} Tho' nothing was so dear to him as her Presence, he now wish'd for a handsome Excuse to take leave, he long'd for an Opportunity of Reflection; he could not for his Soul know what to make of her Behaviour, or whether he should interpret it to his advantage or the contrary; and the different Emotions by which he was agitated, rendered it altogether impossible to resolve which way he should proceed. Nor was she inwardly less disturbed, all she said to him was wild, and incoherent; all his Answers distracted, and strangely distant from the Purpose; but both being equally disordered, neither had the power of making any Observation on the other. Company coming in, gave a Relief to both; and the *Count*, glad of the Interruption, withdrew to contemplate on what had pass'd: but not all his Penetration (of which few Men had more) could inform him of the Certainty. Sometimes he flatter'd himself with a Belief that it was to her Kindness he was indebted, for her passing over in silence that which he was not insensible she had from others resented as the highest Affront. Sometimes he imagined it only as a delay of the Misfortune he must expect, and that she forbore taking an immediate Observance, that she might hereafter return what she had received with the Appearance of a more sedate Severity. The Dilemma he was in, was the most perplexing that could be; and the more he consider'd, the more intricate he found it.

The Impossibility of forming any direct Conjecture of her Sentiments, rendered it extremely puzzling how to behave in an Affair so nice and delicate, to desist visiting her, or continuing to write as formerly, he thought might seem to argue a Decrease of that Inclination he would have believed most violent; and to do either, he fear'd would give her an Opportunity of discarding him {164} for ever; but after a long debate in his Mind, he at last resolved to take those Measures which might be look'd on as most the Effects of my Influence, and accordingly writ to her the next Day. The Contents of this Letter being full of a prodigious Artifice, I will repeat to you.

> To the most Adorable *Masonia*
>
> To reiterate the thousand Protestations I have already made you, that my whole Soul is at your Devotion, that my Life and its eternal Peace, are light when balanced with a Moment's Inquietude of yours, and that I chuse to suffer Torments equal at least to what the Damn'd endure, rather than Cause a Frown upon that Face, whose Smiles were made to chear the admiring World. All this, divine *Masonia!* You are not ignorant of; those regardful Bounds in which my burning, self-consuming Passion has been confined, cannot but have convinced a Soul so heavenly just as yours, that nothing is so dear, nothing so sacred to me as your Honour. Unknowing who I am in Quality of a *Lover*, I may perhaps be bless'd with your Commis-

eration, and in the Person of an *Acquaintance* with your Friendship; sufficient Recompence, Great Gods! For the lingring Martyrdom of *Love* ungratified. But if your Bounty thinks the humble Awe, the duteous Respect which to the end of my Life I shall persevere to pay you, worthy of a greater Return; 'tis this I would implore, that if at any time, by any Accident yet urforeseen, you should arrive at the Knowledge of your Slave, you would not, to be severely strict to *Virtue*, banish *Pity*, and drive from your Presence him who finds no Joy in Sight but looking on you. Grant this Request to the Terrors of my Despair, to the Agonies of a Heart which bleeds but at the Apprehension of your Displeasure, and be in Mercy, as in all else divine, and that you may the more easily dispose yourself to favour me in this Particular, {165} permit me to assure you, that not all the Suggestions of ungovernable Desire! Not all the Racks of Nature! Shall even in Death prevail to wound your Ears with one presumptuous Declaration, but as I have liv'd, will die in the most refin'd Purity of zealous Passion ever

Your unknown Adorer.

This Letter fail'd not of the Effect for which 'twas writ, to melt *Masonia* to a Tenderness she ne'er had known before. So humble a Respect in a Man who had ever been accounted in the Affairs of Love the most daring of his Sex, joined to so engaging a Softness; his Behaviour, both as the *Lover* and the *Friend*, so every way agreeable to her Humour; and what she could hate wish'd in the Man who should address her, had she been at liberty to receive any Declarations of that nature; made her readily afford him that Pity he intreated, and indeed a greater share of it than he imagined.

The first Visit he made her after the Adventure of the *Locket*, occasioned a good deal of Confusion in both. He dreaded lest she should now, obeying the Remonstrances of her Virtue, discover her Knowledge of his Presumption, and inflict that Punishment the nature of the Crime required; and she, that in spite of the Declaration of his last Letter, and the distant Observance he had hitherto paid, the Violence of his Passion should burst out in a Declaration. But these Terrors were but of a short Continuance, and each had the pleasure to find themselves mistaken.

Both behav'd in the manner they were accustom'd to do to each other, or if there were any Difference, it was only that his Words and Eyes expressed something of a greater Awe than before, and her's of an Increase of Softness and {166} Good-Humour; tho' mix'd with a certain Bashfulness which naturally arises in a modest Woman, from being in the Presence of the Man whose Wishes, however he may disguise them, she is sensible aim at Enjoyment. Her Proceeding was indeed enough Encouragement for him to hope every thing, had it been given by any other Woman; but he had so high an Opinion of her Virtue, and was so fearful of losing the little he had gain'd upon her, that he let not fall the least unguarded Word to give her cause to repent the obliging Carriage with which she treated him.

While things were in this Position between them, Count *Marville* continued his usual Brutality; and as all Tempers, if they grow not *better*, grow *worse*, his became so intolerable, that it must have been more than human Patience, which could have enabled his Lady to endure it. The severest Rules of Virtue and Duty to a Husband, oblige not a Woman to suffer herself to be abused in the manner she was, and it was not only her own Opinion, but also the Judgment of all her Friends, since his ill Treatment was so publick; and she run the risque of losing not only her Health by his Debaucheries, but also her Life, which in his Fits of Passion he had often threatned, that it would be far from blemishing her Reputation to quit his House.

By the Advice therefore of many discreet Persons, among whom were some of the *Religious*, she ordered Lodgings to be taken for her, and on the first Opportunity went to them. The Obligation there was on Count *Marville* to allow her a separate Maintenance in proportion to the vast Dower she brought him, made him very uneasy at this removal. Lawyers were employ'd on both sides; who finding it, to their advantage, instead of making up the Breach between them, widened it yet more, and the former Indifference they had {167} for each other, was now turn'd to the utmost Detestation. She could not brook the Sight of a Man who had used her so ill, and expressed not the least remorse that he had done so; nor he of a Woman, who pretended a right to inspect into his Conduct; wherever they met, they quarrelled, and scarce was the Royal Presence of force to check the violence of their Hatred from breaking out in Expressions unbefitting the Place.

All this time she was visited as before by Count *Riverius*, and with the same Reserve; he could not venture to declare himself, tho' this Separation from her Husband was of no small service to his Hope's Increase, he could not as he thought yet find an Opportunity sufficiently favourable, and he chose rather to converse with her in a manner less rapturous than he could wish, than to hazard being reduced to the Misfortune of not conversing with her at all. And it was this unassured and fearful way of proceeding, which softened her more than all the Rhetorick his Wit and Passion could have inspired her with; for considering him a Lover not dangerous to her Honour, she avoided not his Presence, thought herself obliged to treat him with a more than ordinary *Civility*, as he did her with a more than ordinary *Respect*; and when alone, indulged that little Vanity, to which all Mortality is incident, of pleasing herself with the Reflection on the Deference he paid her. The Tenderness she had for him every Moment taking deeper Root, spread itself at length through all the Avenues of her Soul, and she became, insensibly to herself, all Love and soft Desire: tho' no Woman ever had more Prudence in concealing what was improper to be talked of, yet the little Knowledge she now had of the State of her own Heart, made it discoverable to others by a thousand unguarded Words and Actions. *Cocona* her {168} Woman was immediately in possession of the Secret, and hugg'd herself with the Advantage she might in time reap from it. To this end she watch'd even her very Looks, and under the pretence of

Duty and Observance, scarce left her alone one Moment; happening to be from her on some Occassion, much longer than usual, she found her in her Closet with a Book in her Hand, on which she seem'd very attentive: coming up to her with the Assurance of an embolden'd Favourite, she saw it was a Translation of a famous old Poet of a foreign Nation, whose chief Perfection was in writing Love-Affairs; You are very tenderly engaged. *Madam, said the cunning Sycophant,* and it is no small Subject of Admiration to me, to see you who without any Concern have seen the noblest Youths of this Island languish for you, be at all affected with the History of an Amour, which probably was never any more than fictitious, or if in reality it ever had an Existence, has long since known a Period. It was the celebrated Epistles of *Ovid*,[94] which so known to all the World, cannot be Strangers to a Person so polite as you, that this Lady was now employ'd in; and the Story she happened to hit on, that of *Helen* of *Greece*, to the enamour'd Prince of *Troy*. *Masonia's* Face was cover'd with conscious Blushes at this Remonstrance from *Cocona*; which that artful Creature perceiving, and inferring from thence, that what she had said, and touched her to the quick, run on this manner: do you imagine, Madam! *Added she,* that any of the Histories contained in that Book, are Truth! For my part, I want Faith to believe there ever were such loving Fools. If Love be Folly, *reply'd the Lady with a Sigh*, I dare swear there are as great Examples in this Age, as any the former could produce. They are but few then, *resum'd the other.* The fewer, the more to be admir'd and valued, *said* Masonia.

{169} That is true, *rejoined her Woman,* but 'tis seldom they are so, even by the Object of their Affections? There is indeed but little Gratitude, *answered the other,* but that is oftener owing to the difference of our times from those in which the Heroes of *Ovid* liv'd and lov'd, than to a thankfulness of Nature. The Crime of *Helen* in forsaking her Husband (tho' a tender and indulgent one) was not accounted of that shameful kind, but that all the *Grecian* Princes thought that to recover her, and bring her back to her forgiving Husband, was a Cause worthy of a ten Years War; whereas in our more nice, and scrupulous Days, should a Woman make an Elopement from the *worst* of Men in favour of the *best,* she would not only be contemn'd by the World, but also abandoned by her nearest Friends what *then* was pardonable, is *now* not so. See *(continued she, letting her Head sink carelesly on her Shoulder, and dropping some Tears which it was not in her power to contain)* see *Cocona,* the Prevalence of Custom! Finding her in a Humour so fit for her purpose, the insinuating Wretch let not slip the Opportunity: but pur-

---

94 Haywood's choice of Ovid is noteworthy because of its comparative, metaphorical nature, but also because Ovid, too, was known as a writer of erotic poetry and therefore functions as an authoritative figure.

suing the Discourse in as warm a manner as she durst take the liberty to do, at last told her she was very certain that she was not less belov'd than any of those Beauties immortalized by *Ovid*'s no less charming Lays. Nor do I think, *said she*, that you could be ingrateful to so much tender Passion, if Circumstances did not make it, as it were, necessary to appear so.

'Tis impossible to represent to you the Confusion of *Masonia*'s Thoughts at these Words; even I who inspir'd the Tenderness she felt, am alone able to conceive it. All the obliging Behaviour of *Riverius*, came presently into her Mind; she reflected what he must endure in the unintermitting Pangs of hopeless, suppress'd, despairing Love, and compassionated his Sufferings by what she felt {170} herself; not that she imagined her Heart was possessed of any part of that Passion which so violently agitated his, but she was sensible of an Excess of Friendship, which she long'd to let him know, but durst not. It was in this soft and melting Disposition easy for the cunning *Cocona* to sift out the whole Secret. In spite of the natural Reservedness of this Lady's Temper, and the Caution she had hitherto observed in speaking of *Riverius*, the Artifice of this Creature now won her to reveal the whole Affair, from the first Letter she had received from him, to that which followed the Adventure of the *Locket*, and the whole Truth of her Sentiments on the occasion. It was nor to gratify her Curiosity, that she had taken so much pain to dive into this Secret: she had other Ends; and being perfectly Mistress of what she wanted, hasted to the Accomplishment of them. She doubted not but the News she had to bring, would make her a welcome Guest to Count *Riverius*, and accordingly went to his Lodgings, and related to him every particular of the Conversation she had with her Lady on his score; giving him also to understand, that it was only the Fault of his too timorous Passion, which had so long made him endure the Torments of Suspence, and advis'd him to declare himself the very first Opportunity. The design of this mercenary Seller of her Lady's Honour, was answered to the full in a Purse of Gold, and an Assurance of further Bounties, as he found the Benefits of her Advice. 'Tis difficult to say which of these two were most transported; the Count to find himself so much more happy than he ever could even hope to be, or *Cocona*, that she had it so much in her power to oblige a Gentleman so vastly liberal; both had their Reasons to be satisfied with the Friendship of the other, and in the Sequel found their Account in {171} proceeding as they had done. But not all the Encouragement she gave him, not all the Boldness which former Successes had inspir'd him with, cou'd prevail with him to follow the Dictates of his Impatience, and declare himself her Lover.

He continued to visit her with his usual Assiduity, but in all his Words and Actions persevered in his usual Caution, never discovering even in a Look the Knowledge of his Happiness, 'till *Cocona*, vex'd to the Heart to see him so timorous, and well knowing that these distant Wishes were of no service to the End she proposed to herself, brought him to her in a Season when it was almost an Impossibility in Nature for him to maintain his accustomed Restraint. It was in a cool and refreshing Evening of a sultry Summer's Day, when the contemplative and languishing *Masonia* had laid herself down on a Bank of Violets in the Garden, that this diligent Tempter was told Count *Riverius* was come to wait on her Lady: knowing in what Place and Posture she was, she trembled lest any of the Servants should dismiss him on the account of her Retirement; she therefore made no delay, but running hastily to the Door, told him she had Business of the utmost Consequence to impart, and that he must come in. It is not to be doubted but that he readily obey'd the Summons of this good Friend, and being brought by her into a Gallery which over-look'd the Garden; Now, *said she*, or never is your Time. This precious Moment lost, may perhaps never be regain'd, and you'll hereafter curse that Backwardness, which is the only Impediment to all your Soul can wish. She then pointed out the Place where *Masonia* lay reclin'd, and used so many Arguments for his Encouragement, that he was at last convinced he had been to blame, and inflicted Torments on himself which it was not the desire of his fair Foe he should endure. {172} Recovering therefore (by the Suggestions of her who he knew was perfectly acquainted with his Charmer's Sentiments) great part of that Boldness which had been wont to arm him on the like occasions, he passed the Alley which led to that delightful Grotto,[95] in which she was reposed. She was fallen asleep, and the Heat of the Day having prevented her from dressing, she was in a loose Dishabillé of green Lutestring flower'd with Silver; which being as it were only carelesly thrown over her Shoulders, and quite unfastened before, discover'd Beauties 'till that ravishing moment he had never seen but in Imagination: the whole Proportion of her fine-turn'd Neck, and heaving Breasts, were now exposed to view, excepting only where here and there an unty'd Lock of the most lovely Hair in the world fell scattering down; and by seeming to endeavour to hide some part of Beauty, disclos'd another by showing of itself. Nor were her Legs and Feet with greater Caution skreen'd, the Bank being rais'd a pretty height above the Ground they hung over it, and her Petticoats being shorter than Ladies generally wear, except in an Undress, the happy Count had a full Opportunity of feasting his Eyes with sight of those Charms so dear to a Lover's Fancy.

In this extatick View how improbable is it he should contain himself from the pursuit of gratifying other Senses besides that of Seeing: the tempting Fruit seem'd to invite the Taste as well as Sight, yet still unable to conquer some Remains of that Awe, which had so long deter'd him, he offered at no more than her Hand, and

---

95 [*grotte*, French; *grotta*, Italian: a cavern or cave made for coolness. It is not used properly of a dark horrid cavern.]

that too, he ventured on but with the utmost mark of Adoration: he threw himself on his Knees by the Bankside; and putting it gently and trembling to his Mouth, designed no more than to steal some Kisses on it; but the fear he had of offending, {173} made him offend the more. The Confusion of his different Agitations entirely took from him the power of Thought, and the Touch of her Hand working that Effect on him which none uninfluenced by me can be sensible of, he fell amist the Extasy of Pain and Pleasure quite motionless upon her Breast.

The sudden Weight broke in a Moment the Bonds of Sleep: she started and awak'd, but how, enquiring Stranger, shall I make you comprehend what 'twas she felt within, at sight of *Riverius!* The Tenderness she had for his long Sufferings, and a just Sense of what she ow'd to her own Honour, rose in her Soul with equal force, and impossible to yield to the Dictates of either different Suggestion, she wanted but little of being in his Condition when he recover'd from it; and perceiving she was sensible of what had happened, and that it was now too late to go back if he had a mind to it, entreated her Pardon for what the Violence of his Passion had transported him to do, and what he still continued to do, (for he remov'd not from the Posture he was in) with Words so soft and persuasive, that it was not in the power of a Woman, who knew what it was to love, to be severe. The Scene indeed was admirable, and worthy my peculiar Regard, never did any two Hearts burn with a fiercer Desire, yet never did any preserve a more untainted Purit: the unaffected Modesty of her Deportment check'd all the wild Wishes *Cocona* had rais'd in him by her loose Prate[96] before she sent him thither; and the Zeal he express'd for her Honour, however prejudiced to his own Happiness, made her look on him as the Wonder of his Sex.

There pass'd between them all that was tender, all that can be conceiv'd of fond and endearing but nothing that was indecent, or that *Masonia* might not reflect on without a Blush. Had {174} *Marville* himself been witness of their Behaviour, he would have found nothing in it to accuse; but by the sight of such an exalted Passion on the one side, and Virtue on the other, might possibly have been reclaimed, and endeavour'd to imitate *Riverius* in his Affection, as the lovely Inspirer of it testified how worthy she was of it. It Was some Hours before the Count could prevail on himself to take leave, or she to bid him do it; but at last to mollify[97] the Pangs of Separation, he had her Permission to wait on her the next day, and every day, and entertain her in the same manner as he had done this; promising never to be angry at any Declarations he should continue to make of his Sufferings, so long as he demanded not a Recompence for them:

---

96 [from the verb: tattle; slight talk; unmeaning loquacity.]
97 [*mollio*, Latin; *mollir*, French: to soften; to make soft.]

which he assuring her he never would be guilty of, they parted with a kind of smarting Satisfaction, a pleasing Anguish on both sides, and which may much more easily be imagined than described, tho' by the Mouth of that Deity from whom alone these sweet Perplexities are deriv'd. I will not therefore, not only for this Reason, but also because it would be unkind, keep your Curiosity (which I perceive is impatient for the *Catastrophe* of an Adventure, whose *Beginning* promises so much) on the Rack of Suspence, so long as it would take to recount the various Turns of Thought which agitated the Breasts of these Lovers when asunder. Count *Riverius* must, with the Boldness which in these Cases was accustomed to be his unfailing Assistant, have thrown off the Nature of a Man, if he had not sometimes repented the little Advantage he had taken of an Opportunity so favourable to his warmest Wishes; nor could he have been my perfect Votary, if at others he had not thought the Condescensions she had bless'd him with, a Recompence sufficient for the utmost he had endured from his Despair. As for her part, she was {175} not without Perturbations, of the two more uneasy to be borne: and if her *Virtue* made her think herself happy, that the Man who of all the World had alone the Power to move her Inclination, made no other use of the dangerous Influence he had over her, than to attest the Purity of his Passion; the Lover, and the Woman in her Soul, seem'd to suggest the Mastery he had over his Desires, was an Argument they were less forcible than she at first had thought them, or than, perhaps, in some unguarded Moments she wish'd they should be. The different Workings of her Fancy were all imparted to *Cocona:* she was now in that Condition which renders the Person involv'd in it incapable of keeping it conceal'd; and as she had already trusted this Creature with good part of her Sentiments, found it no difficulty now to reveal the whole. She made her acquainted with every Particular of their Conversation in the Grotto, and hid nothing of her Thoughts on it from her, every now and then asking her in what manner she should interpret such a Word, or such a Look, or such an Action; which you may believe the other did not want Replies for, which were far from affording any real Peace, and but ferv'd to sooth a while the rising Discontents, that they might hereafter break out with greater Vehemence. She was resolv'd, if possible, to bring this Affair to the Period she wish'd, and on the first Opportunity school'd the Count handsomely for making no better Use of his good Fortune, and related to him all that the unthinking *Masonia* had utter'd by the way of Question, if such a Behaviour were not rather the Effect of a Coldness and Decay of Passion, than a too great Sublimity of it; in fine, she manag'd her Argument so well for her purpose, that the Count got rid of all his Fears, and assur'd her, that in a few days he would put an end to her Theme of Raillery.

{176} Having let you thus far into the Secrets of both their Sentiments, I do not doubt but your Imagination has already postpon'd good part of my Narration. I know you expect the next thing I am to relate, is, that the Count was as good as his word, and that *Masonia*, wholly soften'd by so many and continu'd Proofs of his Affection, had not forever the Power of refusing him any thing. Nor does this Conjecture deceive you; he watch'd a tender moment, when in her Eyes he read the Meltings of her Soul; and e'er the accustom'd Guardians of her Honour cou'd return, and dart repulsing Glances, he seiz'd the glorious Opportunity, rush'd at once on her in a Tempest of Desire, and triumph'd over all the faint Efforts of Virtue. Thus was *Masonia* won, by these Steps she was at last led to give up what was most dear to her; and sure no Woman, who had been with so much difficulty obtain'd, was ever so little dissatisfy'd with what she had been persuaded to condescend to. From the most strict Reserve, she fell immediately into the other Extreme of giving the most inordinate Loose to Inclination; she despis'd the Censure of the World, would scarce suffer *Riverius* a moment from her Sight, shunn'd all other Society, and was so extravagant in her way of loving him, that nothing but an equal Ardency of Passion could have made so unlimited a Fondness agreeable: that Reputation which had been formerly so valuable to her, that she was used to say, she wonder'd how any one could survive the Loss of it, was now so little thought of, that she seem'd not to regard what any one might say of her Behaviour. The Possession of *Riverius* was all she had time to think on, he was the only Object she desir'd to please; and in having him, had all the World could give to bless her Wishes.

{177} By this manner of proceeding, their Amour was soon made publick; Count *Marville* heard it, and rejoic'd in her Disgrace, and since she, quite lost in wanton Pleasure, had no Thought nor Leisure, as yet, from her more agreeable Engagement, to prosecute the Intentions she had of suing out a Divorce; her Elopement, which he imagin'd a Possibility of proving was in favour of *Riverius*, gave him a sufficient Pretence to throw the Odium of their Disagreement wholly on her, and endeavour first to get a Separation by form of Law, which now he doubted not but would decide the Cause much more to his advantage than before.To this end he takes the Advice of Persons the most eminent for such Cases, but they being divided in their Opinions, he defer'd it. In the mean time she lay-in of a Daughter, but that Business, more indeed thro' the Care of *Cocona*, than her own, was manag'd with so much Conduct and Secrecy, that tho' many suspected and whisper'd it abroad, none durst presume to affirm it for a Truth; but soon after, the Continuance of their Caresses produc'd a second, which in due time prov'd a Son. At the Conception and Birth of this unhappy Infant, all ill Planets seem'd to be in Conjunction; she was herself scarce certain that she was with Child, when some busy Demon reveal'd it to the Husband; and taking then especial Care to inform himself of the Truth, resolv'd to proceed against her in the manner he was once about to do before: he had Officers assigned by the Magistrates in search of her, and she was obliged to fly, and screen that undeniable Token of her Fault from the Eye of an unpitying World, and more inveterate Husband. She now liv'd wholly with *Riverius* in Lodgings, which he hired for her in the most private Part of the Town; but it was to no effect, Count *Marville* had Spies, who brought {178} him Intelligence of all that pass'd between them; but he conceal'd his Knowledge till the Day appointed by the Judges for the Decision of the Cause, and then produced Evidences so strong, as quite overthrew all that the Lady had prepared to alledge in Vindication of herself. She was found guilty of Adultery, and an Attempt to bastardize his Family. A Divorce was immediately granted, and she was disrobed of those shining Titles, which had unfortunately tempted her to yield to be his Wife; and all the Favour she found, was to have her Dowry return'd her back without any Diminution.

The Hurry and Confusion of this Affair, wak'd *Masonia* from her long Lethargy of amorous Stupidity; her Eyes were now open, and she saw her Shame writ in the estrang'd Countenances of those who had been her nearest Friends, and who 'till this open Conviction were willing to believe her Accusers in the wrong; every little Prude, saucy on her undiscover'd Faults, now took upon her to advise and reprove this fallen Fair, every Flirt look'd down on her with a scornful Smile; in fine, her *Misfortune* render'd her a mark of Pity to the truly *Virtuous*, and the *Discovery*, of Contempt to the *Pretenders* to it. The loss of Precedence also, though it gave her not that Pain it would have done many other Women, yet she could not avoid feeling some little Alarms at being obliged to give place to those, who, while she was the Wife of a Count, rose from their Seats as soon as she appeared, nor resumed their Places without her Permission. All the Homage, all the Respect which her Titles had commanded, all that more valuable Veneration which the Fame of her great Virtue had made her Due, had now no more a Being, but in her Expectation, when sometimes she forgot the State to which she had reduced herself. With what {179} Stings came now Reflection arm'd! How terrible was now become her once greatest Pleasure, Contemplation! How intolerable were now the Racks of Thought! Yet Thought could not be avoided: she must remember both what she had been, and what she was, and compare the *present* with the *past*, what Shocks soever she endured.

The Misery of her Condition is not to be described; in Company she seemed ashamed, dejected and forlorn; distracted when alone. Nor had the Charms of her endearing Lover, nor all the soothing Arts he was Master of, the Power to make her forego the Sense of her lost Honour. She was perpetually upbraiding him, and testifying her Remorse, either by Tears, Sighs, and all the Marks of sullen Discontent, or loud and keen Reproaches. So unexpected a Change in her Behaviour, made him, who really loved her with a Tenderness, which, but for her lie never had felt, almost as disquieted as herself. For a long time he used his utmost

Endeavours to restore her to her former Softness and Affability of Temper; but when he perceived all he could do was ineffectual, and that this Disposition in her rather increased, than any way abated, he began to grow weary of the vain Attempt; and as the Nature of Mankind is such, that, after Possession, the least disobliging Action creates Disgust, his Passion insensibly wore off, and became colder and colder by degrees, even more swift than those with which it had began. Her Conversation having lost all relish with him, he fought elsewhere the Pleasures she no longer could afford: This added to her other Vexations, the Plague of Jealousy. Every day presented something to increase their mututal Dislike of each other's Proceedings; till at last, he appearing still less regardful, as she was more impatient, the violent Passion which both had profess'd, was {180} converted into an entire Indifference on his side, and Detestation on her's. She hated him for being the Cause of her Misfortunes; and as her *Disgrace* had been publick, thought the least Reparation she owed her Honour, was to make her Penitence so too. She not only desisted seeing him in private, but also shunn'd all Places where there was a Probability of meeting him. Never mention'd him herself; and forbad all others from doing it before her; and if by chance any body named him, it was with the utmost Horror and Remorse she heard them.

It is most certain, that her Repentance for her Crime was no less sincere, than the Passion which had influenc'd her to commit it; and had she confin'd her Hatred within the just Bounds she ought to have done, venting her Indignation only on herself, and the deluding Tempter who had seduced her to an Act so contrary to her Principles, and the natural Bent of her Inclination, the latter part of her Life had been as truly praise-worthy as the first. She would have looked full as lovely in the Eye of Heaven, adorn'd with Penitence, as, before her Fall, she had done in an unspotted Chastity. But, alas! Her Aversion ran to unpardonable Extremes; and the Punishments which ought to have been confined to the *guilty Causes* of her Shame, she extended to the *innocent Effects*, with the most unheard-of and unnatural Barbarity, abhorring, and throwing out to Misery those unhappy Infants, the Pledges of that Tenderness she once had for *Riverius*. The eldest of them she took from the Breast of her who had suckled it from the Birth, and, by the Instigations of the wicked *Cocona*, whose cunning and avaritious Nature made her fall in with all her Lady's Humours, gave the helpless little Wretch to one of those Creatures (of whom there are many in this Island) who for a small Sum {181} of Money, will take the Charge of such unwelcome Children from their Parents, and dispose of them in a manner, that very rarely leaves them the Power of being troublesome. But this poor Babe, in spight of Ill-usage, and the Inhumanity of her who gave her Birth, still lives, though in the most obscure and miserable manner, bred only to fervile Offices, and unpitied, because unknown. The Son has found something a better Fate, for in his earliest Bud, discovering a Promise of something worthy of Regard; a Gentlewoman, who was an Intimate of *Masonia*'s, but very little satisfy'd with her Proceedings, begg'd she might have the Care of him: which, with much Persuasions, was consented to by the Mother, extorting from her first an Oath, never to let him know to whom he owed his Birth. But it was the Pleasure of great *Jupiter* to render this Caution ineffectual; for tho' his charitable Guardianess violated not her Promise, being on a sudden snatch'd from this World when he was about eleven or twelve Years of Age, some Letters hapning after her Death to fall into his hand, which had been written to her by *Masonia*, discover'd to him at once both who his Parents were, and the Inhumanity with which he had been treated by one of them. But before this came to pass, Count *Riverius* was no more; and tho' before his Death, he had often entreated with the utmost Tenderness to see his Children, designing to make handsome Provisions for 'em, especially for the Boy, being the only one he ever had, *Masonia* never would consent; and putting him off from time to time, either under pretence of their being indispos'd, or some other Excuse, at last sent him word that they were both dead, revolving they should be so to the whole World; vainly imagining that her Shame would in time wear off, when nothing remain'd to bring it to remembrance. She after married a most lovely and accomplish'd *Chevalier*, {182} by whom she has two Daughters; she seems as indulgent to them, as she was cruel to the others; and tho' she is now a Widow, these young Ladies seem to know no want of a Father. But how is it possible for a Person, who, like you, are disinterested in the Affair, to comprehend what it was the unfortunate Son of Count *Riverius* felt at so amazing a Discovery. Young as he was, he had a Sense of his Condition, sufficient to make him extremely melancholy: and tho' he wanted not any Necessary of Life, for that good Lady (who protected him from that Destiny to which his Mother had decreed him) had took care to leave him under the Tuition of a Person who fulfill'd her Request, in perfecting him in those Accomplishments her Charity had began to bestow on him; yet it was, for some time, the Fate of this unhappy Youth to lose all those who could, or would be serviceable to him: this Gentleman also died, and he was now left in a wide World unfriended, and without any visible Hope of Support. Where could he now apply, but to her who gave him Being; and being bless'd with a Genius far above his Years, he writ to her, intreating her Permission to attend her, in Terms so moving, as would have melted any Heart but hers: but this relentless Mother was so far from answering his Wishes, that, distracted to find the Secret of his Birth was known to him, and believing his Appearance in the World would revive the Discourse of her Fault, she endeavour'd to stifle the Remembrance of that, by committing a much greater. She agreed privately with the Master of a Ship, for a much larger Sum than would have made her unhappy Son easy in his Circumstances, to decoy him, by some Stratagem, on board, and then convey him to some far distant Shore, she cared not whither, so it were where there would not be a Possibility of his Return. But Heaven would not {183} suffer a Design so unnatural to prosper. By some means this Contrivance was discover'd to him for whom 'twas form'd, and he escaped that Misery intended him. This last Proof of her Unkindness, convinc'd him of the Improbability there was of receiving any Assistance from her; and believing himself absolv'd from any Act of Duty to her, who had thrown off all Nature, and even common Pity for him, he now resolved to appear himself; and since by her means, he had been depriv'd of every thing that was his Father's, but the name, would no longer be deter'd from wearing that; and having carefully inform'd himself of the Particulars of the Transactions of those Days, and finding that in open Court he had been prov'd the Son of Count *Riverius*, imagin'd that in owning himself the Person, and being called *Riverius*, he should find some who might commiserate the Misfortune of his Birth, and that more cutting one of a barbarous Mother. Nor did his Hope deceive him, none saw him without Compassion, and few there were, who had it in their power, that did not contribute something toward the Mitigation of his Woes. *Apollo*, to soften the Severity of the other Powers, endued him with the Spirit of Poetry.

Not inconsiderable are the number of Friends which his Genius this way has gain'd him; and had he not been unhappily introduced to the acquaintance of a vile Woman, a Pretender to that Art, he might have deserv'd many more than he has found; but led by her Insinuations, and perhaps instigated by a belief, that complying with her Humour might be of some advantage to his Fortune, he has been sway'd not only to mean Actions, but such also as are unjust and wicked. The Wretch being married to a Gentleman well deserving a more worthy Wife, is not content he should endure the load of Infamy, which taking to {184} his honourable Embraces a Woman who brought for her Dower three base begotten Children, has pressed his Reputation down with, continues to increase the Burthen, by sinning with as many as her now almost antiquated Charms have power to seduce; I grieve to think how often my young Favourite has been betray'd by her Wiles, to further her leud Designs on those of his Acquaintance who appeared amiable in her Eyes. Nor was this Office, shameful and scandalous as in all Ages it has been esteem'd, the worst he has unwarily been drawn into; the Monster whose Soul is wholly compos'd of Hypocrisy, Envy, and Lust, can ill endure another Woman should be esteem'd Mistress of those Virtues she has acted with too barefaced an Impudence to pretend to, and is never so happy as when by some horrid Stratagem she finds the means to traduce and blast the Character of the Worthy: to assist a Disposition therefore so near of kin, and so pleasing to the infernal Potentate, a thousand busy Fiends are always at her Call to furnish Mischief, and new-point Invention; but notwithstanding her Propensity to Malice, Dissimulation, of which she is a perfect Mistress, makes her not insensible that the surest way of hurting a Reputation, is to speak of it with an affected Candor. Nobody in Conversation seems to have more Softness and Gentleness, she boasts of no good quality so much as good-nature, and under that Cover, when ever she does speak a severe thing against any one, 'tis with the more ease believ'd; but it is but seldom she attempts it, 'tis enough for her to lay the Scheme of Mischief, the *executing* it she leaves to others, who if detected, must bear the Blame; while she perhaps shall be the first to *condemn* what she has been the sole occasion of. With how much readiness the easily deceiv'd *Riverius* has obliged her in spreading those Reports, coin'd in the {185} hellish Mint of her own Brain, I am sorry to say: but as his adhering too much to the Interest of so detestable a Creature, has been the only Crime he has hitherto been guilty of, 'tis to be hoped his good Sense will in a short time get the better of her Infatuations It cannot be doubted but that he has lost many Friends on her account, in particular one there was who bore him a singular Respect, tho' no otherways capacitated to serve him than by good Wishes. This Person receiv'd a more than common Injury from him, thro' the Instigations of that female Fury; but yet continuing to acknowledge his good Qualities, and pitying his falling into the contrary, took no other Revenge than writing a little Satire, which his having publish'd some admirable fine things in the praise of Friendship and Honour, gave a handsome opportunity for. The Poem consists but of a few Lines, which because the Character of this unfortunate Youth is fully, tho' briefly comprehended in them, I will recite.

> To the Ingenious *Riverius*, on his writing in the Praise of Friendship
> Throng'd with the Plaudits[98] of a Crowd of *Friends*,
> 'Tis nobler Pleasure when a *Foe* commends:
> When from my injur'd Soul thy moving Lays
> Extort Delight, and force unwilling Praise,
> The World must own the Justice of the Theme,
> And those thy *Folly* wrong'd, thy Wit esteem!
> While with such Force thou plead'st in *Friendship's* Cause,
> We wonder whence thy Muse th' *Idea* draws;
> Or how so well the *Theory* thou know'st
> Of Virtues, which thy *Practice* cannot boast.
> In budding Youth too much to Mischief prone,
> In vile *Thersites'* Mind might'st paint thy own!
>
> {186} Nor could a *Pandarus* thy Strokes escape,
> Who thy late Deeds dost from his Pattern shape,
> A common Artist may with ease describe
> Prospects the Eye doth every hour imbibe:

---

98 [A word derived from the Latin, *plaudite*, the demand of applause made by the player, when he left the stage: applause.]

But to decypher Objects far remov'd,
And absent Beauties bring to sight improv'd,
Is the great Master-piece of human Will;
And puts to shame a more than *Titian* Skill.
When thy loose Pen on Love and Honour turns,
The ravish'd Heart with Admiration burns,
My Wrongs are hush'd, my Indignation dies,
Or lull'd by thy sweet Notes suspended lies;
Some Angel sure descended to inspire.
Thy late enlightned Breast with sacred Fire;
From the long-reigning Fiends set free thy Mind,
Sublim'd each Thought, and every Wish refin'd:
O keep th'instructive Vision still in view,
With zealous Care the shining Track pursue!
Enjoy the Virtues thou'st so well express'd;
Nor blessing others, be thyself unbless'd:
Believe in humble Innocence thou'lt know
Delights, which pompous Vice could ne'er bestow.

He is, notwithstanding what has been said of him, of so excellent a Disposition, that whenever he has been drawn into Mischiefs of this kind, it has been meerly thro' Inadvertency: his thinking Soul would never give him leave to be guilty of a barbarous or unjust Action to any one; and all the Crimes which the Delusions of this worse than *Lais* have involv'd him in, have rather been occasioned by his too great Good-nature to her, than Malice or Ill-will to those who have suffered by them. A remarkable Instance of his Sweetness of Disposition, as well as filial Duty and Regard to a Mother who had not deserv'd it from him, was, that when through the Solicitations of some Friends, who would not be refus'd, she had consented to {187} bestow a small Sum of Money on him, half of which was paid immediately, and the other order'd some time afterwards; he generously declined the second Payment, hearing that she having been like many others, unwarily drawn into the Snare of this cursed *Well*, had lost great part of her Substance. The Letter he wrote to her, alluring her that whatever his present Wants were, or future Misfortunes might arise, he would sustain them with less Impatience, than to be the cause of any trouble to her, was so very tender and moving, that it would have melted any heart, but one so obstinately harden'd as her's.

The *Deity* had perhaps prolong'd his Discourse on this young Gentleman, who, in spite of his Failings, seem'd to be very much his Favourite, if the appearance of a Person of a very august Presence, just then rushing thro' the Croud, had not cut him off from any further Remarks on a History already related, to enter into a new one; which after he had paused a while to give a little truce to the Stranger's Attention, he did in this manner.

The History of Count *Orainos*, and Madam *Del Millmonde*

Never was a Man more form'd to charm than that young Nobleman; his Conversation has that soft persuasive Air, that there is scarce a possibility of knowing him without loving him: *Apollo* has shower'd his choicest Favours on him, he is justly accounted one of the best *Poets* of the Age, and has in all the other Sciences so excellent an Understanding, that those who are esteem'd most skilful in their several Arts, are glad of improving by those Hints he is well able to give: but not all his Learning or his Wit, could {188} defend him from being made the Property of a deceitful and mercenary Woman: but there is indeed a very good reason to be given why the wisest and best are most easily betray'd. That Generosity and open Candor, which is almost inseparable from good Sense, renders the Person possess'd of it, at once incapable of a base Action himself, or of suspecting it in others. Too frequently, to the unspeakable prejudice of his Fortune, has the *Count* been made a Prey to the tame, smiling Savages, which haunt this *Isle*; great part of his Estate, even in his Minority, he squander'd on those Creatures whose only dependance is on the Friendship of a *Jockey*, a lucky Throw of *Dice*, or Run of *Cards*; and a far greater on *Women*, for Purchases yet less considerable. At length beginning to perceive his Error, he resolv'd to share Diversions only with those whose Quality he thought would not permit them to do a mean Action; but he was too late convinced that no degrees are proof against Dishonour. The Wife of the Chevalier *Del Millmonde* had Beauty enough to engage him to a violent Passion for her, and her Rank and Figure to secure him from all Apprehensions of paying for the Pleasures he expected in an Amour with her, in so expensive a manner, as he had done for others. All the difficulty was, how to gain her; to compass which, he omitted nothing of those tender Blandishments which Lovers make use of; but her Virtue, or the appearance of it, for a long time render'd his Endeavours unsuccessful, and he was almost about to give up the Cause, when an unexpected turn of Fortune happen'd to throw her into his Arms, at a time when he was beginning to despair he ever should arrive at that Happiness. Being one day in his Closet full of uneasy and perplex'd Meditations, he was told a Lady mask'd waited in a Hackney-Coach to speak with him; but {189} that she would by no means be persuaded to alight or send her Name, tho' she said her Business was of the greatest Consequence. The Surprize he was in at such a Message, was the more, because he had not of late convers'd with any Women, who probably would come in that manner; but imagining it must be either some old Acquaintance to entreat a Favour from his Liberality, or a Lady in distress for a new one, knowing his Character, desirous of commencing one with hi; was considering in what manner he should refuse: when coming to the Coach-side, she slipt her Mask aside, just to let him see who she was; and clapping it on hastily again with these Words, I beg, my Lord, *said she*, you will give me leave to speak to you for a Moment. I am undone without your Advice; order the Coach to drive where you please, provided it be private.

What were the Transports of this Soul-raptur'd Lover, when he perceiv'd it was his adorable *Millmonde*, who was come in this free and obliging manner to visit him; and how great his Impatience, to know in what manner he could serve her; I need not go about to make you sensible of: for without bringing you to Confession, agreeable Stranger! I can tell, you have felt enough of those extatick Perturbations, not to want any Description of what on such an occasion must be felt by a Heart in *Love*. The Count had not presently the power of answering her; but throwing himself into the Coach, bid the Person who drove it go a little distance from the House; saying, he then would give him directions where they would be carried. It was not easy for him indeed in the present Tumult of his Joy and Wonder, to think on any proper place: and he must first disharge some part of his overflowing Raptures, e'er dull Consideration could have room. All the time he was {190} endeavouring to make her sensible of what she was secure enough of his Affection to know before, she answer'd nothing; but with down-cast Eyes, and Blushes, plainly demonstrated nothing could afford her more Satisfaction than his continuing to declare himself her Lover. The power of Thought at last returning, he directed the Coachman to a House which he knew was perfectly at his Devotion, and where in his days of universal Gallantry he had frequently met the Fair and Kind. She said little of any consequence till they were in a Chamber together; and then looking tenderly on him, Do you not wonder, my Lord, *said she*, at a Behaviour so different from what you ever have seen in me? What is it I ought not to apprehend, from the ill opinion my proceeding in this manner may create in you? You have very little to fear, *reply'd he*, from him who was born only to obey you. I should be more than bless'd, if I could as easily rid myself of the Apprehensions that this Visit has less of kindness in it, than my fond Wishes, at the first discovery it was you, had made me hope. You Men, *resum'd the Lady, with a half Smile*, as you are easily flatter'd, so you are also as easily dejected. But I give you leave to make what Interpretation you will on this Freedom, so you do not construe it so much to my disadvantage, as to think me unworthy of the Favour I come to entreat—Oh Heavens! *Cry'd the transported Lover*, can you be unkind enough to doubt my Zeal in anything that may be of service to you? I hoped you had been sufficiently acquainted with your power, to be assured it must be more than Life I would refuse to your Commands. Depend on this Assurance, I conjure you; and if you would be obliging in your turn, delay not my impatient Expectations already on the wing, and wild to fly where the adorable *Millmonde* shall direct.

{191} After many other Expressions of the same nature had pass'd between them, she told him, that having unfortunately dropp'd a Letter of his, her Husband had taken it up, and was so enraged with Jealousy, that she should receive any Addresses of that nature, that she had good reason to dread the Effects; and that in the sudden Fright, she could think of no other Excuse than that, tho' directed to her, it was meant to another Lady of her Acquaintance; and that she was no otherways concern'd in the Affair than as a Confidant. And has this Pretence, *interrupted the Count*, gain'd Credit? I am not certain, *cry'd* Millmonde, what Effect it has had, for he flung out of the House immediately, and I took that opportunity of coming to you, to conjure you, if any part of that Tenderness you have profess'd for me be real, to second what I have said; and to make it appear more like Truth, you must this Instant write a Note to me, complaining of the Unkindness of my Friend, and entreating me to speak to her in your behalf. I will do any thing, *answer'd he*, that you think will be conducive to your Service. I know no way so proper as this that I have told you, *resum'd she*; and to take away all Suspicion of a Contrivance, the Person who brings the Letter, must do it with an Air of Secrecy, refusing to deliver it to any hand but my own: this will be sufficient to alarm my Husband's already outrageous Fury to oblige me to shew it him, than which nothing can be more to my advantage. You will easily believe the enamour'd Count made no difficulty to comply with a Request which seem'd so reasonable; but entreated she would permit him to defer the Writing of it till she had left him, not being able, as he said, to lose so much of her Conversation as the time in forming it would take up. This was too trifling a Favour, and too obliging to herself, to be refus'd {192} but presuming on the Confidence she seem'd to repose in him, and the Freedom she had taken, he was not of a Constitution cool enough to stop at that: from one Liberty he proceeded to another; and all things conspiring to aid his Wishes, the Lady yielded at length to every thing he ask'd; but still assuming an Air of Modesty, and assuring him, that she esteem'd her Virtue equal with her Life; and that nothing could have prevail'd on her to follow the Dictates of her Inclination, (which she confess'd had long pleaded in his behalf) but the barbarous Jealousy and Ill-usage of her Husband.

The Count thought himself happy to possess her on any Terms, and not much troubled his head what Motives they were that induced her to this Concession, little imagining what in reality they were, or how he had been deceived into an Opinion of her, which she was very far from deserving. They parted not without a thousand mutual Protestations of eternal Love and Fidelity; and, indeed, 'twas hard to say which of these two was most satisfy'd with what had happen'd, though for vastly different Reasons. The Count, whose whole Soul was taken up in Admiration of her Charms, thought of nothing but how to render himself worthy of the Blessing he possess'd; but *Millmonde* had other Views, which in the Sequel of the Story will surprize you.

The Count had engag'd her to meet him again in a short time, and frequent were the Opportunities she gave him of gratifying his Passion at the same House where first he had been happy: but either growing weary of the Amour herself, or imagining that, according to the Nature of his Sex, he might in time become so, she put in practice that Stratagem which she had often found successful on others. One Evening, as they were together entertaining each other with accustom'd Endearments, the Door {193} was on a sudden broke open, and in rush'd her Husband, accompanied by Several Fellows who pretended to be Persons appointed by the Government to inspect into such Affairs. 'Tis hard to say whether the real Concern of *Orainos* for his belov'd *Millmonde*'s Honour, or her seeming Terror, was the greatest. The *Chevalier* swore he would never see her Face more, and vented that Indignation, which 'twas probable, on so shocking a Discovery, a Husband must be possess'd of, in Language suitable to the occasion. The Count offer'd him that Satisfaction, which by a Man of Honour and Spirit would have been demanded; but he refused it, telling him he would take other Measures, which Words the Count could interpret no other-wife, than that he meant to sue for a Divorce with her, and proceed against him by form of Law; and being unwilling it should be made a publick Business, not only on the Lady's, but his own account, and also being press'd by her with all the Tears and moving Expressions imaginable, he condescended to entreat the *Chevalier* that he would hearken[99] to Terms of Accommodation, protesting in the most solemn manner, that he never would make any further Attempts on the Virtue of his Wife, (which he likewise swore was yet unfully'd) if he would again receive her into Favour. And for his own part, as an Acknowledgement of the Injury he had intended him, he would make him a Consideration superiour to what he could expect from the decision of the Law, reminding him at the same time, how much such Affairs, being brought into open Court, redounded to the dishonour of the innocent Husband, as well as erring Wife; and that if she were prov'd guilty, which was much to be questioned, he would be obliged to return her Fortune, or allow a separate Maintenance, which would be much more chargeable than the {194} maintaining her at home. He urg'd this last Article because he believ'd it would be the most effectual one, the *Chevalier* being justly accounted one of the most avaricious Men on Earth. But alas! the deluded Count might well have spar'd himself the Pains of arguing so strenuously, the other was as willing to be persuaded, as he was that he should be so; and tho' at first he seem'd refractory, before they parted he consented to his Proposals; and *Orainos* giving him a Bill on his Banker for three thousand Crowns, and setting his Hand to a Covenant with the penalty of twice that Sum, if he ever writ or spoke

---

99 [*hearcnian*, Saxon: to listen by way of curiosity.]

to Madam *Del Millmonde* again, he took her with him, leaving the Lover to console himself as well as he could for the loss of his Mistress and Money. His Vexation for the former, 'tis probable, he would not very easily have wore off, if some days after he had not happened into the Company of a Gentleman, who related a History to him of having been serv'd just in the same manner.

The Count could not avoid discovering a good deal of Surprize to hear another had happened on an Adventure so very like what he had lately met, that had he reveal'd it to any one, or could have believ'd the other Persons concern'd in it would have disclosed, he would have believ'd this Friend had only related the Story on purpose to upbraid him, and to prevent his being too much shock'd, had taken it on himself. But on discoursing farther on the Affair, he found that it was not only Fact, but also that it was by the Chevalier *Del Millmonde* and his fair Wife they had been both ensnar'd to part with such considerable Sums of Money, and that these Wretches under the pretence of Gentry had drawn several Gentlemen into Inconveniences, and had in reality no Estate nor Dependance but in such shameful Stratagems as these.

{195} This Discovery cured the Count for some time of his amorous Inclinations, nor has he indeed ever since resum'd them, but where Duty renders them a Glory. He afterwards married a lovely and accomplish'd Lady, and has no remains of Chagrin but what arise from the Reflection how much he has impoverish'd that Estate which is to descend on the Offspring he has by her, before he became her Husband, thro' the Insinuations of base Women, and since by being led into the Delusions of this *Enchanted Well*. His Case, however, is not so desperate as that of the Gentleman he is now talking to. He is call'd the Chevalier *Davilla*, is of a distinguish'd Family, and had a plentiful Estate, but has sunk the best part of it in this bottomless Abyss, whence there is now no hope of ever recovering it; but that which is the severest stroke of his ill Fate, is, that having two very beautiful Daughters, the most lovely of them finding their decaying Fortune could no longer maintain her in the Port she had been bred, has lately prostituted her Charms to one of the Managers of this horrid Scheme, in hope that his Affection may return, what her Father's unhappy Infatuation has loft. And the other of these young Ladies is fallen into so deep a Melancholy, that it may be call'd almost Stupidity.

The Mother of them being of an ambitious haughty Spirit, and withal passionately fond of her Children, by her continual Upbraidings, is no small aggravation of her unfortunate Husband's Discontent. He is now solliciting the Interest of Count *Orainos*, to procure him a place at Court, but cannot expect any great Success, at least as yet, for that Gentleman has many Relations of his own in unhappy Circumstances, and 'tis his Care as well as Duty first to provide for them. However, like a true Courtier, he promises everything, and the {196} other has the Consolation to find the loss of his Fortune has not lost him the respect with which he was accustomed to be treated by him. This, tho' a slender Food to subsist on, is yet more than every one in the like Circumstances can find: the good, the charitable, the obliging *Millfond*, who, while he had it in his power, kept up that Hospitality this Island was once so justly famed for, in a degree which made the more narrow-soul'd Nobility blush, perform'd every Office of benignant Humanity with a chearfulness that added to the obligation he confer'd, and in all his Actions prov'd his greatest Pleasure was in doing good to others, is now himself without a Friend, destitute of Support, and in want of even those common Necessaries of Life, which the meanest and most abject born cannot be without. Those whom his too great Liberality has oblig'd, fly from him as the most dangerous of all Duns, and those who never had occasion for his Assistance, think 'tis not their business to regard him; as if to remedy the Distresses of a Fellow-Creature, especially of a worthy Person, were not a Duty incumbent on all who have the means to do it; but this is a Principle so long out of fashion in this ingrateful and tenacious City, that there are scarce any who remember it; or if they do, it is but to preach against it. Honour, Justice, and Good-nature, are banish'd from their inexorable Hearts; and Avarice, Hypocrisy, and Lust, the Demons that inhabit. See there, two Instances of this lamented Truth; they are Sisters, Daughters of the late Chevalier *Byzarr*, endued by Heaven with some Beauty, but left by their Father in possession of that great Charm to conquer Hearts, a large Estate; but Marriage is a state too limited to be agreeable to Inclinations such as theirs, they are for a taste of all Complections, all Degrees of Men; and tho' they boast to {197} be Women of such Frugality, that they never threw away (to use their own Expression) a single Shilling on that useless and pedantick Virtue call'd *Charity*, yet neither of them will scruple considerable Sums in Donations, where they expect an adequate return of Pleasure. A Footman who belong'd to one of them, talks loudly of the Generosity of his Lady; nor is the other less extoll'd for her Liberality in preferring a Porter, who chanc'd to bring a Letter, first to be her Butler, and afterwards purchasing him a place in the Revenue. And indeed it has been observable in their Characters, that those Enamorato's who have been chosen from low Life, have much longer retain'd their Favours, than those, who, according to a disinterested Person's opinion of things, were infinitely more capable of deserving 'em.

There is also another Lady of the same Family, who seems nearer of kin to them by her Actions, than she is by Blood, being undeservedly the Wife of a Gentleman of excellent Parts, an unparallel'd Sweetness of Disposition, a Rank infinitely superiour to what she could pretend to, and a Face and Person without exception; she has thought fit to make a broken Tradesman of mean Birth, and meaner Education, his Rival in every thing she has the Power of bestowing: Twice has this Wretch, who has no Charm, (unless an unequal'd Impudence be one) been set up in his Business by her Bounty; and having been the third time obliged to go aside, she continues to support him out of her private Purse, tho' she is well assur'd his Misfortunes sprung only from his immoderate Fondness of the viler sort of Women; an Article which one would think should render him unpity'd by her, who, if Gratitude were a thing in use, or to be expected in such sort of Engagements, might expect all his Addresses of that nature. But as he is {198} not the only Man who shares her *Bounty*, she has so much Consideration as to pardon his sharing his Person with others. This is the manner, worthy Stranger, (*pursued the* Deity *in a melancholy Accent*) in which these wretched Islanders abuse my Godhead, and prophane my Name; for among all these monstrous Passions, there is not one who lays not all the blame of their Mismanagement on *Love*. My Influence ever was a Stranger to those Breasts, where Lust, Avarice, or Ambition reigns; yet to whichsoever of these *Demons* a Mortal is indebted for his Misfortunes, 'tis I who am condemned by the mistaken World, and the few Votaries I have, ill used and scorn'd on the account of the pretended ones; whereas if there were none unhappy but such as fell a sacrifice to *Love* alone, there would be few, very few indeed, whose Fate would merit Commiseration. Some Examples, I confess, there are, but then 'tis only when the darling Object is guided by one of those detestable Destroyers of human Happiness: as for Example, a Pair first blest by me, and after united by the no less sacred Bonds of *Hymen*, liv'd for more than ten whole Years together in an envied Tranquillity, and mutual Satisfaction; 'till Interest and Ambition, join'd to poison all the Sweets of Innocence and Love, and render their future Days as wretched, as the past had been the contrary. A great and mighty Prince came arm'd with Pomp and Grandeur, and dazzling the Eyes of Reason in my fair Apostate, won her to forsake her real Peace in search of vain and noisy Triumphs. She quitted the Bed of her too indulgent Husband, and by Ambition led, look'd down with Scorn on his heart-rending Griefs, and the wondring World's just Censure. Am I the cause of this? Be judge, discerning Youth! And clear me from those Aspersions which foul-mouth'd Fame may waft to Countries where I am still {199} revere'd. But why should I complain of the Injuries I receive from Mortals, when my own Mother, Celestial *Venus*, too much adhering to the Suggestions of the worst of Fiends, permits that *Demon* who usurps my Shape, to deceive her into Tenderness? She teaches the Wanton her alluring Arts, and sends the Graces to adorn the Looks of those most Rebels to my Power.

The God here relaps'd into his former Musings, not able to endure the Repetition of what was so displeasing to him, without Inquietudes such as Mortals feel when treated with Ingratitude by those they most esteem; nor could the Stranger assume Confidence enough to attempt disturbing the Contemplations of a *Deity*, till three Ladies, all young, handsome, gay, and richly habited, disengaging themselves from the Throng of People, came swiftly by the place where he and his divine Informer stood; the rush of their Garments as they swept along, and the Dust they made, oblig'd as it were the Observation of those they pass'd. There goes, (*resum'd the softning Power, lifting up his shining Eyes*) in one of those Ladies an Evidence of my abused Dominion, and in another how little sway I have with the Fair; but let us follow them, I doubt not but they are either on some Assignation, or gone aside to talk on some Affairs which may let you into their Characters more effectually than a Description given by any other than themselves. In speaking these Words, with steps unheard he pursu'd the way they took, and saw 'em seated on a little Bench which was placed behind the Pillar of *Fortune*, where they could not be seen by any of the Assembly: the Stranger kept some paces at a distance, wanting the gift of Invisibility which the other had assumed during his stay, till his heavenly Guide pointed out a place for him to stand, where he might unseen hear all was said. 'I know not, *cry'd one of* {200} *them*, in what manner I shall endure, or revenge this Affront; if any other than you, had told me he could use me so, I would not have believ'd it; but pray repeat what he said over again, for the Rage I was in, has made me lose great part of it. I do assure you, dear *Flavia*, *reply'd the Lady to whom she spoke*, I urg'd him in the most tender manner I was able, told him there was no hope of your Recovery, and that you could not die in peace without one kind Farewell from him, that his Name was perpetually in your mouth, and that you would pardon all his past Unkindness if he would give you this last testimony of Remorse. I wept too while I talk'd to him, but Prayers and Tears were equally ineffectual; he seem'd to make a Jest of your Despair, told me he wonder'd you could expect a Man, because he had fool'd away a little time when he had nothing else to do, should make a Business of his Conversation with you, that if you had a greater stock of Love than you knew what to do with, there were young Fellows enough in Town, who would be well enough pleased to take it off your hands; but for his part, all his Hours were now employ'd in more serious Engagements. Oh the Villain! *Interrupted the other impatiently*, I'll tear out his perfidious Soul. I cannot bear it. I'll be revenged, if there be Poison or Dagger to be had. Hold, hold, *resumed she that had been employ'd in this Affair*, one thing I had forgot; Tell her from me, *said he*, that I would advise her not to expose herself or me; these sort of Amours, when publish'd, serve but to make the Persons concern'd in them ridiculous to the rest of the World. I'll hear no more, *cry'd* Flavia: I regard not my own Character, that is already ruin'd by my inconsiderate Passion for him; I have too much attested {201} my own *Folly*, and will now proclaim his *Villany*; not one of his false Vows will I conceal, his Flatteries, his Oaths, his dissembling Letters, all, all will I this moment publish, and make him known for what he is, a Monster! In speaking these Words, she rose precipitately from her Seat, and left the place. She was no sooner out of hearing, than the other two she had left behind her set up a loud Laugh: well, *says the Lady Aggravator*, this is certainly the best Jest that ever happened; poor vain unthinking Wretch, to make choice of me for an Advocate in a Love-Affair; the Man must have been strangely stupid indeed, to have return'd to a Dish he had before been cloy'd on, when he saw before his Eyes untasted Fare. I am amaz'd the silly Creature could imagine he would like her after having been in my Company. Then, *cry'd she who had not spoke before*, he made love to you immediately? With all the Passion imaginable, *answer'd the other*, told me he never saw anything so handsome and genteel in his whole Life, that everything about me seem'd as it were made on purpose to charm him; but as for *Flavia*, he protests he never lik'd her, Fortune happened to throw her in his way, at a time when he wanted Amusement, and the Woman was kind, that was all, and for my part I am very apt to believe him: I never thought her agreeable, besides she's old; she pretends to be but one and twenty, but I'll engage she's thirty at least; then she paints abominably, and wears false Hips; and as to her Conversation, 'tis tedious, she talks nothing but Scandal, and is the worst-natured Woman in the World. But dear Girl, *continu'd she, looking on her Watch*, 'tis almost five, and you must know I have promis'd this new Lover to meet him at six. I must leave you, but I'll tell {202} you to-morrow the Subject of our Chat, I suppose good part of it will be laughing at Flavia—'Tis rare Diversion to us both. Then you are not afraid of meeting the same Fate, *cry'd the other*. No, no, *reply'd the tenacious Fair*, not till I have the same Imperfections.' She was in too much haste to say any more; but setting herself in order as she went, tript away full of the thoughts of her new Conquest, and the Triumph she had gain'd over her too believing Friend.

This little Conversation, *said the Deity*, may give you a taste of the Dispositions of both Sexes in this Island; most Women are fond of circumventing each other in their Amours, and most Men are more taken with Novelty than any other Charm. *Flavia* has given a thousand Instances of her Passion for this ingrateful Lover, yet he prefers a new Face to all the Endearments she can bestow, and this Lady can easily absolve herself for breach of that Trust reposed in her, to purchase the vainglory of a heart which perhaps may not be three days at her Devotion. Thus do they spend their days in an eternal Round of Hurry and Confusion. *Pursuit*, which to a Soul truly inspired by me, is full of Fears, Perplexities, and Care, is with them the only Pleasure; and *Enjoyment*, the beginning of a perfect Lover's Happiness, puts an end to the Felicity of these imaginary ones. This is a Humour so near universal, that the few who are of a contrary one, are laugh'd at as Affecters of a Romantick Singularity, and rarely meet with any other return than Scorn from the Objects of their Constancy. Thus am I affronted even by those who plead my Power as the only excuse they can make for the Foibles they are guilty of. The *Young* wear my Name only as an Umbrage for their Faults, and the *Old*, deceiv'd by their Insinuations, despise and hate me for the ruin they imagine I bring into their {203} Familie; but had the latter of these a more just opinion of my Influence, they would not so often by forc'd Marriages, occasion to their Children those Misfortunes they seem most to dread. I have been looking round this numerous Assembly to point you out a late Instance of this unhappy Truth; but I see he is not here, something has prevented his coming, tho' he is not without a considerable share in the Fortunes of this *Well*. But tho' you see him not, I will describe him in such a manner, that if hereafter he should meet your Eyes, you cannot fail of knowing him.

The History of the Chevalier *Beaujeune*, and the Beautiful *Olivia*

He is the only Son of a distinguish'd and wealthy Family, a Gentleman of admirable Parts, and perfect in all Accomplishments befitting a Youth of Quality: as to his Person, it is extremely agreeable, and if his Stature will not allow him the Epithet of Graceful, the Excellence of his Shape, and Genteelness of his Air, very well make up for that Deficiency. His Limbs are the finest proportioned that can be, his Features are regular, his Eyes and Complexion the most lovely in the World; his Manner of Address enchanting, but of a Humour which few can equal, and is infinitely more valuable than all his other Charms. To make his Character compleat, he has always behav'd in so exemplary a manner to his Parents, that it is with Justice they look on him as the Delight and Glory of their Age; but alas! 'Tis his Obedience that has been fatal to him, and by {204} persevering in that Virtue, even in the tenderest part of Self-denial, he has been oblig'd to the exercise of another equally meritorious,[100] but more painful; *Patience* is now his greatest study, and in his Circumstance is one of the severest Tasks which Humanity can undertake.

The old Chevalier, tho' the best of Husbands to a no less deserving Wife, with whom he has liv'd in a continual Series of mutual Happiness, seems to have forgot it was to me he ow'd the Foundation of his Marriage-Bliss; and induced only by the Prospect of a great Fortune, oblig'd his Son contrary to his Inclinations to wed *Olivia*. It must be confess'd indeed that she is one of the most lovely Women on Earth; but all the Affections of his Soul being before engaged, he had no Eyes to see her Charms: the Compulsion which his Duty to those he thought it the highest Crime to disobey, laid on him to marry her, made her appear yet less agreeable; and tho' he knew her to be a celebrated Toast,[101] and that there were few who would not envy him the Possession of her, yet he look'd on himself as exceedingly unhappy. The

---

100 [*meritoire*, French, from *merit:* deserving of reward; high in desert.]
101 [from the verb: a celebrated woman whose health is often drunk.]

Lady not less averse, declar'd to some of her Intimates, on her Marriage-day, that were it in her power to chuse, Death would be more welcome than her intended Bridegroom. But see the Difference of Tempers! *Beaujeune*, tho' in obedience to a Parent's Will he had torn himself from a young Lady who he lov'd above his Life, and given his Hand, where he found nothing to engage his Heart, endeavour'd by the most obliging Carriage in the world to keep her from suspecting his want of Tenderness; while *Olivia*, on the contrary, let the whole World into the Secret of her dislike, was always traducing him *Abroad*, and studying ways to make him uneasy at *Home*. The old Chevalier and his Lady, now too well convinc'd of their Error, wish'd in vain {205} for a possibility of dissolving that Knot they had taken so much pains to tye. The Ill-humour of their Daughter-in-law, extended not only to her Husband, but to all those for whom she thought he had an esteem; she affronted his Sisters, tho' the most deserving young Ladies in the World, and one of them a shining Example for those of her Sex to follow, who would be counted either wise, or virtuous, used his Parents with Ill-manners; in fine, she was civil to none but who would purchase her Favour, by railing at a Family which her greatest Honour was to be ally'd to. Continual Jars[102] made at length their living together intolerable; they parted by Consent, he must have been infatuated to have been dissatisfied with this Separation, and she sought it for Reasons which in a short time after discover'd themselves to her Confusion. Her Hatred of *Beaujeune* was not greater than her Love of *Marsilius*, a young Officer, who taking the favourable opportunity of her Disagreement with her Husband, made his Addresses to her. Never Woman had taken a greater Pleasure in censuring the Actions of her own Sex, nor was more severe on every little Failing; but now the time was come, to prove that the most rigid are not always the most free from the same Faults which they condemn. Now was the time when she was to be ridicul'd in her turn, and suffer for that Self-Sufficiency which had made her triumph in the Misfortunes of others. She was no sooner acquainted with *Marsilius*, than she became enamour'd of him; he was a Man too much accustom'd to Gallantry, not to perceive the Advantage he had gain'd, nor would he take the faint Repulses she gave, as absolute Denials. In short he ask'd, and he obtain'd all that his Passion could entreat, or her's bestow; for a while they revel'd in all the Joys that the Gratification of loose Desire {206} could yield; not a Week, scarce a Day pass'd without renewing their amorous Stealths. The place of their meeting was the House of a female Confidant, who was too well bribed to Secrecy to reveal the Correspondence; but Persons of their Figure could not frequent such a place without notice being taken. *Beaujeune* had Intelligence of it, and plac'd Spies to observe when

---

102 [from the verb: clash; discord; debate.]

they were together, and bring him an account. One day, which happened to be the fatal one, *Marsilius* was told by a Person who wish'd him well, that to his certain knowledge he was suspected to have an Amour with *Olivia*, and that her Husband was a Man of too much Spirit to suffer the Dishonour unrevenged, if by any means he could arrive at the certainty; therefore advised him to be cautious in his Proceedings with that Lady. *Marsilius* thank'd him, and promis'd that he would, nor did he say more than he intended to perform: for being that Evening to meet her by Appointment, he writ to her, desiring she would defer the Happiness she had made him hope till some other time, letting her know the caution had been given him, and the reasons of it. But she, lost in impatient Wishes, and deaf to all but the Suggestions of her Passion, could not support an Interruption of Delight, and sent him back for Answer, that the care of Reputation was alone *her* Business; and if *she* regarded not what the World should say in such a case, she thought it would ill become *him* to be assiduous about it.

After this, there was nothing left for him to urge, and if he had attempted any further Arguments, he thought it would have been look'd on either as the effect of a too little *Inclination* for her Favours, or too great a *Fear* of what might ensue from the Jealousy of her Husband. In fine, they met, and the Spies which the injur'd *Beaujeune* had {207} employ'd, bringing him immediate Notice, he went to the Rendezvous, and taking proper Persons with him to be witness of the Truth of what he should hereafter report, found the amorous Pair in a Posture which would admit of no Excuse: The Detection was evident, and it would have been rather an Aggravation, than an Alleviation of their Guilt, to have attempted a denial of it. *Marsilius* jump'd from the Bed, naked as he was, and flew into another Room to conceal his Confusion. The Lady behav'd with more Courage, and with a Countenance which had in it nothing either of Shame or Penitence; Well, Sir, *said she*, you have taken a great deal of pains to certify yourself of that which you might easily have known long since. I never dissembled the fix'd Aversion I had for you, and you must be a Man of little Penetration, not to distinguish it was not to the Coldness of my Constitution you ow'd the Insensibility you found in me. This manner of Behaviour so unusually met with in a transgressing Wife, and so little to be expected from a Lady who had been accustom'd to boast of the severest Virtue, astonish'd her Husband to that degree, that he could scarce believe himself awake, or that his Ears and Eyes had not deceiv'd him: he made not, however, the least Reply to what she had said, prevented from doing it, either by Rage or Grief, or that there were no Words proper to reproach her Crime, and insolent Vindication of it, but such as he would not make use of; therefore turning to the Persons who had accompanied him thither, and desiring them to take notice of what they had seen and heard, went hastily out of the Room, leaving her to reflect on what her ungovern'd Passion had reduced her to, and the Consequences which must infallibly attend it.

{208} Marsilus remov'd himself the next Day, and if *Beaujeune* harboured any Tnoughts of calling him to an account for the Injury he had done him, in the manner which is most common, the least allowable both by the Laws of Heaven and Earth; he found himself without the means, and he was obliged to take another and more publick Method of proceeding. What an unhappy Change has this Lady's Mismanagement created in her Affairs! Lately she was the Pride and Glory of her own Family, and (but for a few Failings in her Temper, which 'twas hoped Time and Consideracion would make her repent) the Desire of her Husband's. Her Beauty render'd her an Object of Love to all that saw her, and the Reputation of her great Virtue, of the Esteem of all who heard her Name. What is she now! Is she not by so much more contemptible, as she was formerly more revere'd! The Voice of Praise, is now turn'd to Reproach and Infamy; the Eye of Admiration is for ever clos'd, and the keen Looks of Scorn and Detestation meet her where'er she goes; Disdain *Abroad*, Remorse at *Home*, haunt her perpetually; how truly wretched *is* she, how perfectly happy might she *have* been. Thus is it, (*continued the God, sighing as he spoke*) that most People mistake the way to Bliss, and follow that which leads to Wretchedness and endless Woe. Had *Olivia* been of the Temper of the Dutchess *De Marbien*, or were her Lord of the Disposition of *Beaujeune*, how compleatly felicitous would be the State of both? But to make you comprehend my Meaning in this *Contrast*, I will give you some Particulars of this unhappy Pair, whose Greatness serves only to make their Misfortunes more conspicuous.

{209} The History of the Duke and Dutchess *de Marbien*

The Duke *de Marbien*, when he was very young, imagin'd himself violently in love; that is, had a vile Passion for the possession of the Daughter of a Chevalier, who had it not in his power to render her any other way worthy the Addresses of a Man of his Quality, than by an extraordinary Education; neither had her Person any of those killing Beauties, which, at first sight, subdue the Hearts of Men; her greatest Charm lies in her Mind, and that most noble Part, Heaven has endow'd with Graces which are not to be exceeded by any of her Sex, nor indeed equall'd but by a very few. She has an unaffected Modesty, which the most malignant Tongue of base Detraction never yet had power to fully, a Prudence far above the promise of her years; and to temper, as it were, the Austerity of the severer Virtues, a Sweetness of Humour, an obliging Affability of Behaviour, which endears her Conversation to all who are happy enough to enjoy it; all, I say, but him, who most she wishes to engage. Such as she is, however, the Duke was once so much enamour'd of her, that he declar'd to all the world, and at that time spoke his true Sentiments, That if he did not obtain her, he should be the most miserable Man on Earth. At first indeed, he sollicited her but for a Mistress, but her Behaviour soon convinc'd him of his Error, and made him see she knew the value of her Virtue better: his Addresses were then converted into the most honourable ones, and it was a long time, that even on those Terms she would consent to hear him. He had then a Father living, {210} who was not only one of the most avaricious, but most cunning Men of the Age; she doubted not but his Indignation, that his Son should marry without a Fortune, would prompt him to take all the Measures his inventive Policy could form, to render her unhappy; and had too much Penetration not to fee, that the Son had not a liability of Nature sufficient to defend his Passion from those Artifices the other would practice to subvert it. She was not indeed without feeling the most tender Regard for him; the prodigious vehemence of Love, which he profes'd, inspir'd her with a desire of making him a grateful return, if any prospect had appear'd of doing it without rendring herself unhappy by yielding to her Wishes; but she was too wise to make any one the Confidant of her Iclinations, and from him who had created them, most carefully conceal'd them. 'Tis to be believ'd, not all the Efforts of his assiduous Passion, nor all the softning Pleas of her own secret Wishes, would have oblig'd her to marry him, if her Father had not, prompted by Ambition, forc'd her to be miserably Great. The Nuptials were celebrated with the utmost secrecy, for fear of an Interruption from the Parents of the Duke; but from the first night of her becoming a Wife, she may date the Æra of her Misfortunes. The morning was but in its dawn, when the Endearments of this new wedded Pair received a dreadful Disturbance. The Duke's Father having Intelligence of what was done, accompany'd by a great number of Gentlemen, broke into the Chamber where they lay; and after loading them both with Reproaches, forc'd the trembling Bridegroom to quit his Scene of Bliss, and go with them. All manner of Stratagems were made use of to annul the Marriage, but in vain; and the Chevalier had this Satisfaction for the ruin of his Child's Repose, to think that, in spite of all their {211} Endeavours to the contrary, he was the Father of a Dutchess: but the Soul-torturing Anguish of that unfortunate Lady is not to be express'd, and should I, I, who was witness of her secret Pangs, her agonizing Complaints, heard by no Ears but mine, aim at a Description, it would but wrong the unutterable Woe she labour'd under But think, generous Stranger! think what it must be to lose at once all that the Soul holds dear to know one's self clear, even in Thought, of Sin, yet to be upbraided as the most guilty Criminal; to have the name of Wife, yet be depriv'd of all can make that Title pleasing. Form, if it be possible, an Idea of such a State, and judge what she endur'd. She saw her Husband no more in many Months, he was carried down to a Country Seat, where he was debarr'd even from the privilege of Writing; and to estrange his Affections, the artful old Politician had placed in the House several of the most beautiful Courtezans the Island afforded. At first he was like one distracted, rav'd incessantly on his dear Bride, and exclaim'd against the cruelty and injustice of his Father; but absence, and the allurements of those Wantons, soon made him forget her, and he became pleas'd with those riotous Delights he was permitted to indulge in. It was not, till he cou'd hear her spoke of with all the Contempt imaginable, and not defend her, that he was permitted to return to Town; and by that time, Grief had made so great a change in her, who I have already told you was never Mistress of any extraordinary Charms, that she was scarce to be known. He made her a Visit, but how different, Oh great *Jupiter!* How vastly distant from what it had been, was his Behaviour now! Those Extasies at meeting, those Pangs at parting, those melting, dying Tendernesses which had been accustom'd to convince her that he lov'd, were now no more. He {212} excus'd his Silence indeed, and told her, that nothing cou'd give him so much Affliction, as the fears he should not be able to live with her in the manner he could wish, till the Death of his Father should leave him sole Master of his Aftions; but whenever that happen'd, he would compleat his own and her felicity, and in the mean time conjur'd her to be easy. But in what a manner did he say all this! His Words, his Air, his Gestures, seem'd all forc'd and study'd; too well, alas, she saw, that my enlivening Fire had left his Breast, and nothing now but cold Indifference reign'd. She was several times about to reproach him with so visible an Alteration, but he put it out of her power by some constrain'd Endearment, whenever he found by her looks, that she design'd any such thing. The little time he slay'd with her, which did not exceed an hour, he kept talking so fast himself, that he gave her not the liberty to utter much; and the hurry of her Spirits, between joy and hope, fear and surprize, join'd with his Intentions, depriv'd her of presence of Mind to speak and act as otherwise she would have done. She fretted after he was gone, that she had said no more, but console'd herself with the thoughts of what she would say when next she saw him, which he had told her should be in a few days. With Emotions suitable to the Circumstances she was in, did she expect him days, weeks, months, but found his Promises and her Hopes were vain. The natural Mildness of her Disposition made her endure this treatment with more Patience than most Women would have done; and tho' none could love with greater Ardency, wish with more Passion, nor feel the unutterable Tortures which spring from Tenderness abus'd with a nicer Sensibility, yet she chose rather to support 'em all, than make any Complaints which should be to the prejudice of his Reputation, who had so {213} cruelly inflicted 'em. But the *Chevalier* was of a different Humour; he resolv'd, tho' against her Will, to procure a Remedy for some part of the Misfortune she sustain'd. He knew there was a Method to be taken to enable her to live like the Wife of a Duke, and to that end, sent Persons proper to be employ'd in such Cases, to give him notice, That if he did not make a fitting Provision for her, the Law to which she should have recourse, would oblige him to do it. Such a Remonstrance both by the Father and Son had been long expected, and having before consulted what answer to make, assured those who were charged with the Commission, that every thing should be done becoming the Honour of the Duke, and that the Lady should be satisfy'd in all reasonable Demands, but insisted on having ten days time before any Prosecution should be enter'd: this was assented to, but they had other Views, which, designing as he was himself, the *Chevalier* saw not into. Before the expiration of the time, the Duke sent privately to entreat to speak with his Wife; he had contriv'd it so, as to be certain of the *Chevalier's* being abroad when his Messenger should arrive with a Billet, the Contents whereof were these.

> To the Dutchess *de Marbien*
>
> Tho' I know there are a thousand Appearances which may justly make you suspect my want of that, Tenderness I ought to have; yet I do not quite despair, but that a day will come, when you shall allow my Passion to be rather increas'd than diminish'd by the Obstacles it has met with. You know, my dearest Angel, that I ran the risque of everything to make you my Wife, and sure I have not had long enough the Blessing of calling you so, to be weary of it already. No, by the immortal Gods, you are dearer to me than my Soul, and were it {214} possible for you to guess the Torments I endure in an enforc'd Absence, and constrain'd Neglect, I am certain your soft, your gentle Nature, would more pity than condemn me. I could not live, were it not for the Hope of passing a thousand days of Joy with you, in recompence for those I linger out in fruitless Languishments without you: but why do I waste that precious time in writing to you, which may be much better employ'd in your dear, your wish'd for Society. I have an opportunity of seeing you unknown to my watchful Father, I beg therefore you will come with the Messenger, who will conduct you where I am—I die to see you, and to convince you, if possible, how much I am
>
> Tour most passionately Tender,
and ever Faithful Husband,
Marbien.

In a Postscript, *continu'd the Deity*, there were these Words.

> Fearing the News should by some means reach my angry Father's Ears I durst not venture to the *Chevalier's*, therefore entreat nothing may prevent my Happiness this opportunity. Heaven only knows when I shall gain another. Once more, till I see you, adieu.

Tho' there are few Women of more Penetration than this unhappy Lady, yet she saw not into the Snare laid for her—Surprize and Joy had blinded her. She went, transported with the recover'd Kindness of her dear Lord; these few and ill-dissembled Lines of Tenderness, were sufficient to chase from her Bosom all the Despair and gloomy Cares that had so long inhabited it. She was now all Rapture, even Doubt was now no more, so easy is it to deceive a Mind unpractis'd in Deceit, and so liable is Humanity to credit what they wish; nor did she in his presence entertain the least suspicion of his Truth. Her own excessive Rapture took {215} away the power of discerning if his were feign'd or real. After a thousand seemingly tender Protestations, and renew'd Vows of never changing Love, which his Father (too perfectly skill'd in the Art of Dissimulation) had instructed him to make, he at last told her, that not being able to command any part of the Estate till his Father's Death, he would settle all upon her which was allow'd for his own Subsistence: 'tis indeed, *said he*, but a trifle, but it is better than nothing, and is indeed my All; were it ten thousand times as much, I should with pleasure resign it to you; but the implacable Temper of my cruel Father makes him resolve to stand a suit of Law with yours, and I much fear his Interest at Court will weigh down the Justice of your Cause. Besides, *continu'd he*, should you proceed against him by those means which are threatned, it will add to his Inveteracy, and, perhaps, make him cut us both off; but in accepting this small moiety, which is in my own power to give you, he will discover not only the greatness of my Passion, but also the Generosity of your Temper, and be convinc'd, which yet he never was, that it was not on any mercenary score you consented to be mine. He clos'd his Insinuations with Pressures so tender, and so engaging to her who lov'd, that if she hesitated at all before she comply'd, it was only to return those delusive Caresses she receiv'd from him, with the sincerest and most ardent that a modest Bride could give. In fine, she readily acquiesced to every thing he said, and she had no sooner pronounc'd the Grant, than giving a Stamp with his Foot there came into the Room a Lawyer, and a couple of Persons for Witnesses, who had been plac'd by him in readiness, to draw up the Writings. She could not help being a little alarm'd to find he had dealt with so much Artifice, but having given her consent, would not recede from it. The {216} Settlement being made, there was no farther occasion for Dissimulation: The Duke immediately bethought him of some urgent Business, which he had till then forgot, begg'd her pardon, and took his leave.

The *Chevalier*, at her return home, was almost distracted, to find she had suffer'd herself to be so much impos'd on; and to her other Anxieties, had that of being perpetually reproach'd by the Family, for her too great Fondness and Easiness of Belief. They led her so ill a Life, that she was oblig'd to leave their House. She took private Lodgings in a retir'd Corner of the World, and contented herself to live (now she was the Wife of a Duke) in a more obscure and frugal manner, than she had done while only the Daughter of a private Gentleman: but the inward Disquiets of her troubled. Mind are not to be express'd; and what render'd her Agitations more perplexing than the worst of certain Evils could have done, was the racking Suspence her Thoughts were continually involv'd in; her Affection for her Husband would not permit her to judge of him with that Severity his Actions merited, and yet she could not, when she consuited her Judgment, believe he meant her fair. She writ him several Letters of Complaint; which, because she doubted an Interception, were not directed to his Father's; and the Stratagems she was oblig'd to contrive, to have them deliver'd into his own hands, were not only very expensive, but also difficult to be accomplish'd. She had sometimes Answers which seem'd so obliging from him, however, as made her not repent the trouble she had taken.

At length the Crisis of her Fate arriv'd; the Dukes Sincerity and Constancy was now on the proof. His Father yielded to Heaven a Life which had been the most remarkable, both for Good and Ill, of any Statesman of his Time. There was {217} now no longer a Pretence for living a-part; and, the Funeral over, she did not doubt but he would give her that Testimony of his Esteem. But, how did all her golden Expectations vanish! How, on a sudden, did all her high-rais'd Hopes sink down for ever, and leave to Misery and Despair all her succeeding Day! When she was indulging Contemplation on the Happiness she imagin'd herself about to enjoy when every Knock she heard at the Gate, she fancy'd was her dear Lord coming to fetch her from her obscure Retreat, and place her in his Arms and Palace; when every Pulse beat high with warm recruited Spirits—then! then arriv'd the killing Disappointment! Being told a strange Gentleman desir'd to speak with her, she made no question but he came from the Duke, because she admitted no Visiters, but such as were known to the House; and, ordering he should be admitted, was saluted by a grave Person, but one in whose reserv'd and gloomy Countenance she read part of her Doom. She receiv'd from his Hands a Letter, which, by the Superscription knowing it came from her Husband, she open'd with a mixture of Joy and Fear, and found in it these Lines.

To the Dutchess *De Marbien*

Next to the never having done an Injury, the best thing we can do, is, to repent of having been guilty of one. I am too sensible how infinitely I have sinned against the Obedience I ow'd the best of Fathers in my Marriage with you, ever to make my Crime become my Pleasure. As I cannot deny but you are my lawful Wife, I hope it will be a sufficient Punishment, that I have it not in my power to make choice of one whose Birth might be more agreeable. I could wish there were a Possibility of Happiness with you; but when I consider the prodigious Disparity between us, it cannot be. I {218} would have you, therefore, be as easy as you can in this Separation; and to make you so, as far as is consistent with my Quality, or Peace of Mind, I shall add considerably to your Allowance; and if I do not raise it to an Income which may support you as the Dutchess *de Marbien*, it shall, however, be more than the Daughter of a *Chevalier* could expect. This is all I can do for you, and desire you will not disturb the just Grief I am in for the loss of so excellent a Parent, by any of those fond Complaints you have hitherto been so full of Tenderness, either ill-time'd, or undesir'd, is always unwelcome; and that the continuance of yours ought to be so to me, is the Opinion of the World, as well as of him, who has no other Misfortune, but what his Unadvisedness has drawn on him, in becoming

Your Husband,
Marbien.

Had an instant Flash of Lightning darted upon her, it could not have blasted her more than the sight of this. It seem'd so grosly rude, as well as barbarous and unjust, that scarce could she believe 'twas in the power of Man to act with such Brutality; much more him who she had always look'd on as the most polite, and best-natur'd of his Sex. She read it again, and again, unwilling still to trust her Eyes, till he who brought it, told her, in a very abrupt manner, that she ought not to be surpriz'd at the Contents of that Letter, that she could not but be sensible how much the Duke had demean'd himself by marrying her, and that she must expect the daily Remonstrances he had from his Friends, for the Imprudence he had been guilty of, would, in time, open his Eyes to see his Misfortune, and oblige him to throw off a foolish Passion, which had been so much to the disadvantage {219} of his Reputation among People of true Sense. Here, not all her Stock of Patience could enable her to hear him run on in this manner, without Interruption. How, *cry'd she*, would it be to his Disreputation, to love the Woman he has made his Wife? A Woman who, both before and since her Marriage, may challenge the whole World to tax her with an Action that could taint her Fame? 'Tis vile! 'Tis monstrous this Affection! And below the Dignity of a Man of Sense or Honour to make use of! I woo'd not him; and if I was of a Birth inferiour, as I confess I am, why did he so strenuously press to raise me? I had been content in humble Meanness, nor had a Wish to know the envy'd Torments of the Great. O! Wou'd, (*continu'd she, bursting into Tears*) wou'd the Day which join'd our Hands had laid me in the Grave, I had been happier far. What am I a Gainer by these Nuptials, but knowledge of Disquiet?—A happy, happy *Maid* I was—am now a wretched *Wife.*

The Agony with which she utter'd these Words, would have mov'd any Heart less savage than his to whom they were directed. But he had Interests of his own, which took from him all that little Compassion he receiv'd from Nature, and was not one of those who are capable of being influenc'd by Honour or Justice: and tho' she condescended to entreat him even on her Knees, to move her Lord in her behalf, he quitted her without any Intentions of performing her Request.

The distress'd Dutchess, afterward, made several fruitless Attempts to come to the Speech of her Lord. He had order'd his Servants to deny her admittance to him; and she could never hear any thing from him for a long time, but by the Hands of the Person who had brought her that distracting Letter. At last, finding all her Endeavours {220} for a Reconciliation were in vain, she suffer'd her Friends (for she was now grown incapable of managing any thing herself) to procure the signing of that Addition to her Settlement which he had promis'd her. She then return'd to her Father's House, and was brought into so deplorable a Condition with continual Grief, that they employ'd all their Cares to comfort her.

But Passions the most violent, are seldom, if ever, immortal: time, and the Impossibility there appear'd that ever she should know a better State, made that she was in fit more easily on her. She grew more sedate, and at length gave hopes to those about her, that she would once more regain her former Tranquillity. But while she had been struggling with Afflictions, which none but those who *feel* can *comprehend*, the unthinking Duke was roving round the World in search of Pleasures. The Messenger which had brought her that cruel Letter, and had still continu'd to go to her while there was occasion for an Ambassador, was the chief Promoter of his Revels, and Partaker in them; not that he was of a disposition so sensible of Pleasure, but an indigent Fortune, with a mercenary Soul, made him find Advantages in the Riots of this young Nobleman, which he would never have reap'd from his good Sense, and cool Confideration.

After some Years of one continu'd Extravagance, the Duke, either thro' the natural Inconstancy of his Temper, or the Reflection how much he had been drawn in by his unworthy Companion to embezel his Estate, made him grow weary of it. He began to think there were Comforts in Retirement; and falling into the Conversation of the sober Part of Mankind, more than he had done, was persuaded by them to take home his Dutchess. He sent for her just at the time that she was {221} beginning to live easy without him: but that unhappy Lady is doom'd to everlasting Inquietudes; her Duty told her she must obey the Pleasure of her Husband. He brought her to his House, but Love had no part in his Resolution. He liv'd with her indeed, but she is with him as a House-keeper, as a Nurse; she manages his Affairs, attends him when indispos'd, and is the perpetual Subject to vent his Spleen on, when dissatisfy'd. Her Life is one continu'd Scene of Affliction; and tho' she bears it without complaining, she could not be able to support her Sufferings with Life, if the omnipotent *Jupiter* did not lengthen her Chain of Days, on purpose for an example to those Wives who think themselves unhappy, and fly out into Extravagancies for trifling Wrongs, when balanc'd against her's.

Thus, *pursu'd the Deity*, you see the Difference between Men: these two Stories are of unfortunate Matches, and yet the Persons the direct Opposites of each other. The accomplish'd *Beaujeune* used with the greatest *Civility* the *worst* humour'd of her Sex, whom he married but by *Compulsion;* the Duke *de Marbien*, with the utmost *Barbarity* one of the very *best*, whom his *own Inclination* and Sollicitations alone had made his Wife.

But having related the Misfortunes which these two Families have brought on themselves, I cannot pass over in silence those of a *third*; which, if possible, exceed the others, and will give you an Example of Mutability, such as perhaps you have not often heard of.

{222} The History of the Chevalier *Blantier, Olimpia*, and the unfortunate *Silenia*

Blantier was left, by his careful Father, in possession of such immense Riches, that, tho' he was descended from no more than a Race of Citizens, he had a good pretence to match among the Nobility; and it was his Mother's Hope, as well as her Ambition, that he would do so. But the fair *Olimpia*, a Nymph of his own degree, but far inferiour in Wealth, appear'd to him to have Charms far beyond any he could find at Court. She is indeed very handsome, and before she grew fat, was perfectly well shaped, and genteel, has a good deal of Gaity in her Humour, and a great Share of Wit. At first he address'd her but in private, and was not quite resolv'd whether he should prosecute his Pretentions so far as Marriage, or not; but the Affair soon took air, and his Mother, to her very great Vexation, was inform'd of it. I will not prolong the little Account I have to make you, by any Repetitions of the Remonstrances[103] she made him: I shall only tell you, that, beside the Disappointment, she consider'd such a Marriage would be to the high Expectations she had form'd to herself; she had also an extreme Aversion to the Father and Mother of *Olimpia*, and was withal, one of the worst-temper'd Women in the World.

You may therefore judge with what Inveteracy she set herself to cross his Inclinations there. There was nothing she could invent of ill, but she reported it of her; and join'd to her Commands, Insinuations so artful and well prepar'd, that in a {223} short time she brought him off, not only from visiting her at all, but also to carry his Addresses elsewhere.

Had she liv'd, 'tis probable she might have seen him marry'd according to her wish: but how ridiculously industrious are Mortals, who *waste* the precious Time they might *enjoy*, in racking Cares and Schemes, which, 'tis a thousand to one if they live to see accomplish'd! And how vain is it to think to disappoint the Decrees of Fate! When she had most business, as she thought, for Life, Death put a period to her Stratagems, and robb'd her busy, bustling Spirit of the power of farther Action: yet preserving her Resolution to the last, even when the convulsive Pangs,

---

103 [*remonstrance*, French, from *remonstrate:* show; discovery.]

which parted Soul and Body, shook her unyielding Heart with the greatest Violence, she order'd her Son to draw near the Bed: and taking hold of one of his Hands, and eagerly pressing it between her's, after having prepar'd him for what she had to say, by reminding him of the Duty that was owing to a Parent, and that their Commands ought no less punctually to be obey'd after their Death, than when alive and bringing to his memory some tender Instances of the Indulgence with which she had treated him. I fear, *said she*, that, when I am no more, you will return to *Olimpia*, and that unworthy Woman will at last triumph over all the Care I have taken to prevent your Ruin. He assured her, That he never would think of her, and begg'd her to be satisfy'd: but that was impossible to make her; and she told him, she could not die till he had taken an Oath never to marry her. This he scrupled not to do, and imprecated ten thousand Curses on himself and Posterity, if he broke it.

Now I am easy, *resum'd she*; I could not resign my Soul till you had given me this Satisfaction; may the Vow you have taken be register'd in {224} Heaven, and while you keep it, may all the Gods conspire to make you bless'd: but if you swerve from it, or endeavour by any Equivocation to evade it, may you be more curst than Fiends can wish you, eternal Disappointments be your Lot on Earth, and all the Horrors of the Damn'd hereafter.

These Words were her last; she died, and was lamented as Parents generally are by their Children, thought on with extravagant Grief at first, but in a short time forgot to be no more remembred. In how little a while she was by her Son *Blantier*, you may guess, when I shall tell you, that she had not been laid in the Earth full three Moons, before despising or not reflecting on the Vow she had extorted, he married *Olimpia* with a Pomp and Magnificence, which prov'd how happy he thought himself in being her Husband. They lived for some time together indeed, in a manner which could call the Conduct of neither of them in question; and one would think, that if either was ordain'd to fail in Duty to the other, it must have been *Olimpia*, for it seems scarce credible that he, who to make her his, had broke thro' a dying Parent's Request, had sacrific'd his Interest, and dared all the Punishments which wait on Perjury, should not love to a more than ordinary degree. For a time I must acknowledge he did love, at least had all the Symptoms of my Influence; but Nature never form'd a Man of so inconstant and wavering a Disposition. *Olimpia* marry'd, *Olimpia* enjoy'd, there remain'd nothing for him to desire; and in the fair *Silenia*, her Sister, he imagin'd there was a hoard of Charms with which he never should be cloy'd. *Silenia*, who was not the thousandth part so lovely as her Sister, and whom, till he had obtain'd the other, he never sent one single Sigh for, was now the Goddess of his Affections; and the impossibility there seem'd {225} of gratifying his Passion, made it blaze more fierce; he burn'd, he languish'd, he almost dy'd with the consuming Violence of Wishes in

Revulsion, (for long it was before he durst to speak his Anguish) and poor *Olimpia* found, without being able to guess at the reason, an Alteration in his Behaviour, which gave her Disquiets pretty near those he felt: she took the liberty of complaining to him sometimes of a Coldness which she hoped she had not merited; but whenever he found her beginning on that Theme, he flung from her, and would return no Answer. At length perceiving he express'd an extraordinary Affection and Regard to her Sister, she entreated her to talk to him about it; for tho' she lov'd him not with that Passion which he had profess'd for her, yet being a Woman of Virtue and Good-nature, she could not well endure to see the Man who was become her Husband under any Anxieties he should refuse to make her Partner in; she thought it her Duty so far to pry into his Troubles, as to enable her, if possible, to console them, or endeavour to remedy them if in her power. *Silenia* willingly undertook the Office, having a kind of Tenderness for her lovely Brother, which even I, the God of soft Desire, scarce know how to account for; it was more warm than that of Kindred, yet free from any Wish to have him other. She thought her Sister infinitely happy in having such a Husband, yet thought of it without Envy; she felt a secret Pleasure whenever he took the freedom of kissing or embracing her, yet suffered no Uneasiness whenever she saw him do it to others; she had none of those pleasing tingling Thrillings, which in the dawn of my Influence play round the throbbing Heart, and make it bound with Rapture. Nor had she any of the Inquietudes which attend Desire; she knew nor Hope, nor {226} Fear, nor Jealousy; what she was possess'd of, could properly be term'd no more than a tender Friendship, but then it was such a Friendship which the Charms of his Person and Conversation more inspir'd than the Nearness of his Alliance. In fine, it was a Prepossession which rendred it extremely dangerous for her to see or hear him; but as she was wholly innocent and ignorant of what she felt, she could not be expected to be on her guard. The delight she took in discoursing with him, made her prodigiously satisfied that *Olimpia* had made choice of her in this Affair: and being told by her, that he was in a Summer-House at the farther end of the Garden, she tript hastily to him with a Pleasure in her Mind, which no Expression can describe. She found him reclin'd on a *Safoye*; he was in a thoughtful melancholy Posture, and saw her not, 'till she was come very near him; and giving him, with an innocent Freedom, a little childish Pat on the Shoulder, cry'd, What ails you, my dear Brother? Why do you leave us? As I have sufficiently explained to you of what nature were his Desires, you need not be told what kind of Agitations he felt at this Salutation: he started up; and returning her Kindness with a strenuous Embrace, made her sit down by him, holding her fast with one hand, and with the other supporting his Head, which he lean'd on it, the better to have the opportunity of gazing on her Face, and catching that Breath she was employing in the Business she came about. But when she entreated him to tell her the occasion of his late Chagrin, and from what Source his late love of Solitude and Contemplation had arose, it was not in his power to restrain letting loose all the tempestuous Emotions of his Soul.

He could nor, tho' Death had been the Consequence, prevent his Passion from discovering itself: {227} And is it you, *he cry'd,* my too lovely Sister, who enquire the Cause of my Disorders? Can you, who are the Cause yourself, be ignorant of it? Me! *Interrupted she, (with an unaffected Innocence)* alas! what have I done? I never even in thought offended you. Yes, *resumed he, (and while he spoke his Eyes shot Glances, and his Limbs trembled with such Convulsive Agaries, as might have inform'd her what it was he meant, had not her Youth and Unexperience kept her still in wonder)* yes, this lovely Mouth, these Eyes, *continued he,* this Shape, this Air, all this Heaven of Beauty, has offended me beyond Forgiveness, and I must be revenged, my sweet *Silenia,* I must upon your Charms, or die in the Attempt.

With these Words he clasp'd her at once to his Breast; and joining close to her's his burning Lips, prevented her from making any Reply to what he had said, if she had been Mistress of the Power: but his Behaviour so unexpected, so strange, so different from all she had ever been accustomed to, either from him, or any other Person, rendred her incapable of Speech; and when he had given her Mouth the liberty of opening, by removing to her Bosom his furious Kisses, she had no Voice to utter more than, Alas! what is it you mean, my Brother? Oh! Call me not, *said he,* by that detested Name; that Bar to my Desires, too long has rack'd me with the Tortures of the Damn'd; but I will now surmount it, and give my self to *Silenia* by a Tye more near than that of Relative.

He staid not for Consent, but taking the advantage of her Surprize, perpetrated his horrid Wishes, and compleated her Undoing. Being bred in too great an Ignorance of the World, is often equally fatal with a too great Knowledge; for if the latter lays a young Maid more open to criminal Desires, {228} the former renders her incapable of defending herself against 'em, she is betray'd and lost before she knows she is in danger: Poor *Silenia,* at least, prov'd this Truth, ruin'd by her unwary Innocence! The cruel Rapture over, Horror, and Grief, and Shame, made her as incapable of Speech as Astonishment had done before. A stream of Tears were all the Reproaches she could utter, and those fell down her Cheeks in such abundance, that the cruel occasion of them fearing he should be betray'd by her Sorrows, omitted no Argument which might console her: the Tenderness she ever had for him, and which this Action had not eras'd, made her willing to listen to every thing he could say in his Vindication; and where the Heart takes part, the weakest Allegations appear forcible. She began to think, because he told her so, that it would be unjust to hate him for that which nothing but Excess of Love had forc'd him to commit; and suffered herself to be convinc'd by him, That the Action they had done was not a Crime in reality, but only represented as such to the World for the advantage of the Priesthood, that all the Shame lay in the discovery, and that if she would be as careful in concealing what had happen'd as he would be, they might pass their time in an eternal round of Pleasure. The greatest difficulty lay in the account her Sister would expect her to give of their Conversation. At last it was resolv'd, that she should say he had told her, his late Uneasiness had sprung from some dispute he had lately had with his Brother concerning some part of the Estate, which, by their Father, had been left between them. This seemed the least liable to detection, because that Gentleman was a little before that time gone some Miles into the Country, and *Blantier* very well knew, at his return, would easily be persuaded to confirm what he had said, if any questions should be ask'd.

{229} Thus all Parties for a while were easy; *Olimpia*, not in the least suspecting the Truth of what her Sister told her, was satisfy'd that her Husband's Chagrin proceeded rather from any Cause than a misunderstanding of her Behaviour, as her Fears had at first suggested. He was perfectly happy in the gratification of his unlawful Wishes, and the freedom of indulging them as often as opportunity would permit. *Silenia* contented herself with the thoughts of being belov'd by the Man who appear'd to her the most charming of his Sex, and all remorse being overcome by his Reasons, had no stinging Reflections on the Injury she did her Sister, or her own Undoing, but persevered in her Crime without the least consideration that she was guilty of any.

But divine *Justice* would not permit the poor *Olimpia*'s Wrongs always to go unpunish'd, nor would the chaste *Diana* pardon a Maid who had so easily been brought to violate her Honour; the hour came on apace which was to plunge the guilty Pair in Misfortunes equal to their Crime, or those Transports to which they gave a loose.

Their Amour had not been of any long continuance, before *Silenia* found herself with Child; she was not more alarm'd at it than was *Blantier*; he dreaded with reason the Consequence such a discovery would produce, and reflected more deeply than she, wholly taken up with her Passion, had the power of doing. He therefore thought it convenient to remove her, before any notice could be taken of those disorders incident to Women in her Condition; but as they all liv'd together with her Father and Mother, there was no such thing as a plausible Excuse to be made for her leaving them: it was therefore concluded, that she should go away by stealth, and that he should hire a House for her in the most distant part of the Town, where changing {230} her Name, she might live unfound by those she belong'd to, or unsuspected by those she should be among.

The House they all liv'd in, was about three Miles distant from town, and *Silenia* being the Darling of both her Parents, was never suffered to go out without one of them, her Sister, or Brother, or some of the Servants with her, so that it seem'd one of the greatest Difficulties in nature how she should make her escape: at last *Blantier* contriv'd the means in this manner. There was a Woman who had been often serviceable to him on the account of some former Amours, and having good Experience of her Fidelity to him, ventured to trust her with this. It was by her advice he hired a Chariot and Six, which the was to go in, and at an appointed hour wait with it in a little Lane near the House. He was privately to acquaint *Silenia* with it, and the time and place, and to stay at home himself the whole Evening, to prevent any suspicion of his having a hand in her flight, and to observe how the Family took it, and by what method they would endeavour to recover her. All succeeded according to their Wishes; *Silenia* watchful of the hour her dear Undoer had told her, she would find the Chariot, drest only in her Nightgown and Slippers under the pretence of standing at the Gate for the Air, when she saw nobody near, flew from all which ought to have been valuable to her. The punctual Confidant was ready to attend her, and away they drove with all possible speed to Town.

She had not been an hour departed, before she was miss'd; the Gardens, the Fields, all the neighbouring Houses were search'd for her, but no Intelligence could be heard. Old *Meriton*, (for so was her Father call'd) and his Wife, rav'd like Persons wholly void of Reason or Consolation; *Olimpia* was under a very great concern, and young *Meriton* {231} her Brother seem'd stupify'd with Surprize and Grief. *Blantier* affected an Affliction equal to any of them, and ask'd a thousand incoherent Questions, as, *How was it possible she should be gone? And who could it be that had seduc'd her to such an Elopement?* But there were none there capable of satisfying his Curiosity, if he really had been prompted by that to interrogate in this manner. Old *Meriton* at last bethought him of breaking open her Cabinet, to search if there were any Letters that might give some light into the Affair; but there were none, only in tumbling the things that were in it over, a little piece of Paper fell out, which *Olimpia* taking up, found it to be her Sister's writing, and contain'd these Lines:

> If Love's a Deity uncontroll'd and free,
> As all who have experienc'd it agree;
> How is't a Crime when Power supreme compels,
> If the fond Heart from Reason's Laws rebels?
> That arbitrary Passion laughs at Sin,
> And bears down all the Bars of Bleed and Kin!

She read this over several times, and knowing her Sister not to be very poetically inclin'd, was certain that she wrote them in some very extraordinary Agitation of Mind; she doubted not but she was in Love where Reason had not warranted her Passion; but the Words *Blood* and *Kin* gave her some Alarms, which she knew not well how to interpret, nor declar'd till a long time after: she put up the Paper carefully, however, and could not get it out of her head, but that she should, some time or other, discover the Meaning more clearly than she wish'd to do.

The Search for *Silenia*, by her careful Family, was extended to as many places as they cou'd have a Hope, tho' never so distant a one, of hearing of {232} her, and continu'd for many Weeks; but no Intelligence arriving, the Affliction of her lamenting Parents is not to be conceiv'd: but *Olimpia* to the Grief for the Misfortune of a Sister she had lov'd so well, had other Disquiets, which were, if possible, more terrible to endure. The Verses she had found in *Silenia*'s Cabinet, the many Tendernesses she had seen between her Husband and that unhappy Maid, and the little opportunity she ever had of conversing with any other Man, came all at once into her Mind, and she trembled with the apprehension, that she should, one day, find her Suggestions had been but too justly grounded.

Yet how dreadful soever the *Certainty* may be, *Suspence* is what no Mortal can sustain when there's a possibility of being resolv'd; and being one day full of jealous Emotions, it came into her thoughts to make a little tryal of *Blantier*; and as they were talking of *Silenia*, and he, according to his custom, bitterly condemning the Man who had betray'd her from her Honour and her Friends. He deserves, indeed, all the Reproaches we can load him with, *said she* and the more, because it is most certainly one, from whom we cou'd not expect such treatment, one, I fear, too near ally'd to be suspected. She look'd earnestly in his Face while she was speaking, and perceiv'd a visible Alteration in it; but taking no notice of it to him, I can show you, *resum'd she*, a little piece of writing of her's, which allows sufficient room for my conjecture. How! *cry'd be, with a faultering and confus'd Accent*, Has she left in writing any Testimony of her Folly? Yes, *reply'd* Olimpia, (*as much confounded to find by his disorder so much reason to believe the truth of her Suspicions, as he had been at her Assertion*) she has left something which is methinks too plain. With these Words she pull'd the Paper out of her Pocket, and gave it to him. 'Tis impossible to represent in {233} what manner he look'd, when reaching his hand, which trembled as he took it; but all that can be conceiv'd of Horror, of Shame, of Guilt, was too conspicuously delineated for his unhappy Wife not to perceive it. He doubted not but the Secret was discover'd, and that in this fatal Scroll he should read his own Name, and was ready to fall on his Knees, confess the Crime he had been guilty of, and implore her Forgiveness and Secrecy; when casting his Eyes on it, to see in what manner she had betray'd herself and him, and finding nothing of what he expected there, he immediately recover'd his Assurance, and instead of acknowledging he was the Person had occasion'd its being writ, ask'd *Olimpia*, what she meant by imagining this could unravel any part of the Mystery? But she who had observ'd all the Changes had been in him from the first of her mentioning it, was, by this time, work'd up to a pitch of

Rage too high to admit restraint or dissimulation, and plainly let him know her Thoughts. Fear of detection being over, he now asserted his Innocence, seem'd to resent her suspecting him of an Act so vile, and wish'd ten thousand Curses on himself if guilty. All he could say, however, was ineffectual to persuade her to believe him, and he flung out of the Room, as he said, to prevent his Passion from rising to any excess; but in truth, to conceal the disorder this Discourse had rais'd in him. Tho' *Olimpia* had no longer the power to conceal her Doubts from him, she had been ever most careful not to give a hint of what she thought to her troubled Parents; but her Discretion now was render'd fruitless: her Mother hapning to pass by the Room they were in, and hearing 'em pretty loud, had the Curiosity to listen, and heard distinctly all the latter part of what had been spoke between 'em of this Affair. *Blantier* had no sooner left the Chamber, than she {234} enter'd it, and demanded of *Olimpia* what had been the subject of their Conversation; but that Lady thinking it utterly improper to let her know, both because she thought it would be a considerable addition to the Grief she was already in, and that she was too well acquainted with the Duty of a Wife to divulge the Faults of her Husband, as artfully as she could evaded what she ask'd: but the other, who had but for form sake desired her to repeat that which she knew before, acquainted her with what she had done, and that she could not help joining in her fears, that it was indeed by no other than her Brother-in-law, the indiscreet *Silenia* had been betray'd. They had a long and melancholy Consultation what was best to be done to make a perfect discovery, and at length it was agreed, that a trusty Servant should be employ'd to watch him wheresoever he went; not doubting but by that means, they should find out where she was plac'd, in case he were the Person for whose sake she had made this Elopement. Accordingly one who they could depend on was made choice of, and the very next day *Blantier* going abroad, the Fellow enter'd on his Commission: but the artful Transgressor was now upon his guard; his Wife's Behaviour, and the suspicion the Verses had created in her, was sufficient to make him think he should be observ'd: he therefore after his coming to Town, chang'd Coaches so often, called at so many places, and frequently took the advantage of going thro' Houses which had Passages in them to other Streets, that it would not have been in the power of all the Eyes of *Argus*[104] to have discover'd the end of his progress; and the unavailing Spy was oblig'd to return as ignorant of what he was to learn, as when he set out.

The next day he did the same, and the next to that, and so on for many succeeding ones, till, tir'd with the fruitless Expectation, they resolved to {235} desist sending him; yet persevering in the Opinion they had conceiv'd, that *Blantier* was

---

104 [Reference to Ovid, Hera transferred *Argus's eyes* to the tail of the peacock.]

really the Man to whom they owed this Misfortune, and the more confirm'd in it, by the Caution he took, they resolved to proceed with him by other Measures; and one Evening, when there was no body in the Room but himself and them, the old Gentleman and his Wife told him, without any Evasion, that they were certain he was the Person who had brought this Dishonour on their Family; but if he would restore their Child to them, and by his future Kindness to *Olimpia*, make what reparation was in his power for the Injury he had done her, they would forgive what was past. They persisted in their Accusation, he in his Denials, with equal Violence; and the Contest grew at last so high, that it ended in a Quarrel; the next day he remov'd from their House, taking *Olimpia* with him; so that that afflicted Lady, to her other Causes of Disquiet, had the addition of being separated from the most endearing Parents, and obliging Brother in the World: the latter of whom in a short time afterwards fell sick of a Distemper, for which Physick had no Cure. This young Gentleman, being of a most soft and gentle Disposition, was struck to the Soul at this unhappy Disunion of the Family, who were all equally dear to him. One Sister ruin'd and dishonour'd, as it was probable, by him who was the Husband of the other; and she also torn from the Embraces of her Friends, by him to whom Duty exacted this Obedience; both his Parents in an Agony of Grief, which wanted but little of bringing them to their Graves. All this, reflected on too deeply, threw him into a Consumption, of which in less than too Moons he expir'd.

Silenia was all this time as happy as the continu'd Fondness of the Man she love'd could, make her, {236} and being very young, and of a Temper not much addicted to Consideration, felt very little regret, at the Sufferings which she could not but be sensible her Family endur'd. *Blantier*, indeed, always conceal'd the worst part of it from her, fearing to throw her into a Discontent, which to a Woman in her Condition might have been fatal; designing as soon as she was eas'd of her Burden, to make some plausible pretence for her returning home, not only because he found it an Expence more than his Estate, large as it is, could well enable him to support; but also that he found it would be very much for his own Ease otherwise: for this passionately enamour'd Lady expected him to be every day with her, without considering how impossible it was he should be so, without creating suspicion at home. And indeed it was his being so often abroad, where no body could find out, that had made the Family at home so positive he was with her: but she either not consider'd this, or not regarded it, and was distracted when she saw him not, tho' I have already told you with what Caution he was oblig'd to proceed, when he did visit her. All these Reasons join'd to another, without which the rest would have been of no effect, his Passion satiated, made him resolve to quit her, tho'he carefully conceal'd his Intentions till after she was deliver'd; which, when she had been about twenty days, and she, as 'twas believ'd, entirely out of danger, he came to her, and having a Countenance of exceeding Melancholy, she ask'd the Cause: young *Meriton, said he,* your Brother, is dead. Dead! *cry'd she, (prodigiously alarm'd, for living in that obscure manner, she heard little of the News of the World; and he, as I have already taken notice, conceal'd all that he thought might give her any Uneasiness)* of what Distemper? *Pursu'd she.* A broken Heart, *reply'd he*; they say the Grief he took at your {237} Departure has been his Death. There was no need now for him to let her know what he design'd concerning her Return, of which this Account was but the Preparative: *reflection* ever till this moment a Stranger to her Mind, now rush'd upon her in the most dreadful Form! She now thought as she ought to have done long before she saw the Crime she had been guilty of with open Eyes, and acknowledg'd the Punishment to be just. Oh my unhappy Brother! *Did she cry*; has my Dishonour been so fatal to thee? What, Oh what must not I, the cursed Cause, expect? Perhaps my Father too, and wretched Mother, will fall like Victims to *Silenia*'s Shame. With these words she fell fainting on the Bed, where she was sitting, and tho' the Care that was taken of her soon brought her to herself, it was but to renew those Agonies, which threw her into Convulsions too fierce, too violent, for her not yet recruited Strength to struggle with, she expir'd within the space of twenty-four Hours. *Blantier* seem'd like one distracted when the News was brought him (for he was not present at her last moments) but her Death brought him too many Conveniences not to render him consolable. He now thought himself secure from all Detection that he was the Person who had ruin'd her; and tho' he was sorry the Catastrophe had proved so fatal, yet he would never have enjoy'd much Ease of Mind, had it happen'd otherwise. He gave orders for her Funeral to be celebrated with a Magnificence suitable to the first Tenderness he had for her, nothing being omitted befitting a Woman of Quality but *Escutcheons*; and those were wholly improper, because there was more than a possibility the *Herse* might be seen by some who might be acquainted with the *Arms*.

But as much as he hugg'd himself in an assur'd Security, the Secret he had been so fortunate to {238} preserve in her Life-time, was after her Death reveal'd at full, and by a way which should, methinks, deter offending Mortals from persevering in their Crimes, when what is most conceal'd from human Sight is to the Eye of Heaven explored, and by the most unthought-of means oftentimes discover'd. Divine *Astrea* would not permit the mournful Parents of this undone Departed to remain for ever in an uncertainty so perplexing; but, to the holy Priest, who, unknowing who she was, had ministred the funeral Rites, appear'd in her own heavenly Form, and told him all the Mystery, commanding him to visit that afflicted Family, and let them know the Crime and Punishment of their unhappy Child. Full of the Goddess, the venerable Father repair'd immediately to the House of *Meriton*, and disclosed the Sacred Mandate; the wretched Pair knew well his Character, and doubted not the Truth of what he utter'd; but to convince the unbelieving World, they accompany'd him to Town, and being directed by him to the Tomb where the unfortunate *Silenia* was laid, had the Stone remov'd, and the cold lifeless Corse expos'd to view; Tho' vastly chang'd from what she was, who ever had seen her in her Life, might easily have known her now; and besides, she happen'd to have a Ring on at her Death, which being too small, could not be easily taken off, and was bury'd: this was a Jewel too well known to have belong'd to the Family, and serv'd as a Demonstration to those who at first seem'd to make a doubt if it were she. It would be needless to repeat to you the Cries and Lamentations of these unhappy Parents at finding their Child; but finding her for ever lost to them and to the World, you may believe their Grief was proportion'd to the Cause: but resolving to revenge those Injuries which had brought her to so untimely an End, as far as was in {239} their power, after having by diligent Enquiry trac'd out the Truth of every thing, they commenc'd a Suit of Law with *Blantier*, which was near being the Ruin of his Fortune, as it was of his Character with all Men of Honour, Virtue, or common Morality. The little Infant, that Product of his and the unfortunate *Silenia*'s Passion, old *Meriton* took home, *Blantier* being compell'd to give it a Portion large enough to compensate for its unhappy Birth. But I must not forget to mention the Behaviour of *Olimpia* in this Affair, who show'd an Example of conjugal Duty, which can never be too much admir'd. Her Husband convicted of the Guilt, she was commanded by her Parents, on the pain of their eternal Displeasure, to forsake the Bed and House of a Man who had so grosly wrong'd her, and dishonour'd her Family; but she endeavour'd first, by mild Answers, to dissuade them from insisting on her doing an Action so unbecoming the Title she had now taken on her, and finding they were still resolute, chose rather to disobey them, (a thing she had never done before) than fail in that, which her Marriage-Vow had made her Husband's Due, and which no ill Usage can justly afford a Pretence for cancelling; tho' how terrible it was to her gentle Nature to incur the Curse of those, whose Blessing she was born to hope, can only be conceiv'd by a Soul equally tender, equally virtuous. But what return has she for this forgiving Goodness? *Blantier* having ended his Law-Suit, soon forgot *Silenia*, the natural Inconstancy and Mutability of his Temper, made him not capable of even thinking for any long time on the Misfortunes his Amour with her had brought on him. A new Object happen'd in his way, he was charm'd with her, Desire taught him Eloquence, and Eloquence inspir'd her with Gratitude; with her he now passes the greatest part of {240} his Days and Nights, and *Olimpia*, still maintaining her first Maxim, that nothing ought to provoke a Wife against her Husband, is a Pattern of Patience, which there are but few will imitate.

I applaud her heroick Virtue, *said the* Stranger, and think there is infinitely more Greatness of Soul in suffering well, than in resenting Injuries, tho' in ever so justifiable a manner: had *Olimpia* quitted her transgressing Husband, she could not have been condemn'd, his Perjury and Inconstancy seem'd to deserve no less; but in continuing with him, her Superiority of Genius enabling her to look down rather with Contempt than Anger on the Injuries done her, seems, methinks, to demand a Statue of Gold to be set up in memory of such transcendent Goodness.

And yet, *reply'd the* God, there are People vile enough to put an ill Construction on this exalted Virtue; she is frequently represented as a Woman that has her Designs in what she does, that being addicted to Pleasures herself, the best way to have her own conceal'd, is to take no notice of her Husband's, that doubtless there were Faults on her side, or a Man who married her only thro' Inclination, would not so suddenly have withdrawn it and a thousand such like *Innuendo's*, to lessen the Brightness of a Character which would eclipse their own. *Envy*, and her cursed Offspring *Detraction*, have here so many Votaries, that few can 'scape their prevalence; they bear down all before them, not even the noblest Sons of Fame, back'd with a thousand Glories, and their Heads adorn'd with Wreaths form'd by the hand of the immortal *Pallas*, have Defence against the Venom of those encourag'd *Fiends*; aloft they soar, and with *Titanian* Boldness combat *Heaven* in the Persons of its Favourites. Too much of this sad Truth you will discover, when I anon shall lead you to those {241} proud Palaces, whose gilded Spires seem'd to o'erlook the World. *There* shall you see the busy Courtier kneeling for Preferment, and while he sues to obtain his Suit, mingle with his Intercessions some vile Invective against the Man, his *Patron* looks on as a Foe, tho' perhaps only so to his Vices, and has more real Worth, tho' less Power, than the great shining Nothing he addresses. *There* shall you see a General cover'd with honourable Wounds, and loaden with his Spoils after a long Campaign, returning home, and (while on his Chariot-Wheels Millions of Wretches, whom his Valour has preserv'd, hang clinging to the Spokes, and almost deifying their Deliverer) some stand in Corners grinning as he passes, and laughing loud at the deluded Multitude; then turn aside, and say he has fought well, indeed, but better had it been for his Country, if he had ne'er been born: and then run on, enumerating Vices, which perhaps he is infinitely more free from than his base Accusers. *There*, what will raise your Wonder more, you'll see the Father envy the Son, and seek to blast his rising Glories; you'll behold a Mother half mad with Rage, because her Daughter matches to a Title above her own, and claims Precedence of her. You'll see a Statesman, full of Ambition and a Thirst of Grandeur, refuse a proffer'd Coronet,[105] lest his Co-

---

105 [*coronetta*, Italian, the diminutive of *corona*, a crown: an inferiour crown worn by the nobility. The coronet of a duke is adorned with strawberry leaves; that of a marquis has leaves with pearls interposed; that of an earl raises the pearls above the leaves; that of a viscount is surrounded with only pearls; that of a baron has only four pearls.]

equal in Authority should also be alike distinguish'd. You'll see a celebrated Beauty deform those Graces she receiv'd from Nature, to introduce a Mode, which takes from others all their power of charming. So strangely does *Envy* influence the Soul, that those possess'd of it, with pleasure quit their own Designs and Views, to ruin those of others, but I will not postpone your Admiration, you will discover Purposes, which, unseen, would not gain credit. In the meantime, let us return to this Assembly, and if there be any Persons {242} in it worthy of your Observation, besides those I have already pointed out, I shall acquaint you with their Characters.

The *Stranger* prostrated himself on the Ground in thankful Adoration, and had continued in that Posture much longer, if the benignant Power had not suddenly rais'd him, and commanded him to cast his Eyes on a Gentleman of a very graceful Appearance, but in whose Face all the Characters of Despair and Grief were imprinted in such lively Colours, that whoever look'd on it, might read his Mind labour'd under some irremediable Woe. That, *said the Divine Bestower of the supremest Bliss*, is the Count *Casseville*; he married, without consulting me, a young Widow, whose vast Jointure he expected would support him in a fashion suitable to his Birth, (having lost great part of his Estate in this enchanted Well;) but mark the Consequence of Matches, where Interest is the only Inducement! she consented to be his Wife, only as a Shelter for her to pursue her amorous Engagements with another with more Security. On this young Favourite she lavishes all that Wealth which had induc'd the Count to marry her; and in the room of advancing himself by her means, he is forc'd to retrench even those necessary Expences, without which a Man of Quality makes but a very indifferent figure in the World: for without suffering him to receive any Support from her Income, she obliges him to pay out of his, for even her wearing Clothes and Jewels. The Misfortune, indeed, is justly fallen on him; for being before contracted to a young Lady of more Beauty than Fortune, he barbarously quitted her for this Widow, tho' he knew the loss of his Affection would render her the most miserable Woman in the World; she is now in a Melancholy, which is pretty near Frenzy. He pities her too late, and has this addition to his {243} unhappy State, to think that he deserves no better. Quite different is the Circumstance of yon gay, well-dress'd Spark;[106] he is married to a Woman of much the same Constitution as that of the Count's Lady, but she is so far from diminishing the little Fortune of her Husband, that being beloved by a Person who is a Favourite at Court, has made a very considerable Post for him, the Purchase of her Favours. But hold! I see two Gentle-

---

106 [*spearca*, Saxon; *sparke*, Dutch: a lively, showy, splendid, gay man. It is commonly used in contempt or for a lover.]

men, who by their Gestures seem to be greatly incens'd with each other ; the one is the Marquiss *de Bon-Cœr*, the other the Chevalier *le Brune*; they quit the Crowd, and take their way toward the Fields—let us follow and observe them; I know the occasion of their Quarrel, and it may be worth your pains to be a witness of the Issue. They are both Men of good Sense and Spirit, and the provocation given by the Marquiss, is a justifiable pretence for the other to call him to account.

The *God* here cast about the *Stranger* a Vapour, which rendered him invisible to mortal Eyes, and in a moment, by the incomprehensible Power of Divine Transition, they were on the Ascent of a little Hill, whence they could easily discern all that pass'd below. Immediately the Antagonists appear'd, and having chose the Vale for the Decision of their Contest, were near enough for the attentive Youth to hear every word of their Discourse; the Marquiss was the first that spoke: in compliance with your Request, *le Brune, said he*, I have accompany'd you thus far; but as we have been Friends, would willingly know for what reason you throw off that Name, before we proceed to Extremities, which may be fatal to one or both of us. If there were a possibility, *cry'd the* Chevalier *fiercely*, to add to the Injury you have already done me, it would be trifling with my just Revenge, in counterfeiting an Ignorance of the Cause. Have you not, in the most {244} base, ungenerous manner, forfeited all the Respect my Soul once paid you? Have you not wrong'd me in the most tender part? And by violating the Honour of my Sister, thrown an eternal Stain on a Family, which if less enobled than your own, is yet as brave, as worthy, and more ancient. 'Tis you alone, *reply'd the Marquiss coolly*, who stain your House's Honour, and are the Ruin of your Sister's Fame, by this inconsiderate Passion. Her Virtue never has by me been sully'd, and I believe her pure as Innocence itself; nor did I ever hear her but by you accus'd. What need of Accusation, when Conviction's plain? *Interrupted* le Brune; she has herself confess'd the Folly of her easy Nature, and your undoing Arts? Herself confess'd it! *Cry'd the Marquiss, strangely alarm'd.* Yes, *pursued the other*; a Letter of yours, directed to her, fell by accident into my hand. I knew the Writing to be yours, and a little surpriz'd at the Privacy with which the Messenger would have deliver'd it, and not being able to imagine what Affair could induce you to send to her in that manner; I broke it open, and found, what I could have wish'd never to have known, Rage and Grief were near depriving me of my Senses; o'erwhelm'd with both, I flew to her Chamber, and. partly by Menaces, partly by Persuasions, at last wrung all the shameful Secret from her. The Marquiss, who had been far from imagining the other knew he had so much reason for what he had done, stood speechless for some moments; then coming out of his Study, with a deep Sigh, Well, *le Brune, said he*, it would be vain for me to persist in a Denial of what my ill Fortune and Imprudence has made so plain a Discovery of. I own I have been to blame, but which of us is always Master of his Wishes? If Love be an Excuse for what I've done, I love your adorable Sister with a Passion {245} which would not have permitted me to have lived if not gratified, and still burns in my Breast so strongly, that I scarce repent the heights to which it has transported me. All I can do, is to wish your Sister had appear'd less charming to my Eyes, or that it were in my power to repair the Injury I have done her, by making her my Wife; but you know I am married, the indissoluble Knot was tied before I saw her Eyes, and therefore can make no return but with—None, *interrupted the Chevalier growing more enrag'd*, but with your Blood; that's the Amends her injur'd Honour asks, and mine will take. Yet hold! *Resumed the Marquiss, with a melancholy Air*; you are sensible, *le Brune*, that I dare fight, and cannot chink I hold this Parley, because I fear your Sword. No, I am well assur'd you know me better, but should I fall by you, or you by me, your Sister would be so far from reaping any advantage by the Conquest, which soever gains it, that 'tis probable the Triumph would be only her eternal Hate. Sure I am, she would detest the Man by whom her Brother fell; nor do I think it Vanity to say, I am certain she would but ill endure the Murderer of him whom she has vow'd she lov'd. Her Reputation, which is now unblasted, that which you call a Crime being known but by us two, might then, perhaps, by her Despair and Grief, be blaz'd abroad. Besides, *le Brune*, if possible, give Truce to Rage, and call Reflection home. Then tell me, if in your Life's whole Course, you ne'er were guilty of that very Fault, you now think so unpardonable in me. Tell me, was you ne'er so much subdued by the Almighty Power of Love, as to forgo all other Considerations, would those Soul-torturing Pangs, those agonizing Racks of Nature, which Desire creates, refuse that Ease the darling Object could afford, only because she was the Wife, the {246} Daughter, or the Sister of a Friend? Oh no, and you have never known what 'tis to love, if you deny this Truth. These words had such an effect on the late furious *le Brune*, that he sheathed his Sword, which he had out all the time of this Discourse, and at the same time disarm'd his Eyes of all that Rancour[107] they had worn: too much, *cryd he*, my Soul avows the Justice of this Assertion, to aim at a Contradiction. Yes, too well, my Lord! I know the Force of that Tyrannick Passion, to wonder at the Effects of it in you. Pardon the sudden Heat with which I have been inflamed, and I forgive my Sister's Ruin. Call it not so, *said the Marquiss*, by Heaven her Reputation shall be ever safe; and if the Gods e'er make me in a Condition, and she continues single, as she has vow'd to do, the Priest shall authorize our future Joys. I doubt not the Performance of this Promise, *reply'd the* Chevalier, I know you have *Honour*, and you say you have *Love*, and either of these is a sufficient Motive to induce you to repair your Passion's Fault. To compensate for that I have been guilty of

---

107 [*rancoeur*, old French: inveterate malignity; malice; stedfast implacability; standing hate.]

to you, I will let you into an Adventure, which will make you cease to wonder that I so soon relinquish'd all that Fire of Rage, which, at the first Discovery of this Misfortune, was kindled in my Soul; the Place where we are, is private. I am now full of the Remembrance, and I think I cannot take a fitter Opportunity to relate it. The Marquiss told him, he could not oblige him more, and having thank'd him, the new-made Friends sat down together at the foot of that Hill, on which the attentive Stranger and his heavenly Guide had listen'd to the former part of their Conversation, and with an equal Curiosity waited for the Remainder.

{247} The History of the Chevalier *Le Brune*, *Cleander*, and the fair *Euphelia*

You know, my Lord, *said he*, that I spent some time in viewing the Curiosities of foreign Courts; as I was on my Return, I made my way thro' *Utopia*, a Land famous for remarkable Adventures, and certainly that which happen'd to me there, is not the least worthy Observation. Travelling along the Road, accompany'd only by one Servant, I was set upon by a Gang of the *Banditti*, they were five in number, well arm'd, and admirably mounted, so that you may believe I could not expect to defend myself for any long time against such odds: I attempted it however, and kept them in play, hoping the Approach of some Passengers might relieve me: I saw my Man kill'd before my Face, and had my own Horse disabled in such a manner, that I was oblig'd to dismount; I leap'd off as nimbly as I could, still keeping the Villains at the distance of my Sword's Point: after which, I got my Back against a Tree, and in that posture laid two of them dead, and very much wounded another. There were now but two of them capable of prejudicing me, and I began to think I should have the better, when my Sword unluckily broke; they were just about to plunge both theirs in my now defenceless Breast, when the sudden Tread of Horses Oblig'd them to turn. Those whom Heaven sent for my Deliverance, were a Gentleman and two Servants, who seeing at a good distance the latter part of my Distress, came galloping to the Place where we were, and thinking {248} it no Dishonour to take the advantage he had of those, who by their Habits and Behaviour he knew to be Ruffians, set upon 'em so vigorously, that they were glad to be oblig'd to the Swiftness of their Horses for their Safety. It was not till after I thought myself out of danger, that I found I was not so; I had receiv'd many Wounds, tho' the Hurry of my Spirits had prevented my feeling the Smart of them: but they now began to pain me so vehemently, that together with my Faintness, occasion'd by the Loss of a great quantity of Blood, made me little able to return those Thanks to my Perserver, which the Action he had done demanded from me. He did not, however, seem to expect much from me at that time, and perceiving my Condition, entreated I would accompany him to his House, which was not above a Mile distant from thence, and assur'd me nothing in his power should be wanting for the Cure of my Wounds, and Recovery of my Strength. The Offer was too obliging, and, as the Case stood, too necessary for me, to be refus'd: I endeavour'd to mount that Horse my Man had rid on, but was not able; the obliging Stranger therefore order'd one of his Servants to get up behind me, and hold me round the Body till we got to the end of our little Journey; and, indeed, had it been farther, I should have had no more occasion for his Civilities, for by that time we had reach'd the House, I fell in all appearance dead, and lay some time as such; as I afterwards found, he took the same Care of me, as if I had been a Brother, or, if possible, something that had bore a dearer Tye to his Affections. He sent immediately for a Surgeon, and order'd his Wife that the same Diligence in everything should be used about me, as tho' it were himself had wanted it. And indeed, had I been in my own House, with my nearest Friends and Kindred about me, I could not have been regarded with a more sincere, {249} or ardent Tenderness. I came not to myself in spite of all their Endeavours till the Surgeon had search'd my Wounds and dress'd them; and when I had Sense enough to know what was done about me, I wanted Voice to thank him for his Favours. It was several Hours before I recover'd my Speech, but I saw so great a Joy in the Face of my Deliverer, when the Surgeon told him, I was in no other danger of Death than what was caus'd by my executive Weakness, that as often as I have reflected on it since, it has been surprizing to me: but certainly the whole World never produc'd a Gentleman of more Good-nature, Honour, and Generosity, than *Cleander*, for that was his Name. There pass'd not a day, scarce an hour, in which he did not come himself into my Chamber to see how I was attended; he was not one of those, who think they do a great deal if they give Orders for a good Action, he would see every thing done himself, and the Servants acquainted with the Sincerity of their Master, imitated his Zeal, and seem'd to endeavour to outvye each other in Complaisance and Care. I give you this particular account of the uncommon Humanity and Friendship which, while a Stranger, I found from *Cleander*, that I may make you sensible how very much I ow'd him, and how vastly different from what I ought, the cruelty of my Stars oblig'd me to deal with him.

When I began to be well enough to sit up, he would needs have Dinner serv'd in my Chamber, believing Company would be a Diversion to me, and contribute something coward my recovering; but alas! How fatal, how dreadful was the effect of this last testimony of his Goodness? By frequent opportunities of discovering the Perfections of his too charming Wife, the adorable *Euphelia*, I lost that Liberty I so long had boasted, and grew the most enamour'd, and most ungrateful of Mankind.

{250} I struggled indeed with the all-conquering Dart, but Love and Death are equally resistless. no *Reasons* are of force to repel the *one*, no *Physick* can withstand the *other*; in vain my Obligations to *Cleander* pleaded, in vain her Virtue, and their mutual Fondness, check'd my aspiring Hope. I saw no Prospect but Despair, yet was compell'd to tread the Road which led to it. I design'd not, indeed, at first, to have discover'd what I felt, and form'd a resolution to die in Silence rather than be guilty of attempting so monstrous an Injury to the Man to whom I ow'd my very Life. This was, or I deceiv'd myself, the reason why for some Days, nay Weeks, I stifled the secret Wishes of my Soul; but I have had sufficient Cause since, to believe it was rather the Impossibility there seem'd of succeeding in my aim if disclos'd, than a Principle of true Honour which restrain'd me; and that there is no such thing in nature, as a Lover who can restrain the Impatience of Desire, when Hope receives Encouragement from the Object of his Passion.

To have follow'd the Dictates of my Honour, as soon as I had been able to travel, I should have remov'd from a place so dangerous for me to continue in, and I did make some faint Efforts to take my leave; but the Goodness of *Cleander* would not suffer me to leave his House till I was perfectly recover'd. He press'd me strenuously, and I, too willing to be persuaded, suffer'd myself to be overcome; nay, when my strength was so perfectly restor'd, that nothing but the remembrance remain'd that I ever had been hurt, the ill Genius of this unhappy Gentleman made him take so great a liking to my Conversation, that he could not hear me speak of leaving him without expressing a vast deal of uneasiness, and at last, being continually sollicited to it by him, and her who was not born to be deny'd any thing by me, the fatally fair {251} *Euphelia*, I obey'd the Instigation of my own burning Wishes, and gave my Promise to stay till the Spring of the Year (it being then the depth of Winter) should facilitate my Passage over some Icy Mountains, which I was obliged to cross before I could take shipping for chis Island.

You'll say, my Lord, that these continued Obligations should have made me chuse to do a violence on my own Life, if Death alone cou'd have prevented my doing an Action which should render me unworthy of living; and indeed I know not but that had been the Remedy to which I should have had recourse, had not an unexpected Revolution hapned in my Affairs—A Turn so unforeseen! Unhoped! And, in my Hours of just Reflection, almost unwish'd! Arriv'd, as put me past the power of listening to the Calls of Honour, Friendship, Virtue, Gratitude, or ought but Love, triumphant, overbearing Love!

An Accident hapned to call *Cleander* some Miles distant from his own House; he was oblig'd to stay about a Week, his lovely Wife and I were left at home with no other Company than the Servants; who never entering uncall'd, I had all the Opportunity I could have wish'd, had my Designs been vicious, to have attempted the perpetration of them; yet still I bore the Torture unreveal'd, persisted in my Resolution of being just to Honour and *Cleander* in the despite of Love: but with what Pangs, what convulsive agonizing Racks, I need not go about to represent to you, who, you say, have felt the same, and was but by them enforc'd to wrong a Friend who lov'd you. This difference there was indeed between those Conflicts which Honour rais'd in both; you burn'd in an unlawful Flame, but for the Sister of a Man to whom Good-nature only made you to have some regard; *I* for the *Wife* of him, to whom I was bound by all the Tyes which ought to link Humanity. When {252} compar'd with *Mine, Yours* was a petty Crime; nor was I insensible how monstrous it was to sin against him, even in Thought: but I will not lengthen my Narration by any Remarks which would be but impertinent to one, who has it in his power so easily to form a Judgment of the Sufferings I endur'd; so I shall only say, that I still flatter myself, Virtue had gain'd the day, and wild Desire ne'er found a Voice to speak its horrid meaning, had it alike been silent in *Euphelia*. But that destructive Charmer sympathizing in my Wishes, and unable to imitate my Resolution, had long since read, unknown to me, my Passion in my Eyes, and expecting when I would declare it, had consulted within herself in what manner she should reply. At first she resolv'd to treat me with that disdain an offer of that nature would have merited, but soon threw aside that Severity, and long'd for nothing more than that I should declare myself her Lover. Finding I still was dumb, the Pain it gave her made her know she was herself a Lover, and what she thought she had desired only as the effect of Woman's Vanity, she now found proceeded from a quite different Cause. She wish'd I should address her, not to have the pleasure of *refusing*, but of *granting* my Request; and perceiving I made no better use of so favourable an Opportunity as her Husband's absence, took a time to upbraid me for it, when she thought I must be of a Constitution very different from my Sex, if I endeavour'd not to make ample reparation for the Fault I had been guilty of. I relate this part of my History, my Lord, in a gay manner, because the Expressions I make use of, being most of them her own, it may serve to let you into the Humour of this Lady, which was far from being answerable to the seeming solidity of her Wit, or modesty and innocence of her Behaviour. But as I was telling you, *Cleander* {253} had been gone three Days, when on the third Night being in Bed, full of those perplex'd Cogitations which were my ordinary Companions, I heard my Curtains on a sudden undraw, and by the light of a Candle which was burning on the Table, saw it was *Euphelia* who had open'd them. Judge my surprize at such a Visit, it put me so far from the power of making that use, which, as she afterward confess'd, she expected from me, that it render'd me even incapable of Speech; which she observing, What *Le Brune, said she*, are you so little accustomed to the Conversation of Ladies, that you are at a loss to entertain them? These words, utter'd with a sort of Air which I know not how to describe, and so different from that Reserve which I had seen her always wear, if possible, heighten'd my Astonishment; but getting over it as well as I could, An Honour, *reply'd I*, so extraordinary as that which the adorable *Euphelia* now confers on me, may well excuse

{247} The History of the Chevalier *Le Brune, Cleander*, and the fair *Euphelia* — **195**

my want of Words to thank her, since there are none in Language to reach the Sense I have of it. I would have you, *said she*, take this Visit as the effect of the sublimest Friendship. I have observ'd a growing Sadness on you, and I would have you believe so well of me, as that I may be a trusted Person. the severest Woes find ease in real Pity, and that mine is so, you will easily be convinc'd, if you make me the Confidant of your Misfortunes. I must have been more *Dull* than some are *Vain*, not to have seen both into the meaning of her coming, and her pressing me to explain my Sentiments, and yet I know not how I was by some inward Agitations prevented from letting her see I understood them; and she was oblig'd to urge me farther yet. I fancy, *pursu'd she*, you are in Love; tell me if you have not left behind you in any of the Courts you have travell'd through, some favourite Charmer whose absence gives you Pain?

{254} My Amazement a little lessen'd, and Extasy taking place, I now had Courage enough to answer her in this manner. No, Madam, *cry'd I*, the Heart of *Le Brune* might have defy'd the force of Love, had Charms no more resistless than all I have seen in Palaces, not invaded it: free as the chearful Birds that wanton in the Air, I came into this Country, and with the same liberty should I have left it, if *Euphelia*, divine *Euphelia* ne'er had bless'd my Eyes. While I was speaking these Words, she gave me a Look so passionately tender, so ravishingly soft, that had I been possess'd of all those Sentiments of Honour and Gratitude for her Husband, which had debarr'd me from attempting a reward of my Passion, and which, in that sudden surprize at her Behaviour, I really was not; they would all have vanish'd, and my whole Soul would have dissolv'd in Love and Fondness. She made me no other Answer than a gentle Sigh, nor did I wait for one from her Tongue, her Eyes had sufficiently declar'd all I cou'd wish; and snatching her to my Breast, without any farther Ceremony, explor'd each Beauty of the unresisting Fair, and rioted to the height of Extasy in those luxurious Joys, which ne'er till then, durst I indulge Desire so far as even to hope. Oh how is it possible for me to make you sensible of the Transports of this dear guilty Moment, the unlook'd for Blessing left me scarce Sense to taste it, I was all madness; the amazing Joy gave Thought no room, and had we separated after the first Embrace, I should not, when alone, have believ'd it real, but that I had been deceiv'd by some Infatuation, and cheated by the fury of my Zeal into Enthusiasm; but the kind, melting Author of my Raptures, indulg'd 'em still, and suffering me to reap repeated Pleasures, made me at last to own 'em perfect, and that I had indeed *Euphelia* in my Arms, that very *Euphelia* I so long had languish'd for, yet {255} never hoped, nor aim'd to enjoy. The Wildness of our Bliss so far abated as to allow breath for Speech, she told me, that from the first Moment I had been brought into the House, she had regarded me with an unvanquishable Affection, that I had her Virgin *Heart*; for tho' a Wife, she never knew what it was to love before that Duty to her Parents had been the only motive which had induc'd her to give her Hand to *Cleander*, and by a thousand such like Arguments endeavour'd to excuse what she had done for me.

She staid with me the whole Night, and you may believe, amidst those tumultuous Emotions which her Presence gave, I had but little time for Reflection; but when the Dawn of Day oblig'd her, tho' unwillingly, to take her leave, and Consideration had resum'd its Power, with how fevere a *Bitter* were the Remembrance of the *Sweets* I had enjoy'd, accompany'd! The Idea of *Cleander*'s Merits, my Obligations to him came fresh into my Mind, and I could not help thinking myself the most guilty Wretch on Earth. These Cogitations detaining me in my Bed much longer than I was accustom'd, *Euphelia* sent a Servant to know if I were not well. I could not hear her Name without a Mixture of Delight and Horror; but as we are all willing to indulge ourselves in the former, when we have an Opportunity of doing it, I endeavour'd as much as I could to get over the other, by reconciling my Conscience, as well as I was able, with that Opinion I had often heard maintain'd, That Passions being involuntary, the Consequences of them were rather to be pity'd than condemn'd; And the more to enable me to stifle a Remorse, which at the same time that it afflicted me, gave no manner of reparation to the Person I had injur'd, I made what speed I could in dressing me, and hasted to her Sight, whose excessive Charms {256} were my only Vindication; I found her in her Drawing-Room, adorn'd with all her Graces, to which were added a certain Air of Languishment, an Enchanting, Soul-dissolving Softness, which render'd her, I thought, more lovely than ever I had seen her; her unequal'd Tenderness, her thousand inexpressible Endearments, made me again forget my Guilt, renew my Crime, and yield myself the Slave of Pleasure! Racking! Insupportable! Sense-destroying Pleasure! Never did any two indulge Desire to a greater pitch of Extasy than we; but so different was my Passion from that with which most Men are animated, that Possession rather added to its Vigour, than any way abated it. Thus mutually loving, thus mutually bless'd in uninterrupted Raptures, how dreadful were the Thoughts that the expected Approach of *Cleander* would put an end to 'em, when he must seize my Treasure in his Arms, clasp her before my Face; nor she dare to resist, or seem unwilling to accept his Ardours! What Torture, what an unutterable Idea of Horror, did this Reflection present to both! I could not bear it, and my Charmer even died at the Apprehension The Day in which he was to come, being arriv'd, full of distracted Thoughts, and wild Impatience, she ask'd me if I truly loved her; which I having protested with all the Imprecations I could invent, Well then, *said she*, what I have to propose will not seem displeasing to you. I have too nice a sense of what I owe to Honour, and to Love, to be the Property of adulterated Joys. Having been *Your's*, I can no more consent to be *Cleander*'s, but will this moment, if you'll agree to be the Partner of my Flight, be gone forever from his Sight and Bed. I was already gone too far in Ingratitude to stop at this, and accepted the Offer of taking her away with a Joy proportionable to the extreme Passion I had for {257} her. This being concluded on, no time was to be lost; she went to her Chamber to pack up her Jewels, and what Ready-Money she had; I to the Stable, to order my Horse should be made ready. Both being agitated by the same Desire, neither waited for the other; and having told the Servants that we design'd to meet *Cleander* on his way, we left the House, as we thought, unsuspected by anybody in it.

Euphelia was perfectly acquainted with the Road her Husband was to come, and you may be certain took a different one. Our Design was not to leave *Utopia* immediately, not doubting but the Elopement of a Woman so considerable as *Euphelia* would make noise enough in the Country to occasion all the Ports being search'd, and perhaps an Embargo on the shipping for some time, to disappoint which, we laid the Plot to go no farther than the next Town, (believing, as 'tis common in such Cases, the nearest Home would be the least liable to Suspicion) and changing our Names, pass for Husband and Wife, till the Season of the Year should be more favourable for Travelling. We pass'd thro' that very Wood, near which I had been in such danger, when the Valour of *Cleander* preserv'd me: and the Sight of it reminding me of the ungenerous Return I was now making him, gave a sudden Shock to all that was honourable in me: I grew so exceeding thoughtful, that my fair Companion took notice of the Change, and ask'd the Cause of it; I made no scruple of consessing the Truth; but she, who had the Art of soothing beyond all her softning Sex, would not permit me long to continue in these perplexing Cogitations, she would needs alight, and have me do so too, and accompany her in a little Walk in that Wood. 'Twas in vain I represented to her the Danger of delaying our Journey so near her own House, or that of being set {258} upon by Ruffians in the manner I had been; her Fondness, or rather the fatal Influence of her Stars, would suffer her to take no denial, and I could not, without appearing guilty of a Coldness, which would have seem'd but an ill Return for her passionately ardent Affection, have offer'd any farther Arguments against what she seem'd so bent on. I, therefore, attempted no more in contradiction to her Humour, but tying my Horse to a Tree, led her into that shady Covert, which, in spite of Winter, still maintain'd its green, and which at a distance she had been so much taken with. We sat down in that part of it, which was most fenced from Wind and Cold, and the dear Inviter used her utmost Endeavours to make me forget everything but Love. She could not move in vain a Heart so disposed to obey her, Rapture soon took up the place of Melancholy, and every anxious Thought again was hush'd; nor should we, perhaps, of a long time have remembred we were not to take up our Abode in that Place, had not an Interruption which we least expected, happen'd to remind us of the inconsiderate Folly, which Excess of Fondness had led us to commit.

As secure as we imagin'd ourselves from Suspicion, *Euphelia*'s Excuse of going to meet her Husband gave great occasion for it. Had we, indeed, been going on such an Errand, she would certainly not have gone without Attendants; but such an Infatuation sure was never known, nor had I the power of advising better, till it was too late. An old Servant, who had lived long in the Family, and fancy'd he discover'd some Glances more than ordinarily kind between us, guess'd at part of tho Truth of the Journey we were pretending to take, and, unknown to any of his Fellows, watch'd at a distance which Road we went; and finding it directly opposite to that which he knew *Cleander* was to {259} come, made no doubt but that his Master was abus'd he therefore returned not home, but crossing the Fields with all possible speed, struck into that where he might meet his Master. He did, and inform'd him of all he imagin'd, and all he had discover'd. The injured Husband, confounded and amazed at what he heard, could scarce give credit to what he thought an utter Impossibility, (so kind an Opinion had he of both myself and her) but being by his faithful Servant press'd to satisfy himself, by the same way he had arriv'd to bring him that Intelligence, he suffer'd himself to be conducted by him to the Wood we were in; my Horse he saw and knew, and easily found where we were sitting. The wild Amaze, the Grief, and mingled Rage which sat on the Brow of this unhappy Gentleman, could be equal'd by nothing but the just Shame and Confusion on ours; tho' *Euphelia* retain'd not Sense long to endure it; the Shock was too violent for her Weakness to sustain, and giving a great Shriek, she fell in a Swoon at his Feet. I, who had not been much inferiour to her in Guilt, suffer'd almost as much, and tho' my Eyes were open, my Tongue had lost its Use; I had no Words to excuse or vindicate a Crime, at once so base and plain, till he, after having cast a furious Look at me, turning to his Servant, said, Take up that Woman, and convey her home, but watch that at her returning Sense, Shame makes her commit no Violence on herself. You may, perhaps, my Lord! expect that I could not see the Fellow do as he was order'd, without an Endeavour to hinder him; but I protest to you, that the Sight of *Cleander* made a very Coward of me, and it was as much as I could do, to regain Presence enough of Mind to say to him, as the Servant was taking her up, and mounting his Horse, with her in his Arms. If what you have seen be a Crime past Pardon, leave the {260} offending Beauty with him who has most reason to take care of her. I need not your Instructions, Sir, *reply'd he*, and shall act both with her and you as best becomes my Honour: tho' I know not, by the little you have made use of to me, if I should not be excus'd to deal otherwise; yet one of the Things which are out of my power, is to return a vile Action in its kind, therefore desire you will prepare to answer me as a Man of Spirit should, before the coming of my Servants, who will immediately be alarm'd, gives me the odds against you. In Speaking this, he drew his Sword, and making a full Pass at me, obliged me to put myself in a Posture of Defence;

but nothing being more terrible to me than the Thoughts of fighting with a Man to whom I was so highly obligated, and had so greatly injur'd, I stood but on my guard, and endeavour'd, by all the Arguments I could in such a Case, and at such a Time, make use of, to persuade him to take any other Revenge, than forcing me to lift my Arm against him, who had preserv'd me: but the just Rage he was possess'd of, was rather increased than abated by my Remonstrances, and aiming only at my Life, and mad that I answer'd not the Thrusts he made, flew directly on me, and thinking to reach my Heart, receiv'd my fatal Weapon in his own, before I had time, or thought to drop the Point; he ran so full upon it, and with such Force, that when he fell, above an Inch appear'd out of his Back. He died that moment, and to go about to represent the Horror I was in, would be to give you an Idea of it infinitely short of what I felt; I rav'd, I tore my very Flesh, and mourning over the Body, seem'd to have forgot what was owing to my own Safety, till the Approach of *Cleander*'s Servants reminded me of it, who I saw at a distance running in a little Troop; they were on foot, believing, I suppose, {261} the Danger their Master might be in, would not allow time for getting on their Horses. The Sight of 'em, and the Reflection that all the Punishments that could be inflicted on me, would not have the Power to re-animate that Body, whose Soul I had dislodg'd, made me jump on mine with all possible Dexterity, and make the best of my way thro' the most unfrequented part of the Desert. I stop'd not till I was at least fifteen or sixteen Miles from the Place, and then but to change my Horse, who not being accustom'd to such Journeys, began to flag. By Night I reach'd a little Village pretty near the Seaside, where I design'd to go the next Day, and, if possible, embark for homewards; but this Resolution vanish'd on my Pillow, *Euphelia* return'd with all her Charms to my enamour'd View, I fancy'd that lovely Creature might have some need of my Assistance or Advice, and could not persist in an Intention to abandon her to the Fury of her Husband's Relations, and Insults of an unpitying World, without a Comforter; and not all the Remorse which I felt for the Wrongs and Death of *Cleander*, yet flagrant, could stifle the Memory of what I ow'd her Love. I procur'd a *Hermit's* Habit, cut off my Hair, and disguising myself with a false Beard and Wrinkles, travelled on foot back to the fatal Place; I contriv'd to be lodg'd at a little Cottage, which stood very near the House, and without the trouble of asking any suspicious Questions, was inform'd of everything I was covetous of knowing. I saw the Body of the unfortunate *Cleander* carry'd to be interred in the Tomb of his Ancestors, which was not above two Furlongs from his House. I heard his Widow had been examin'd concerning his Death, and that she had clear'd herself with an Assurance and Self-Interestedness which I could never have believed, if not too fully convinc'd of it, for being accus'd of a criminal {262} Correspondence with the Person by whose hand he fell, she took the most solemn Oath, that I was the greatest Villain in nature; that deluding her abroad, under the pretence of going to meet her Husband, I had carry'd her a different Way, and attempted to ravish her in the Wilderness: and. to confirm the Truth of what she had sworn, offer'd a Reward to any one who should apprehend and bring me to Justice, large enough to excite a great many to an Endeavour to obtain it. I heard the very People, with whom I was, daily express how gladly they should undertake the Search, if they could entertain the least hope of discovering where I was conceal'd; there was no Person, whom her Insinuations had won to believe what she said, that did not detest my Name, unnumber'd Curses met my Ears wherever I went, and even those most inclin'd to Mercy, said I deserv'd the worft of Deaths. Such a Character, tho' in a Place where I was utterly a Stranger, and had no design of continuing in, was insupportably shocking; but the Consideration how much *Euphelia* had contributed to give it me, made it more dreadful yet. Tho' I could not blame all she alledg'd in defence of her own Innocence, yet the setting a Price upon my Life, convinced me, that she not only seem'd to wish me dead, but in reality did so, or at least thought the Punishment the Law would have inflicted on me, if taken, a trivial Misfortune to that of being suspected to have been false to her Husband's Bed. How vastly different was this to the Passion she had pretended? How prodigiously had she deceiv'd me twice, first in the Opinion of her *Virtue*, and afterwards of her *Love?* I now gave over all thoughts of shewing myself to her, not being able to trust the Protestations she had made, so far as to assure myself she would not carry her Affectation of Innocence and Fidelity to {263} *Cleander* so far, as really to expose me to the Judges. Therefore, tho' I would have given my Eyes almost to have had the liberty of upbraiding her, I found it more prudent to deny myself that Satisfaction: and in the same Disguise that I had left it, return'd to the Sea-Port Town, and soon met with a favourable Opportunity of leaving a Kingdom, which had I never enter'd, my Mind had been free from those Inquietudes the Death of *Cleander*, and my Ingratitude to him, make perpetually to haunt me.

Thus, my Lord, have I let you into the secret History of my Misfortunes, that you may see the Justice of all-ruling Fate, which has punish'd the injury I did *Cleander*, by that you have done my *Sister*; and it is the remembrance how unfit a Person I am to use my Sword in revenge of affronted Honour, since it has been so fatal when drawn in the Defence of a *wrong* Cause, that has made me give over the intention of taking that Satisfaction of you, for a *justifiable* one, which else it would have been mean-spirited to have neglected.

Le Brune here finished his Discourse, and after the Marquiss had made some few Remarks on it, they broke up Conversation, and walk'd forwards toward the *Enchanted Well*, which, tho' it was now near Evening, was as much throng'd as ever. The God of tender Inclinations seem'd bury'd in Contemplation at the Story which this *Chevalier* had been relating. He spoke not for some time, and the Stranger finding in it something extremely surprizing, took the boldness to say, the Misfortune of *Le Brune* has given me much concern, and an adequate desire of knowing what happen'd after his departure, to the fair inconstant *Euphelia*; and as I am sensible nothing of this kind can happen unknown to thy Divine Omniscience, intreat that the same condescending Goodness which has made me {264} sharer in so many Wonders, will also inform me by what Power she was influenc'd to act in the manner she did, since I cannot think it was thy Inspiration which led her either to the Bed of the *Chevalier*, or the return of *Virtue* in her Breast, which made her seem so regardless of his Safety after. You judge most truly, *reply'd the Deity*, there is an humble Fear, and awful Respect, to the Person belov'd, which induces the real Lover to act with Modesty and Caution, thereby to render him, or herself, deserving the Esteem of the admir'd Object; my Influence never yet led the bold Ruffian to *ravish* what he wish'd to enjoy, nor gave the Woman confidence to *own*, unask'd, the secret Fire which burn'd within her Breast; 'twas I indeed who actuated the Faculties of *Le Brune*, the Symptoms of my Deity were apparent in the humble Adoration he paid her, not daring, till authoriz'd by herself, to utter what he wish'd, or give Desire a name: but 'twas that hateful *Fiend*, who is so often mistaken for me, who fill'd her Soul with such ungovernable Fires, and made her after as careless what became of the Man she had profess'd to love, as before she was of her Reputation. She soon became involv'd in an Engagement with another, and regarding no more than a *present* Satisfaction, neither thought with any tenderness on the *past*, or gave herself the trouble of consulting what sort of Prospect presented for the future. The Person she made choice of, had not the Generosity of *Le Brune*; he boasted of the Favours he receiv'd, and she was the most expos'd and wretched Woman in the World. 'Tis pity, *said the Stranger*, that the *Chevalier* is not by some means appriz'd of it; to know her Inconstancy had drawn on her the Punishment it merited, would doubtless be no small Consolation for the Injustice she did him. It would doubtless, *reply'd the softning Power*, afford him a vast deal of Satisfaction, but you must {265} consider, that he himself was guilty of the highest Injustice, and the divine *Astrea*, to whose Counsels the whole Hierarchy of Gods submit, cannot consent he should have any mitigation of that eternal Chagrin his Remorse for the injury he did *Cleander*, must perpetually involve him in; and to show you how exact that heavenly Dictatress is in paying Wrongs in kind, I will give you a little short History of a Gentleman, who, but for one Infidelity in Love, had been the most eminent Example of Virtue and strict Honour, that for many Ages Humanity has boasted.

The History of the Count *Montreville*, *Martasinda*, and Madam *de Fautmille*

Never was mortal Man endued with greater Perfections both of Mind and Body than the accomplish'd Count *Montreville:* He has a Person which the nicest Eye can find no Blemish in, and an Understanding so extensive, that it is scarce possible to talk to him on any Topick, or in any Language to which he is a Stranger; yet is he never absolute in enforcing any Argument: and, tho' perfectly convinc'd of the truth of his Assertions, endeavours rather to persuade than impose what he would have believ'd. But indeed he is rarely put to the tryal how far he can endure contradiction, because he has that prevailing manner of uttering what he means, that were he to defend even Falsehoods, it would be in such a manner as would put Truth itself out of countenance and unable to reply. More lovely, and more wife than Words can speak, or even Thought conceive, did he, for a long race of Years, triumphant scorn my Power, admired by all, himself admiring none; till at the {266} last, my watchful Darts found one revenging moment, and pierc'd him to the Soul. *Martasinda!* The brightest Maid *Utopia* could ever boast, forsook her native Shore, to gain new Conquests here! A thousand noble Youths confess'd her Power of charming, and night and day offer'd incessant Orisons[108] to me: Never was I more fervently implor'd than on the account of this transcendent Beauty, nor ever did I with more reluctance deny Requests so humble and sincere; but Fate assisting the ill Genius of this unhappy Charmer, compel'd me to be unjust and cruel to the most faithful of my Votaries, and give the Prize to the all-conquering *Montreville*. But he, ungrateful for the Bounty, no sooner found my Inspiration in her Eyes, heard it in her trembling Accents, and grew assur'd I had dissolv'd each bar which might oppose his Wish, than he abjur'd my Influence, banish'd me his Breast, and, in my room, receiv'd that hateful *Demon*, that Foe profest to Innocence and Virtue, who by the undistinguishing World is call'd *Love*, but by *Montreville* could not be mistaken for me. While I maintain'd my Empire o'er his Soul, he thought of *Martasinda* as the supremest Joy that Heaven cou'd give, and never aim'd at more than to possess her by those Ways which Honour might approve; her Interest then, her Fame, her Happiness more than his own he wish'd—but now, how vast the Change! The Gratification of his wild Desire, tho' by her Ruin, was his only Hope. Ungovernable Heats, Impatiencies, Deceits, supply'd the place of humble Awe, and a disinterested Tenderness. He like'd, 'tis

---

108 [*oraison*, French, this word is variously accented; *Shakespeare* has the accent both on the first and second syllables; *Milton* and *Crashaw* on the first, others on the second: a prayer; a supplication.]

true, with an extravagancy of Passion, wish'd with an unbounded Fervency for the Enjoyment of her lovely Person, but 'twas a sort of liking whose View was selfish, and had no other regard to the admir'd Object, than as she was form'd to afford Satisfaction to his present {267} Humour. Conscious of the Change, and of the Fiend he had entertain'd, he had however, knowing her perfect Modesty, the Artifice to hide it from her; and it was under my Umbrage, and in my Name, that he still continu'd to improve that fatal Kindness I had rooted in her Breast; melted by his delusive Softness, at last it grew to that unhappy height, of being unable to refuse him any thing he should ask. The charming Traitor soon discover'd and seiz'd the lucky Moment to undo her, and sunk in a Lethargy of sense-enslaving Pleasures, she lost all Memory of what she ow'd to Virtue or to Reputation; while he, of both regardless, waited not Opportunity, nor consulted Secrecy, but gave a loose to Passion, indulging wild Desire at Times and Places, which plainly demonstrated her publick Shame was of less consequence to him, than the disappointment of one intended luxurious hour. There were few Persons who had any acquaintance with either of them, that were insensible in what manner they past their time together; and those who had no other knowledge of them than by report, had also, with the Character of their Perfections, this of their Failings too. The Count was generally condemn'd, but *Martasinda*, by her own Sex, most prodigiously so. Those who had envy'd, were glad of the Occasion to rail against a Rival, too potent for their feebler Charms to vie with; and those who really admir'd her, were angry that a Woman who had been esteem'd in all other things so perfect, should be guilty of a false step, which might give the Men reason to suspect, that those of an inferiour Class of Understanding, would be less able to resist a Temptation, which she, with all her Stock of Wit, had not the power to do. The Intrigue for some time engross'd the Discourse of the whole Town, and indeed was of much longer duration than the thing {268} itself; the talkative part of Mankind certainly find a pleasure in censuring the Actions of others, which nothing else can equal; and had those Reflections made on the amorous Correspondence between these two ceas'd with the Cause, it had after appear'd no more than as a Dream. The Passion with which *Montreville* had been agitated, had too much vehemence to be lasting, it aim'd but at Enjoyment, and in Enjoyment ended; and *Martasinda* with all her Charms, was, after a few Nights, in his esteem, but as another Woman: he continu'd indeed to visit her, but so different was his Behaviour to her from what it was accustom'd, that she could not avoid seeing and lamenting the Error she had been guilty of, which she now found had rendered her too cheap ever to resume her former Value. She resented it as Women commonly do in such Cases, wept, entreated, threatned, rail'd, by turns, but sued and raged in vain. She was now past the power of giving, or denying; she had lavish'd away all her power of creating Hope or Fear, and must submit to that Fate she had often heard, and now experienc'd, was the inseparable Consequence of a too fond belief of the Lover's Protestations, or vainer Dependance on Self-desert. She was forsaken so suddenly, that as I have already said, she was the most unhappy in the want of his Affections, at that time the World said he most indulg'd them. But when at last the Secret was reveal'd, when by his entirely absenting himself from her, and her apparent Despair, it was blaz'd abroad, that he lov'd her now no more; with what a Consternation was all who heard it struck! What strange Conjectures were not form'd upon it! How liable were they both to Calumnies[109] which neither of them merited Some laid the blame on *Martasinda*, others on the Count; but the severest Censures fell on *Martasinda* everybody knew {269} he had address'd her on honourable Terms, that she was a Fortune little inferiour to what he might expect; but that if she had been more so, her Wit and Beauty very well made up for that deficiency; it was therefore generally believed that he had discovered some Slip in the dark which she had made, or he would either not have changed the design of his Sollicitations, nor she accepted of any from him beneath those Terms on which he had at first declared himself her Lover.

Thus was this unhappy Lady undone, and for a great while had not so much as the Consolation of being pitied; what she endur'd, or in what manner she supported the Miseries she labour'd under, would take up more of the Evening than I can well spare, having design'd it for the disclosing to you Affairs more surprizing than any you have yet heard; I will therefore only tell you, that her Sufferings were more than she had Philosophy to sustain: and walking one day full of despairing and disturb'd Reflections by the Sea-side, in a sudden Agony of Thought, she threw herself amidst the Waves, and there alone found ease for hopeless Love, and Ruin ill repaid. *Montreville* had a Stock of Good-nature, which never but on this Lady's account had been forfeited, and to hear of so unexpected and so dreadful a Catastrophe, made him ready to do a Violence on his own Life; and in so terrible a manner was he afflicted, that to have exchanged Conditions with her, was a woe infinitely short of what he felt—he saw, or he fancy'd that he saw her ever before his Eyes. He neither could sit, walk, nor lie alone, and he became so altered in a short time, that he was scarcely to be known. His fine and delicate Complexion wore now a death-like Paleness; his sparkling Eyes were sunk and hollow, and all their shining Radience extinct; his once plump dimpled Cheeks were now {270} fallen in, and lank, and had deep furrows such as Age engraves. His ever folded Arms, and drooping Head, seem'd with a weight of Care too heavy for his Body, and bowed it down towards the Earth. Nor was his Conversation any more the same; that gay, and sprightly Wit, that eternal Vivacity which used to accompany

---

109 [*calumnia*, Latin: slander; false charge; groundless accusation.]

his Discourse, was now changed to a heavy Dulness. If he spoke at all, it was rather more displeasing than his Silence; for as before he took care to render every thing he said obliging, he now seem'd fond of creating only Chagrin. In fine, there was nothing remained of the accomplish'd, admir'd *Montreville*, but the Name.

Yet all this severe *Astrea* did not think a sufficient Punishment for the wrong he had done to *Martasinda*; and whatever he suffered, unless he suffered by that very Crime he had been guilty of himself, was too little an Expiation for Justice to allow as such. He had a Mother whom from his Infancy he had lov'd with a Tenderness above the common Level of filial Affection; she was not yet old, he being not more than twenty-eight Years of Age when this Misfortune happen'd, and she not exceeding fourteen when he was born; the advantage of good Features and an excellent Complexion, made her appear younger than indeed she was. A Gentleman of a distinguish'd Rank had address'd her, she listened to him with Pleasure; it was said they were married, they liv'd together as Husband and Wife, and nobody question'd their being such, nor call'd her by any Name but that of Madam *De Fautmille*, which was that of her supposed Husband; one House, one Bed contained them for the space of two Years; at the end of which, taking an occasion to quarrel, he flew from her, declar'd he had only join'd with her in imposing on the World; that the Ceremony {271} of the Church had never pass'd between them, nor should any Consideration oblige him to permit it. The Lady, who had ever been accounted the most virtuous and reserv'd of her Sex, could not support the shame which this Declaration, too just to be disprov'd, had drawn upon her; and in a raging Fit of Passion, after having attempted every thing to bring him back, finding all her Endeavours vain, flew up to her Chamber, and before any of her Servants had the least guess at her Intentions, taking off her Girdle,[110] and fastening it about her Neck, strangled herself. The Odium her Death, and the Cause of it, threw on the Family, joined to the Grief for losing a Mother in that manner, whom he so tenderly loved, increased his former Distraction for the Misfortune of *Martasinda*; and both together were very near driving him to an Imitation of what they did; and being prevented only by being continually watched, he lives in a Condition to which the worst of Deaths would be preferable.

Thus, worthy Youth (*continued the Deity*) you see how the Injuries he had done *Martasinda* were retorted on himself in the Person who was nearest and dearest to him; and there are few Men, who, like him, have been guilty of betraying the Innocent, who do not some time or other feel the Woes they inflict. Nor is it in this alone, all other Crimes bring on their Punishment, and if thro' the Partiality of Interest or Favour, they escape that which is by Law decreed for them, they meet it in

---

110 [*gyrdel*, Saxon: any thing drawn round the waist and tied or buckled.]

a severer manner from the hand of Heaven; Triumph they may a while, but Vengeance, long deferred, falls with the greater weight, and he who thinks himself most safe, is often nearest to Destruction.

The *Stranger* was about to make some Reply, when on a sudden, from a near Vale, there arose a {272} Mist so thick, it darken'd all the Air, even the bright Glories which darted from the God of Love, were for a while obscur'd, and the more dazzling Beams of *Phœbus* robo'd of all their Force; a pale faint Shine, like that of *Cynthia*'s Crescent, was all they had to boast; wondring, and terrified, the trembling Mortal stood; fain would he have ask'd the meaning of this Prodigy, fain have implored Protection of his heavenly Guide; but Astonishment deprived him of the Power, nor had he aught of Speech or Motion left, till the benignant God thus chear'd his drooping Soul; Fear not, my favourite Charge, *said he*, nothing has power to hurt thee, with bold and curious Eyes gaze on! Behold! And see the Wonders of this Day—this memorable Day, which in the Book of Face I saw mark'd down, but am not well assured of the Event; for *Jupiter* from the inferior Powers screens all Foreknowledge of Futurity, and 'tis but by Conjecture we inspire our Prophets. As he was speaking, the Fog gathering itself together, condens'd, and hung in Air; a huge and floating Cloud, then growing more extended, seem'd by degrees to shape a human Form, but of a Size so monstrous and unproportion'd, as made the affrighted Stranger stand in need of all that Courage the Deity had inspired, to enable him to bear the sight of looking on it. But the dread Image lasted but for a moment; from a stupendous Rock, whose snowy Top seem'd crown'd with Stars, a venerable Form, the *Genius* of the Isle, descended slow, and on a golden Anchor glided majestick thro' the brightning Air; his right Arm by the Divine *Astrea* was supported, clad in white Robes of pure Ætherial Light: *Reason*, the sacred Guide of aw'd Humanity, sustain'd his Left: at their Approach the hideous Phantom flew, and in a distant Chasm, beyond the ken of mortal Sight, conceal'd his horrid {273} Shape. 'Tis done! *cry'd the bright Queen of everlasting Justice*; 'tis done! Pursue the glorious Aim you have began; revenge your helpless Son's long injur'd Cause, and punish these idolatrous Worshippers of *Interest* and *Fortune!* In speaking these words, she gave a Sword into his hand, which when he had receiv'd with becoming Adoration. Take also this, *said* Reason, *presenting him with a Wand*; this will dissolve the Inchantment of yon detested *Well*, and show the infatuated Crowd, to what they have sacrificed their All. To these Favours, they added some Words too mysterious for human Comprehension; then, swift as Thought, or the wing'd Lightnings at great *Jupiter*'s Command, they mingled with the Air, soar'd to the Skies, and bless'd no more the Eye. The aweful *Genius* now left alone, descry'd the God of Love, and prostrating himself low as the Earth, address'd the smiling Power; O Deity, *said he*, justly adored thro' every Nation of the peopled World! Behold the Presents I have receiv'd from Heaven, and be not thou less indulgent than the other Powers; but when the Commands of *Justice* and of *Reason* are fulfilled, in punishing those daring Contemners of the immortal Gods, vouchsafe to reassume thy Throne among us. Unbless'd, and unrefin'd by thy enlivening Influence, Stupidity and uncorrected Dullness would rule o'er the Land; the tuneful Muses fly the uncultivated Waste, all Arts, all Sciences be lost; *Apollo*'s Lays, or sweetly-founding Harp, would fail to charm where thou art not. 'Tis thou alone who inspirest Susceptibility;—the Mind of Man, rough and obdurate, is by thee made gentle, kind, and commiserating. 'Tis thou who art the Bond of all Society, the Life of Conversation, the Improver of Nature, the Reformer of Manners, and the great Source of {274} human Happiness. Had thy degenerate Race, *reply'd the Deity*, believ'd thus justly of me, they had not banish'd from their ungrateful Breasts my Inspiration, nor would those few who still continue to obey my Laws, become the Objects of Contempt and Ridicule. The Name of *Cupid* is despis'd, and *Lust* and *Avarice*, those undoing Harpys, honour'd and rever'd by *one*, the innocent and unwary Virgin is seduced; by the *other*, the experienced Matron is betray'd to a forgetfulness of her first Vows, and yields herself a Prey to mercenary Slavery. Even Nature is depress'd by these two Fiends, and has no more the power to operate. Where sordid Interest points the means of Gain, or Passion actuates the tempestuous Will, Sons against Fathers rise Fathers renounce the Babes they lately blest; Brother with Brother vies with inveterate Strife. The Power of Blood and Kin, all Alliances, all Ties of Relative, or Obligations lose their force; their Desires *self-centred*, aim only at *self-service*, let 'em then enjoy it, 'till *Fate* and *Jupiter* shall, by the glare of some unlock'd-for Woes, force them at once to see their Crime and Punishment. O Doom too too severe! *Resum'd the hoary Genius*; true is the Suggestion of Humanity, that *Love*, of all the Gods, once injur'd, is with most difficulty persuaded to forgiveness; yet was this Isle once thy chief Residence, thy darling Spot of Earth; not thy fair Mother, all-charming *Venus*, took more delight in the blest *Cyprian* Shades, than thou hast done in these refreshing Groves. And can'st thou then, thou who art call'd all Gentleness, hate what thou so much hast favour'd? Too presuming are these Upbraidings, *interrupted the Bliss-dispensing Power, with a Voice, and Eyes of as much austerity as such a Face could assume*; rather condemn thyself, who idly thus hast hid thy {275} sluggard Form, nor once appear'd to animate thy drooping Race some Ages past. What is become of all the mighty Names which used to make this Island Queen of Notions? Where is the Courage, which should awe their Foes? Where the Wisdom, which should invigorate their Counsels? Where's the Hospitality, the open Bounty, the Charity, which made you once so famous? 'Tis lost, 'tis gone; and what is worse, those very Virtues are perverted into Uses the most detestable to

Heaven. All the Remains of Valour are Tavern-Broils;[111] your only Proofs of Wisdom are Artifice, and basely circumventing each other; and your Liberality known but in Brothels, the Benefit of common Prostitutes and Panders.[112] Have not thy rebellious Sons contemn'd, blasphem'd, dethron'd each sacred Power, and on our Altars sacrificed to Idols? and are we to *intreat* that Adoration our Bounties should *command?*

The God here ceas'd and from his sparkling Eyes shot Beams of angry Fire. The trembling *Genius* once more upon his Knees implor'd forgiveness, nor durst to rise till a relenting Look confess'd his Pardon; then with submissive Air. I own, all conquering Power, *said he*, the Folly of those Words my rash ungovern'd Zeal inspir'd; justly, indeed, dost thou accuse a People who have alas too much rebell'd against Happiness and Thee. Their Crimes are heinous numberless, exceeding all Report; but well thou know'st the Fault is not in me. A potent Dæmon by adverse Fate upheld, has driven me from my native Home, exil'd, forlorn, unsought, and scarce remembred by my thankless Offspring; long have I conceal'd my Shame in gloomy Caverns, sculk'd into Dens deep as the Center of the groaning Earth, or on some barren unfrequented Rock, complain'd to the {276} Immortal Gods to change my Doom: unpity'd, unanswer'd, till this happy hour, I pierc'd the Heavens with fruitless Lamentations; but *Jupiter*, at the Intercession of *Neptune*, at length commiserated my Woes, and sent to my assistance divine *Astrea*, who, with *Reason*, ever my constant Friend, just now you saw depart: by them supported, my cruel Foe flew my revengeful Presence, and has no more the power to influence the mistaken World. Soon shall I resume my Force; and Avarice, Hypocrisy, Lust, and every other Fiend, shall cease to actuate the Mind of Man; back to their native Hell they shall be chas'd, and Virtue once again possess her Throne. But give me leave (*continu'd he, after a little Pause*) with all Humility to remind thy Godhead, that tho' too many of these infatuated Islanders have obey'd the instigations of a Myriad of permitted Fiends, I yet have Sons whose noble Minds have never been mis-led, who firm to Honour, and to Truth, no Change of Times or Circumstances could alter; in every state of Life the same, and always Brave, and always Honest; for instance, let me name the great *Argeno*, that matchless *Hero*, and that faithful *Lover*. Have not his unequal'd Deeds reach'd e'en the utmost *Thule? Minerva*'s Wisdom, with all the Spirit of the God of Battle, attend him to the Field, inevitable Deaths fly from his unerring Hand; fir'd by his Example, the chearful Soldiery march secure of Conquest, nor fear the unnumber'd Millions of their Foes.

---

111 [*brouiller*, French: a tumult; a quarrel.]
112 [This word is derived from *Pandarus*, the pimp in the story of *Troilus* and *Cressida*; it was therefore originally written *pandar*, till its etymology was forgotten: a pimp; a male bawd; a procurer.]

Gloriously dreadful in the *War* he shines, but in soft *Peace*, how sweet, how gentle is his Air! Would one not swear that he was form'd for *Love* alone, when he'to *Altezeera* talks, that *Altezeera* whom no disparity of Birth or Fortune could make seem less worthy in his Eyes, whom no length of time, nor absence could erase, {277} whom no Malice could traduce, does not the Soul of Harmony dwell upon his Accenns? Is not his Voice, whenever he addresses her, so languishingly tender, so kind, and so beseeching, as tho' he still sollicited a Blessing which Auspicious *Hymen* has long since authoriz'd him to enjoy? Do not his Words, his Looks, his Actions all denote thy Power, and testify the ardent, the constant Lover?

From the first mention of *Argan*'s Name, the allcharming Features of the God of Love, so lately ruffled with unusual Rage, resum'd their natural Calm and heavenly Sweetness; and when he perceiv'd the *Genius* had done speaking, *Argeno* is indeed, *said he*, the faithful Votary of every Virtue, and my peculiar Worshipper. At the blest moment of his Conception, a general Council of the Gods was held, and every one contributed to make, the favourite Embryo as near divine as Humanity can be. At his Birth the indulgent Heavens put on uncommon Glories, and busy *Fame*, who knew to what he was predestin'd, practis'd a thousand long-neglected Airs, clear'd her hoarse Voice, and tun'd it into Sweetness, to chant his Wonders with the better Grace thro' every Region of the spacious Worlds.

Nor are (*resum'd the Genius*) the Merits of *Cleomenes*[113] less shining, tho' with a different Lustre than those the celebrated *Argeno* boasts. That greatly noble *Patriot*, whose only Care, whose only Aim, is how to serve his Country, shows he despises all those sordid Views by which his Contemporaries are sway'd, looks down on Titles, and chuses to be great in Worth alone. The truly Meritorious ne'er sued to him in vain, nor did the Undeserving, tho' ne'er so near ally'd by Blood, meet advantage by his Favour. The humble Virtuous need but to be known, to be exalted high as his Interest {278} can raise them, but the proud Vicious meet his utmost Scorn. With him no Recommendations but intrinsick Goodness and known Abilities are of force, no secret Bribes, no Flatteries, no Insinuations, ever mov'd him to a forgetfulness of what he owes to Heaven, or to his Country. Nor is his *Capacity* inferior to his *Zeal*; with a Penetration almost infallible, he sees Events long e'er they happen, looks into the Source of things, and turns, with admirable but virtuous Policy, intended Evils on the heads which form'd them. Dear to *Minerva* and *Astrea*, their Aid he constantly invokes, and reaps the Benefit of his pious Orizons. Then, for his strict Obedience to thy Laws, Joy-giving *Cupid!* Well thou know'st his

---

113 [Walpole (King 2012, 37).]

Faith, so often tempted, and yet never false to his first Vows, his sacred *Hymeneal* Contract.

I own (*reply'd the Deity*) his Truth, and have rewarded it, by interceding with the Queen of Heaven, Marriage-loving *Juno*, to influence the fair *Zelinda*'s Breast with all those Virtues which render Conjugal Affection pleasing; and from my Mother *Venus*, I obtain'd this Grant, that she should be ever young, and ever lovely.

Thou also wilt acknowledge (*added the persuasive Genius*) that the intrepid *Clitophon*, and *Nelsus*, worthy to be titled *Heroes*, the former descended of Ancestors more enobled by their Deeds than Titles, the latter bred up to Arts and Sciences, and perfect in all the Accomplishments which adorn; a *Court* or *Study; yet* in the *Field* behaves as tho' enur'd to Arms, and only vers'd in War. 'Tis hard to say, whether *Clitophon* in a *Civil* Employment, or *Nelsus* in a *Military* one, shines most conspicuous; or in which of these *Emilius*, the justly distinguish'd *Emilius*, has most deserv'd Applause, compleat in both, in *War* and *Council* equally serviceable to {279} his Country—all-charming, all-necessary to his Friends, dreadfully terrible to his Sovereign's Foes. *Communus*, rich in the Mind's noblest Virtues, seeks the Distress'd, relieves their Wants with open-hearted Bounty, nor waits to be intreated to do good. The Sick, the Poor, the Captive, the Miserable of all Conditions, feel his tenderest Care; with dewy Comforts he revives their parch'd-up Souls, and robs Calamity of all its hurtful Force. Kind, liberal, hospitable to all, his Quality serves but to render the more dazzling Glories of his unequal'd Mind conspicuous, and is the least part of what commands Esteem. Then for his Wisdom, his Affability, his condescending Goodness—

You may spare the Repetition (*interrupted the sweetly-smiling God*) it is not even in *Apollo*'s Lays to chant *Communus*' Praise as it deserves; there is no Virtue, no Grace, no Charm, he is not master of. Equally dear both to the Gods and Men, all Tongues are full of his Applause. His Actions are accompany'd with such Sweetness, such a resistless Pleasure flows from all he does, that even Envy's self is dumb, and wants a Voice to blast Perfection so divine. His mighty Influence may be known by his Success in this *Enchanted Well*, not like the Wretches, who, prompted by the ruling Demons of this Isle, throw in their All, he sacrific'd a Trifle at the Shrine of *Fortune*, and, unconcern'd what the Event should be, or how repaid, while they, with anxious Eyes, beheld their Hopes sink with their Offerings into the bottomless Abyss; his Agents brought him News of floating Heaps of Gold waiting for his Acceptance: so wonderfully were his superior Virtues distinguish'd by the all-seeing *Jupiter*, that he revers'd even Fate, and this destructive *Well* (permitted but for the Punishment of those infatuated by it) added to the Power he was {280} before possess'd of, of saving and protecting others, who had neither *Vices* sufficient to render them of service to *Lucitario*'s Party, nor Strength enough of *Virtue* to merit so peculiar a Testimony of the Care of *Heaven*, as to be unprejudic'd by the Folly of engaging in it. Hence it was, that many imagin'd the blind Goddess had now the Use of Eyes, and knowing *Communus* the most *worthy*, tho' least *assiduous* of her Worshippers, had given the Prize where best it would be employ'd.

Communus is, indeed, *resumed the venerable Genius*, an eminent Proof my Inspiration has not utterly forsook the Land, nor are his Deeds, with those of the others I have mention'd, the only modern Instances of Virtue; even the soft Sex affords many Examples of excelling Goodness; witness the late incomparable *Mira*, that bright Miracle of Chastity, Fortitude, Magnanimity,[114] Truth and Tenderness; who can sufficiently extol the Greatness of her Mind, who, when her noble Consort, Count *Deleau*, having been unhappily seduc'd to join his Interest with a Party obnoxious to the Decemvirate, was under Sentence of Death, she threw off her Sex's Fears, appear'd all the Heroine! And rather counsel'd him to follow, than dissuaded him from the Dictates of his Honour, in refusing a proffer'd Pardon, on condition of betraying the Persons, by whose Insinuations he had been mis-led. When the Orders came to hurry him to Execution, she took her leave of him with an unparallel'd Courage, and tho' she had long loved him with the utmost extravagance of tender Passion; had been so lately married, that the Name of Bride was scarce worn off; tho' he had return'd her Affection with the greatest Ardency, tho' nothing was equal to the Fondness he had for her, but that with which he was regarded by her, tho' their Sentiments, their {281} Humours, their Opinions, were so much alike, that they seem'd to be animated but by one Soul, and were mutually uneasy even at a moment's Absence from each other; yet did she resign him, never to behold him more, but a bleeding headless Corse, with Temper, with Patience; uttering nothing before him, which should take from the Resolution he had form'd, or render him unfit for the great Task at hand, reserving all her Tears, and her Distraction, till Pity should be useless to relieve her Woes. But when she had took her long, her everlasting Leave, when he indeed was gone, no more to bless her Eyes, her Behaviour soon convinc'd the Standers-by, it was not to the Indifference she had for him, she ow'd that seeming Insensibility of his Fate; now she gave a loose to all the pent-up Passions of her struggling Soul, her Love and her Despair were now sufficiently evinc'd. Never was any Grief like hers, the Restraint she had put upon herself, while in his Presence, made it break out with greater Fury after, nor were her first Emotions less consolable, than those which accompany'd her to her Grave. The little time she lived, she look'd on all who came to comfort her as idle Triflers, and incapable of judging of her irremediable Misfortunes. Oh talk not to me, *would she say*, they never

---

114 [*magnanimité*, French; *magnanimus*, Latin: greatness of mind; bravery; elevation of soul.]

knew the Count *Deleau*, who can believe I can admit of Ease, when he is gone! And then again, bursting afresh into a Torrent of Tears, add, Can *Mira* live without *Deleau?* Oh no, our Souls were too firmly united ever to separate, and when his was driven from the lovely Body, mine lest its Mansion too; in effect, I died when he did; and all that animates this wretched Frame, is but the Spirit of transcending Woe. In this manner did she answer to all who endeavour'd to calm the Tempest of her {282} Grief, which in a short time threw her into a lingering Disease, of which she expir'd; never since the Loss of her dear Lord having allow'd any Intermission of her Sighs and Groans, till she was told she could not survive him; but then long absent Cheerfulness again seem'd to renew its place in her Countenance; she smiled, and waiting the Approach of that only Physician, who could give her Pains redress, receiv'd him with a Welcome, which demonstrated how much she desir'd to remove from a World, which, wanting *Deleau*, had nothing in it but what was odious to her.

Here was a Constancy which I confess, indeed, there are too few Examples of; yet sure thy Godhead will approve and praise it: nor canst thou but acknowledge the fair and virtuous *Amabella*, tho' compell'd to the Embraces of the Man she hated, and torn from one she loved with the greatest Fervency of fond Affection; does she not set a shining Pattern for her Sex to imitate? To be just to Duty, she abandons all that's dear, treats him with Scorn, with seeming Detestation, and to her unloved, unloving Lord, omits no modest Testimony of Conjugal Affection, to make him know his Happiness; while he, insensible of all her Charms, of all her Goodness, maintains a Woman he took from a Brothel, in infinitely more Pomp than his to deserving Wife. Yet does she still remain unmoved from her first Principle, That no ill Usage from a Husband, can be Sanction for that of the Wife.

Saphira too, that blooming Beauty, for whom, before the Misfortunes of her Family, the noblest Youths have vainly languish'd, condemn'd to Age and Wrinkles, Deformity and Ill-Nature, preserves her Honour and her Fame, with a Resolution which was not to be expected, or Scarce hoped, from her {283} tender Years: we are, indeed, to suppose she is in great measure indebted, for that admirable economy in her Conduct, to the wife Instructions, and constant Admonitions of her excellent Mother, the never too much extoll'd *Cornelia*, that wondrous Woman, who beheld without Concern the greatest part of those vast Possessions, which she once was Mistress of, confiscated thro' the imprudent Management of her Husband, who behav'd not so exactly as he ought to have done in a publick Affair, supported the Death of a beloved Son, whose great Heart could not survive the Ruin of his Fortune, with a Magnanimity scarce to be credited by those who knew the Tenderness of her Nature,–and saw her darling Daughter thrown into the Arms of a Person, rather capable of creating Horror than Love, meerly because he had an Estate, and she had lost one. All these Afflictions, tho' each great and heavy, Patience, and

Strength of Mind, enabled her to bear, without venting any extravagant Exclamations of the Severity of her Fate; but when the News was brought that her Husband had ended his Days in a foreign Clime, where he had been obliged to shelter, the Shock was more than all her Fortitude could sustain. Her Affection was so sincere and constant, that all the Misfortunes she had suffer'd thro' his unhappy Proceedings, had not the power to alienate; she continu'd for many Days, in a Condition, which gave those about her sufficient reason to believe she would not long survive him; but Fate preserv'd her even in this, the most terrible Calamity (in her Imagination) that had ever befallen, her. She lives, but lives only for the Comfort of others, herself being incapable of receiving any.

{284} Infinite is the number of Examples, *continu'd the Genius*, which I could bring to testify this Isle is not so far debased beneath what it has been, but that it still may claim thy Patronage and Care; but that the Work is needless, since nothing is conceal'd from thy omniscient Sight; that Dæmon who assumes thy Shape and Voice, and borrows from thee so much in all beside, that those who feel his Influence know not their Error, till by Experience convinced, cannot copy thee in this, and my mistaken Sons worship an Eyeless *Cupid*. Besides 'twould too long, much too long delay the destin'd Punishment of yon vile Blasphemers of the immortal Gods. The Will of Heaven obey'd, I will return, and once more supplicate Remission for those Offences, which my too guilty Race has been ensnar'd to act.

This said, high on a shining Cloud he tower'd away, the Sword of Justice not yet unsheathed, required not present use, and was girded on his Side; but the sacred Token of Almighty Reason, his right Hand, with firm and steady grasp, held out extended; and as he rode thro' the refulgent Air, seem'd from its beamy Point to scatter Suns, and bring redoubled Day. The Titulary Priests from far beheld the dreadful Radience, and trembled at approaching Fate; but few of them being permitted presence enough of Mind to offer at an Escape, they gather'd hastily together in Clusters, as tho' Consultation would avail; but before they had well time for either, the Ruin they apprehended fell upon them. Swift the commissioned *Genius* reach'd, with his Fraud-disclosing Wand, the Shrine of Fortune, then that of *Pecunia*. Down fell the wooden *Deities*, with all their Trophies, Inscriptions, Altars, Offerings, on the Heads which form'd them, the {285} Rabble's Sport and Prey, who scrambled for the gaudy Baubles that adorn'd them. Then, descending lower, he touch'd, with the same forceful Gift, the secret Springs by which this great Machine was set in motion; strait to their native Springs the unguilty Waters flew, and showed to the amaz'd Spectators Eyes, not Gold and Gems, not Ambergrease and Coral, but naked Mud, and long-drench'd reedy Ooze. A general Howl of Terror, Anguish, and Astonishment, such as we may imagine will be heard from the affrighted World at the dissolution of Nature, ran thro' his confus'd Assembly, some of whom had lavish'd their All in this fatal Abyss, and had no dependance, no hope of Support, or even Sustenance for themselves and miserable Families, but from the Returns these pageant Priests had made them believe would shortly give them back their own with tenfold Usury. What was now the Estate of these unhappy Wretches! How truly dreadful their Condition! Long beguil'd with pleasing Dreams of coming Happiness, Prosperity, Plenty, to be waked at once to such a Certainty of Penury, Disgrace, and all the Miseries which make consummate Ruin. To have no hope, no expectation left, and to know that they had lost all this by an Infatuation, a wilful Blindness, which took away even the Consolation of Pity for their Woes, and rendered them condemnable even by themselves; was, if possible, an Aggravation of them: with Guilt and Shame opprest, with Fear and Wonder stupified, they stood as riveted in Earth, and seem'd so many Monuments of Misery, known but by their horror-darting Eyes to have any Remains of Life. Fain would they have pray'd, but to whom should they address their Orisons? The Heavenly Powers they had despis'd, contemn'd, {286} blasphem'd; Despair *there* check'd their too late rising Piety: and for the *Idols* they had worship'd, they now saw how little capable they were of hearing or relieving them. But those thus penitently dispos'd, were but the smallest part of that prodigious Number of People who had throng'd to the *Enchanted Well.* Those of 'em who were not so far undone, but that they knew how to live in the fashion they had been accustom'd to do, if no Returns were made, as they were less disturbed at the downfall of it, they were also less touch'd with remorse at the Offence they had been guilty of to the *real* Gods, in their Adoration of *imaginary* ones. So certain is it, that Want is the Mother of Devotion: the young gay *Coquette,* tho' she lost great part of her Pertness, still flirted her Fan,[115] and perhaps *affected* more than *felt* a real Terror. The well-dress'd powder'd *Beau,* shaking back his Ruffle, and gently rapping with his ring'd Fingers his Snuff-Box-Lid, cry'd, *Gad,*[116] tis wondrous strange! But 'tis highly probable, had he been ask'd, would have been extremely at a loss how to have reply'd to any Question of what had happened: for these kind of Animals, of both Sexes, are certainly of a Species by themselves, Nature sent 'em into the World animated only by a little Spirit of her own; they have no Souls, are incapable of discerning any thing farther than the Senses direct them. Thought, Penetration, Reflection, are what they know nothing of—they are a sort of *Butterfly*; pretty, lit-

---

115 [The Victorian act of flirting with a hand fan where different gestures could imply different interests. As an expression of this flirting method, the "Fanology or the Ladies Conversation Fan" was sold for specifically that reason and had flirting language imprinted upon the paper part of the fan.]

116 [Derived by *Skinner* from *gadfly*; by *Junius* from *gadaw,* Welsh, to forsake: to ramble about without any settled purpose; to rove loosely and idly.]

tle, unhurtful, insipid Insects, who when they have play'd away their Season here, are translated into some other World to buzz about, incapable of meriting either Heaven or Hell. But the Politician, who from a supplicating *Courtier*, hoped to be made a *Count*; a Count, a *Marquiss*; a Marquiss; a *Duke*; and in the {287} Expectance of future Grandeur had submitted to traffick as an humble Cit;[117] how did this total Disappointment shock the Ambition of his thinking Soul! Yet, hardned in his Crimes, he not repented those he had committed, but was already beginning to rack his inventive Brain by what new Stratagem he should arrive at those Honours he was so covetous of wearing, tho' unworthily. The *Miser* too, who, tho' he had still enough, would sooner have sold himself to everlasting Perdition, than have parted with one of those dear Pieces he esteemed of more Value than all Heaven, was ready to lay violent hands on his own Life, for this overthrow of his Hopes; and was prevented from it, only by the remembrance, that the Store he had at home might, when he was no more to guard it, be lavish'd in Expences by his less covetous Heir. He was too full of Regret for what he had lost, and Care how to preserve what he had sav'd, to have the least corner of his Soul taken up with Contrition for those Sins which had brought him into the Misfortune he lamented. All were, indeed, disorder'd, all confus'd, a wild Distortion sat on every Face; but it was not that kind of Discomposure which the *Genius* had hoped to find: and looking on 'em with a Countenance in which 'tis hard to say if Grief or Anger had the greatest place; but the latter gaining the Preheminence, as he more perceived their Inflexibility, with awful Frowns and stern majestick Air, he thus address'd them:

> O Race unworthy of your noble Lineage! Did your brave Ancestors live to see this Day, their Souls, their very Souls would shrink as mine, who animated theirs, does now, at your Disgrace; your Fall from all that's truly Noble, Great, or Good—Degenerate Wretches! How have you lost that Sense of Honour you were once {288} so fame'd for? A Prey to Avarice the worst of Vices, because the gratification of it leads you into a thousand others Hypocrisy, Deceit, Perjury, Murder, Treason, Lust, Witchcraft; for gain you'll forgo your very Gods, betray your Prince and Country, prostitute your own Wives and Daughters, plunge a Dagger into the Breast of her that bore you, or him you have begot, nay, even give up that Gold, which to purchase, you have, perhaps, been guilty of the most detested Crimes, and ran the greatest dangers; even that you will give up, led by a hope to have it doubly paid—and justly are you serv'd! O may you still meet the same Fate, and Disappointments ever be the Consequents of Attempts which Honour has no share in. If you have any Sense of Shame, or just Remorse be not extinguish'd in you, fly this detested Scene of Villany and Fraud, and in your Closets implore forgiveness of the offended Gods. Go ye Reproaches to your Name and Country!

---

117 [contracted from *citizen:* an inhabitant of a city, in an ill sense. A pert low townsman; a pragmatical trader.]

Hence! Nor show your abject Heads, till Time, and Prayers, and Penitence, in part shall expiate your Crimes!

These Words, coming from the Mouth of a Being whose Influence, tho' few receiv'd, all were proud to acknowledge, had the power of shocking Hearts, who before had been harden'd to every thing; none had the Courage to reply, but every one making what haste he could to be gone, those heaps of People, which had compos'd this late numerous Assembly, was, in a moment, melted away; and at the end of his Speech, the *Genius* found himself alone, but did not long continue so. The well-pleas'd God of soft Desires, who while these things had been transacting, inform'd the Stranger of the meaning of some of those Passages which he had seen, but were too mystical for human {289} Understanding to fathom; by the same incomprehensible Means that he had convey'd him to the Hill, now return'd him to that place which he had left so crouded, but now found no more than a wild and dreary Waste.

With words befitting the Deity of Love, he congratulated the good *Genius* on his Triumph over his long potent Adversary. I hope, *reply'd the venerable Being*, thy Godhead is in part appeas'd by what I have done; the Demon most obnoxious to thy Power is Avarice, and him I have sufficiently scourged in the Persons of his Votaries. The tender Nymphs, and faithful Swains, whose Injuries have cried to thee for Vengeance, now will receive ample Compensation; sordid Interest, and Love of Gold, no more shall triumph oe'r their Charms; Beauty and Virtue shall henceforward be the great Attractives, Marriage shall now join *Hearts* as well as *Hands*, and cease to be the Bawd of *Fortune*.

Had'st thou the Power, *resumed the Deity somewhat gravely*, to execute the same Authority throughout the Isle, as thou hast done in this small Part of it, my replenish'd Sway again might shine with former Force and Lustre; but O they scorn me still in yon rebellious Towers, from my lov'd Throne among the Great and Fair, I yet am driven, and that Monster, *Lust!* Is treated like a God, feasted with my Incense, and adorn'd with all the Trophies due alone to me.

Long it is, *answer'd the Genius*, since last I made my Tour thro' those luxurious Palaces—but in thy Presence, if thou shalt condescend to accompany me, will I now revisit them. 'Twas my Design to go, *added the God*, tho' painful to my Eyes to look on Objects so ungrateful; and here, *continu'd he, presenting the Stranger*, behold a noble Youth, the {290} partner of our Progress, by *Fate* and *Jupiter* decreed to be a Witness betwixt Gods and Men. But mortal Sense cannot sustain incessant Toil, his Faculties already drooping with the visionary Wonders of this Day, require Repose; let him in some of yonder odoriferous Recesses enjoy that Rest which Nature asks, then rise refresh'd, and wait us in the remaining and more surprizing Incidents of our next Stage.

The *Genius*, with an humble Bow, gave his assent; and strait the God of Bliss wasted the weary'd Youth to a close Bower, where oft his charmful *Psyche*, in pleasing Dreams, had felt his softening Power, there left him to recall his wandering Spirits, and by enjoying the benefit of Contemplation on what he had seen, refit him for what he was yet to see.

The End of the First Volume.

{291} A. Key

Pag.
7.	Lucitario,	C—gs.
9.	Conbree,	D. P—d.
11.	Marcus,	L. G—ge.
	Mirazaida,	Mrs. Le—n.
12.	Lady,	Css.C—y.
	Marthalia,	Mrs. Bl—t.
13.	Gratiana,	Miss Ch—ld.
14.	Romanus,	M. T—rd.
17.		Col. M—y.
19.		Dss. S—y.
21.		E. P—gh.
		Mrs. Th—n.
23.	Miranda,	Mrs. M—r—n.
33.		Mrs. Br—nt.
34.		Mrs. H—ll.
35.	Constantius,	Mr. G. H—ll.
	Lauranus,	Mr. A. H—ll.
39.	Somerius,	Mr. So—rs.
	Philarchus,	Mr. Sy—s.
	Burtonius,	Mr. B—n.
	Arthario,	C—r H—tt.
	Mersus,	H—rl—y.
43.	Gloaticia,	Mrs. S—ns—m. {292}
	Chevalier	Major F—e.
45.		D. R—d.
	Rutho,	Mr. S—ns—m.
	Her Lodgings,	A Gardener's House at *Fulham*.
47.	Certain Duke,	R—d.
	Bookseller,	C—rl.
	Young Officer,	Captain N—s.
49.	Clarismond,	Lday H—
55.	Salvida,	Lady F—w—r.
56.	Antoinetta,	Wid. G—.
58.	Dutchess.	Dss. N—d.
59.	Count Almont,	L. H—v—m.
60.		D. N—d.
110.	Duke de Ulto,	D. M—e.

111.	P. del Carmel.	D. *M—lb—gh.*
	Ct. Hermio,	D. *Gr—n.*
113.	—	Dss. *Gr—n.*
115.	Melanthus.	Young *C—gs.*
119.		Singer at the Opera.
121.	Cesaria,	Css. *J—s—y.*
122.	Damias,	Mrs. *D—k—ns.*
	Juditha,	*Cesaria*'s Woman.
126.	Hortensia,	Lady *B—rl—w.*
129.	Serpentius,	Sir G. *C—l.*
130.	Bellario,	*E—ce B—l.*
135.	Clione,	Mrs. *W—ns—d.*
137.	Luina,	Mrs. *L—nn.*
146.	Bellimante,	Mrs. *C—ll—ns.*
149.	Alma,	Lady A. *L—.*
	Prince del Ponto,	D. *B—n.*
150.	Bellingar,	Mr. *W—k—ns.*
151.	Masonia,	Lady *M—.*
	Marville,	L. *M—.*
	Riverius,	L. *R—.* {293}
167.	Cocona,	Mrs. *C—*
181.		Mrs. *Fl—yd.*
	Accomp. Chevalier,	Col. *B—t.*
182.	Young Riverius,	Mr. *S—e.*
183.		Mrs. *S—ns—m.*
187.		L. *L—nsd—n.*
		Mrs. *S—sf—d.*
195.	Davilla,	Capt. *H—k—s.*
196.	Sisters,	Lady *H—re's* Daughters.
197.		Mrs. *L—.*
198.		Mr. and Mrs. *H—wr—d.*
		Prince of *Utopia.*
200.	Flavia,	Lady *J—D—gl—ss.*
203.	Beaujeune,	Mr. *Y—* and Wife.
205.		Mrs. *As—t.*
	Mersilius,	Col. *N—t—n.*
209.	Marbien,	D. and Dss. *W—n.*
210.		His Father.
209.	Chevalier,	Col *H—s.*

222.	Blantier,	Mr. *H—t.*
	Olimpia, Silenia,	The two Mrs. *Al—w—y.*
236.	Meriton.	Y. *Alw—y.*
238.		Parson of *C—v—t—G—d—n.*
242.		Sir *Tho. D—r—g.*
		Mrs. *H—wk—ns.*
243.	Le Brune, Boncœur,	Major *B—n,* Ld.
		B—y.
247.		Vander *H—t,* and Wife.
265.		L. *R—s.*
		Lady Dowager *R—s.*
		Mrs. *M—yt—n.*
277.	Argeno,	D. *Ar—le.*
	Cleomenes,	Mr. *W—e.*
278.	Clit and Nelsus,	*De—y,* and G. *W—s.*
279.	Communus,	D. *Ch.—s.* {294}
280.	Mira,	Lady *D—r.*
281.	Count de Leau,	L. *D—rw—tw—r.*
282.	Saphira,	Mrs. *C—rs.*

Index of Names

Astell, Mary   5, 28, 41

Barbauld, Anna Letitia   8
Behn, Aphra   2–4, 26
Bowman, Walter   1, 25
Burke, Edmund   10

Campanella, Tomasso   18
Cavendish, Margaret   19
Cicero   29
Conbree, Duke de   27, 30, 48, 218
Cragg, James   13, 46

Descartes, René   4, 27–29
Dover, Lord   7

Fielding, Henry   8, 16, 25, 39 f.
Fowke, Martha   8

Hill, Aaron   3, 8, 15, 25 f., 189, 191, 216
Hobbes, Thomas   22, 29, 31
Hume, David   10, 28, 39 f.

Locke, John   28 f., 39 f.
Longinus, Cassius   26 f.

Mallet, David   25 f.
Mandeville, Bernard   28, 39
Manley, Delarivier   3 f., 16, 39
Montague, Lady Mary Wortley   15

Ovid   144 f., 183

Plato   19, 30
Pope, Alexander   7 f., 15 f., 39

Rapin, Paul de   10, 40

Sansom, Martha, *see also* Fowke, Martha   8, 15, 25
Savage, Richard   7 f., 15, 25, 39, 156
Scudéry, Madeleine de   28
Smith, Adam   28
Swift, Jonathan   7, 10 f., 16, 39, 213

Temple, William   22, 45
Thomson, James   25
Trenchard, John   10 f., 51

Walpole, Robert   13, 16, 22, 34, 39, 209
Whitehead, Charles   8

Index of Subjects

activity 30, 48
affectation 23, 200
– affecters 164
– affection 28, 50, 55, 58, 64 f., 67, 75, 84, 86, 88, 91 f., 94, 97, 106, 121 f., 125, 129 f., 139, 144, 147, 149, 157, 160, 165, 170, 173 f., 177 f., 188, 192, 195, 197, 204 f., 210 – 213
alchemy 13 f.
angel 60, 91, 124, 128, 155, 171
avarice 18, 20, 22, 34, 47, 49, 52, 56, 88, 161 f., 207 f., 215 f.

Bank of England 12 f.
beauty 19, 44, 49, 51 f., 57, 60 f., 64, 73, 75 – 77, 109, 111, 119, 121, 133 f., 136, 146, 156, 161, 168, 179, 188, 195, 198, 202, 204, 212, 216
body 27, 44, 90, 97, 103, 105, 109, 114, 117, 122 f., 131, 137, 151, 177, 184, 192, 199, 202, 204, 212

community 9, 29, 33
compassion 62, 69, 77, 83, 94, 98, 116, 153, 174
conscience 71, 77, 93, 98, 131, 196
constancy 30, 32 f., 45, 49, 52, 57, 64 f., 77, 85 f., 111, 121, 164, 173, 212
Cupid, *see also* deity of love 15, 18 – 23, 30, 32 – 34, 45, 56, 207, 209, 213

deity of love 30, 44, 216
demon 19, 30, 45, 50, 53, 111, 126, 149, 161 f., 202, 210, 216
desire 4, 15, 18, 20, 22, 25, 28 – 31, 33 f., 45, 48, 53, 56 f., 59 – 61, 63 f., 72 f., 75, 78, 80, 85, 87, 90 f., 93, 95, 97, 101, 105, 107, 111, 120, 124 f., 128, 134, 139, 142 f., 146 – 149, 166, 168 f., 173, 177 – 179, 186, 190, 193 – 198, 201 – 203, 207, 216
dishonour 95, 97, 156, 159, 167, 184 – 186, 191
divine 18 – 20, 22, 30, 44, 46, 60, 63, 87, 109, 123 f., 128, 141 f., 162, 185, 188 f., 195, 201, 206, 208 – 210
– divine historian 24, 31 f., 54
– divine justice 23, 45, 180

duty 53, 73, 143 f., 153, 155, 160 f., 165, 175, 177 f., 183 f., 186, 195, 212

emotions 26, 28, 44, 51, 141, 170, 179, 182, 196, 211
enamorato 72, 80, 118, 139, 161
envy 44, 66, 110, 122, 137, 153, 165, 174, 178, 187 f., 203, 210
essence 63

factions 9 f.
force 7, 14, 17 f., 20, 22, 44, 77 f., 93 f., 96, 106, 111, 114, 123, 127 f., 134, 136, 143, 147, 154, 190, 192, 195, 199, 206 – 210, 216
friendship 1, 24 – 26, 30, 52, 57 – 61, 67 f., 76, 83, 91, 99, 126, 131, 139, 142, 145, 154, 156, 178, 192 f., 195

genius 8, 21, 25, 56 f., 61, 71, 117, 152 f., 187, 193, 202, 206 – 211, 213, 215 – 217
Goring Pamphlet 5

Hillarian Circle 1, 3, 7 f., 14 f., 24 f., 39
history 1, 4, 6, 13 f., 16, 26, 28, 31 – 34, 39 f., 42, 51, 72, 86 f., 109, 116 f., 120, 128, 131, 137, 144, 155 f., 160, 165, 168, 176, 191, 194, 200 – 202
honour 19, 22, 44 – 46, 48 f., 52 – 56, 58, 60 f., 71, 75, 80 f., 83, 85, 90, 95 f., 99, 104, 106 f., 109, 113 f., 121, 123, 131 – 134, 136, 138, 140 f., 143, 145, 147, 149 – 151, 154 f., 159, 161, 166, 171, 174, 180, 182, 186, 189 f., 192 – 196, 198, 200 – 202, 207 f., 211 f., 215
hypocrisy 56, 60, 63, 88, 109, 128, 153, 161, 208, 215

idea 3, 7, 9, 25 f., 32, 89, 154, 169, 196, 199
imagination 2, 43, 89 f., 94, 100, 127, 146, 148, 213
impatience 45, 74, 77, 83, 88, 101, 145, 155, 157, 193, 196

Jacobitism 5 f.

Index of Subjects

justice   21f., 54, 71, 86, 99f., 108, 111, 134, 154, 161, 165, 172, 174, 190, 200, 205–207, 213

love   4, 7f., 18, 21f., 26f., 30–34, 39, 41, 48f., 52, 55–57, 59f., 62f., 67, 71, 73–79, 81–100, 104–112, 114, 117, 120f., 124–128, 130–133, 135, 138–148, 150, 155, 157f., 160, 162–164, 166, 168–170, 172, 174f., 177, 179, 181, 184, 188–190, 192–197, 199–202, 204, 206–209, 211f., 216

lust, *see also* demon lust   22, 30, 33f., 78, 88, 99f., 111, 153, 161f., 207f., 215f.

Macclesfield Scandal   35
mind   8, 34, 45, 47f., 50f., 56f., 59, 61, 64, 73f., 86, 90, 93, 96, 101, 105, 108, 115, 121f., 126, 128, 131, 137f., 141, 145, 147, 154f., 168, 172f., 178, 181f., 185, 188, 196, 198, 200, 202, 207f., 210f., 213
– presence of mind   109, 140, 170

nature   10f., 22f., 26, 28, 30, 35, 43, 51f., 56, 59, 61, 66–68, 70, 72, 75f., 80f., 84f., 87, 90f., 94, 96–98, 100, 105, 108, 111, 114, 120, 122, 126, 128–130, 132f., 136–138, 142, 144, 146, 148, 151, 153–155, 157–159, 161f., 169, 171, 174, 177f., 181, 186, 188–190, 192–194, 199, 204, 207, 212–214, 216
necromancer   10, 13, 20, 46, 50, 112, 122

party politics   10f., 22, 24
passion, *see also* compassion   3f., 18, 21f., 24, 26–31, 33f., 48, 51–53, 55–57, 59–61, 64, 72, 75, 80f., 83–95, 97, 99, 102, 104, 106, 111, 113–115, 118, 120, 124, 129f., 132, 136, 139, 141–143, 145, 147–149, 151, 156, 159, 162–164, 166–172, 174f., 177–181, 183f., 186, 189f., 193–197, 200, 203, 205, 207, 211
patriot   11, 16, 22, 34, 36, 112
– patriotic   11
patronage   14–16, 213
person   5, 7f., 11, 16, 21, 29, 46, 50f., 54f., 57f., 63f., 66f., 70f., 73–75, 79, 84, 86, 90, 93, 96, 104, 108–111, 113f., 120–122, 127, 133, 137–139, 142–144, 148f., 152–163, 165–168, 171–175, 178f., 181–185, 187f., 195f., 199–203, 205, 211f., 216

pleasure   18, 27, 34, 43, 48, 56–58, 60, 65, 68, 70f., 75–78, 83, 86f., 90, 97, 114, 120f., 127, 132–135, 142, 147, 149–152, 154, 156, 161, 164, 166, 172f., 175, 178, 180, 187f., 194–196, 203, 205, 210

reason   4, 10–12, 15, 21, 24, 29, 32, 42, 48, 58–62, 69, 83–85, 93f., 96, 98, 100f., 103f., 106, 111–116, 119, 124, 126, 129, 132, 137, 145, 148, 156, 158, 162, 166f., 178, 180–182, 184, 189, 192f., 198, 203, 206–208, 213f.

satire   17, 41, 90, 154
scandalous fiction   6, 29
science   1, 19, 22, 43, 58, 118, 156, 207, 210
security   15, 51, 60, 83, 88, 102, 185, 188
self   1, 5f., 9, 22, 26f., 30, 32f., 49, 51, 62, 92, 94, 111, 120, 129, 141, 165f., 169, 179, 199, 204, 207, 210
sense   7, 44, 46, 56, 69, 74, 80, 92f., 96, 106, 114f., 118, 123–125, 127f., 136, 146f., 150, 152, 154, 156, 174f., 189, 192, 195f., 198, 203, 214–216
sex   4, 16, 30, 49f., 54, 57, 59, 61, 64, 73, 75, 77f., 81, 83–85, 94f., 102, 106, 108, 111, 115, 117, 124, 126–128, 131, 133, 136f., 142, 147, 159, 164, 166, 168, 174f., 180, 194, 197, 203, 205, 211f., 214
– fair sex   49, 56, 122f., 134
Sign of Fame   2, 5
slavery   22, 207
soul   4, 24, 28–30, 45f., 49, 51f., 54, 56–58, 60–62, 64, 66, 72f., 75, 77f., 80f., 83–88, 90–93, 95, 97f., 108f., 111, 114f., 118, 121f., 124–128, 131, 133f., 138–141, 143, 146–149, 153–155, 157f., 161, 163–165, 169, 171, 175, 177, 179, 184, 186, 188–191, 193, 195f., 199, 201f., 206, 209–212, 214f.
– of soul (greatness of)   186, 211
South Sea Bubble/South Sea Company/South Sea Crisis/South Sea Scheme   10–14, 24, 35, 39
sovereignty   97
speculative desire   34

spirit 21f., 29, 31, 62, 71, 77, 94, 110, 123, 125, 133, 153, 159f., 167, 170, 173, 176, 189, 191, 198, 208, 212, 214, 217
Statute of Anne 17, 24, 39
sublimity 24, 27f., 31, 48, 52, 91f., 148
– Longinian sublime 26, 33

theory 26, 28, 154
Tories 10f.
Tulip Mania 13
tumult 9f., 43, 107, 157, 208

understanding 17, 24, 28f., 40, 64, 74, 85, 121, 156, 202f., 216
utopian 17f., 20, 23, 27, 33, 35, 41, 51
utopia, *see also* utopian 14, 16–19, 33, 42f., 191, 197, 202, 219

vice 1, 18, 20, 22, 30, 33, 47, 57, 63f., 68, 109f., 119f., 128, 136–138, 155, 187, 210, 215

virtue 1, 18, 22, 28, 30, 33f., 45, 48f., 52, 54, 56, 58–63, 72f., 90–92, 95, 109f., 113, 121, 130f., 133, 137f., 141–143, 147–150, 153–156, 158f., 161, 165, 167–169, 178, 186f., 189, 193f., 200–203, 207–211, 216
vitalism/vitals 56, 107

Whigs 10f.
will 2, 15, 20–22, 25, 34f., 45, 50–52, 54, 56f., 59–61, 64, 69, 76–78, 83–86, 90f., 95, 97–102, 105–109, 113f., 116, 122–128, 131–133, 136f., 141f., 148, 151, 154f., 157f., 161, 163–166, 168, 170–173, 176f., 179, 185–188, 190f., 194–196, 198, 201, 204, 206f., 212f., 215f.
world 17, 19, 23, 43f., 52, 54–56, 58, 60, 62, 64–66, 68, 70f., 73, 79–81, 84, 108, 110, 112–115, 119, 121, 123, 129, 131f., 135–137, 141, 144, 146, 148–150, 152, 154, 162–167, 169, 172, 174–176, 179f., 184–188, 192, 199, 201f., 204–206, 208f., 212–215